THE UNITED NATIONS ORGANISATION
HANDBOOK

THE UNITED NATIONS ORGANISATION HANDBOOK

BY
ANDREW BOYD

PILOT PRESS INC
NEW YORK

First Published 1946 by
Pilot Press Inc., New York,
and The Pilot Press, Ltd., London

TO FRANCES

Printed and bound in Great Britain by
W. & J. Mackay and Co., Ltd., Chatham

19083

CONTENTS

We, the peoples of the United Nations, have created a new world organization. The future of our civilization hangs on its success or failure. But the most carefully constructed machine cannot produce results unless it is watched over and directed by human intelligence. How well do we understand our machine, its potentialities and its limitations?

This book sets out the essential facts about the United Nations Organization. It does not seek to prove that it is perfect; but it does try to show why some kind of world organization is necessary to our threatened society, and how any such organization must draw its real driving powers from the common man.

I have to acknowledge the generous co-operation of officials of both the United Nations Secretariat and the United Nations Association, to whom I am indebted for much valuable information; but I must make it clear that I write from a completely independent viewpoint, and that the opinions expressed are purely my own.

ANDREW BOYD.

CHAPTER I

WHY DO WE NEED THE UNITED NATIONS ?

THE INTERNATIONAL ANARCHY

WE need the United Nations Organization for precisely the same reasons that we need a police force, judges, and a code of law. We have found that we cannot live as civilized human beings unless we have policemen and judges and laws. We know that if we lost these three essentials, our society would become a savage chaos in which no man would be safe ; in one word, an anarchy. No civilized man could contemplate for one moment the idea of living in a community of men and women without laws or officials to enforce those laws ; and if we examine the most primitive of " uncivilized " communities, we will always find laws and a general acknowledgement of their supreme authority. Yet the great nations of our twentieth-century world have yet to learn what the remotest fishing village perched on the edge of a mangrove swamp has known for thousands of years. For in the great community of nations there have never been laws or authorities capable of enforcing them. Instead there has been, as Mr. Lowes Dickinson pointed out several years ago, an international anarchy.

This anarchy is due to the theory of the absolute sovereignty of the nation-state. A nation which holds this theory not only refuses to tolerate any interference in its private affairs, but reserves absolute freedom of action in its relations with other nations ; and " freedom of action " naturally includes freedom to make war. Yet no sovereign state would permit its individual citizens, or any group of them, so much as to claim a tithe of the absolute freedom of action which it automatically demands for itself. Indeed, the survival of absolute sovereignty in an age in which the individual citizen is bound to his particular community by stronger economic and social ties than ever before is one of the supreme paradoxes of our time.

The effect of the doctrine of absolute sovereignty is that when a dispute arises between two states, there is no way of settling it except by force. True, it may not be necessary for the stronger state to use force, for the weaker may yield to mere threats ; also there is the possibility that other less directly interested nations may intervene and compel the two disputants to agree on a compromise. But, however the dispute is settled, the final settlement can only represent the balance of force between the various nations concerned. If it happens to be a reasonably just settlement, the justice is purely coincidental ; the basic principle is still force.

A*

Being fully aware of this, the governments of all sovereign nations have to shape their policies so as to achieve and maintain an international balance of force favourable to themselves and their friends. And quite obviously no international balance of force can ever be so nicely adjusted that both parties are satisfied that they are the stronger. Inevitably, then, there is a ceaseless jostling and manœuvring between nation-states all of which are trying to improve their positions. No nation can afford for a moment to relax its efforts ; and so the vicious circle of rival sovereignties continues to rotate. There is no way of breaking out of it. If in any one country a government which is altruistic enough to conciliate other governments comes to power, the domestic opposition will have little difficulty in unseating it on the grounds that it has betrayed the national interest.

Small wonder that in the whole of recorded history there is only one known case of a sovereign nation voluntarily and unconditionally yielding up territory which it already possessed.[1] The tendency is rather for all the nations which have claims in any given area to attempt to forestall their rivals by a sudden *coup de main*. And so all national governments are compelled to exist in a state of constant tension, haunted by the uncertainty which may be summed up in the two questions : " If X attacks Y, will we be strong enough to force X to withdraw ? " and " Shall we occupy Y ourselves, and will our position then be strong enough to deter X ? " Meanwhile, of course, the race to keep ahead of one's rivals in armaments goes on, until finally there are so many weapons about, and so much fear of being outstripped in next year's production, that " the guns go off on their own accord."

So whatever the detailed course of events may be, we can be sure that the international anarchy will always produce one identical result : war. There is then only one cure for war : the limitation of the absolute sovereignty of the nation-state. If nations can be brought to acknowledge the supremacy of law and made to fear the punishment which will follow any breach of that law, the majority of the quarrels which lead to war between sovereign states are likely to be settled without bloodshed, just as in a civilized community most quarrels are peacefully composed because neither party wants to be accused of breaking the peace. And even when passions have flared to such heights that an aggressor nation proceeds to war in defiance of international law, the fighting can still be stopped if there is a concentration of overwhelming force which can be brought to bear upon the aggressor.

In other words, to limit the absolute sovereignty of nations we must create something like an international police force capable of enforcing the law between nations and of suppressing any outbreaks of violence.

That is why we need the United Nations.

---

[1]The transfer of the Ionian Islands from Britain to Greece during Palmerston's ministry.

At the head of the Charter of the United Nations we find it stated that the first and most essential purpose of the Organization is :

" To maintain international peace and security, and to that end to take effective collective measures for the prevention and removal of threats to the peace, and for the suppression of acts of aggression or other breaches of the peace, and to bring about by peaceful means, and in conformity with the principles of justice and international law, adjustment or settlement of international disputes or situations which might lead to a breach of the peace."[1]

How do the United Nations propose to do this ? And what are the prospects of their being successful in such a vast undertaking ?

Before we examine these questions, we should pause for a moment and consider briefly the fate of mankind's previous attempts to eliminate war.

EARLIER SUPERNATIONAL PROJECTS

The nation as we know it is, of course, a comparatively recent develop-ment. Until some three or four centuries ago, the political world was based not so much upon independent sovereign states as upon cosmo-politan empires, each of which dominated a whole civilization and com-manded the allegiance of the embryonic " nations " of those days. Even in Europe, where the Roman Empire had long since disintegrated into the chaos of the Dark Ages, there remained a shadowy unity, based partly on the pseudo-empires of Byzantium and Germany, but more firmly on the Christian Church and the Eternal City of Rome. Haunted by the ghost of the Cæsars, the states of the West continued for over a thousand years to pay more or less dutiful respect to the Popes and "Holy Roman Emperors," and to refer to Rome for a decision on disputes with their neighbours. And if we turn to the rest of the Old World, we find that practically every principality acknowledged at one time or another the suzerainty of the Caliph, the Great Khan, the Grand Moghul or the Celestial Emperor ; and long after each of these potentates had ceased to wield effective power except in the immediate neighbourhood of his capital city, his former viceroys, now independent princes, would still carry on the business of government in his name, and refer to his court for arbitration in any dispute with a neighbour.

Seen in the perspective of time, these ancient empires do not bear much resemblance to world governments. But we must remember that before the opening up of the oceans each group of peoples, whether Christian, Moslem, Hindu or Chinese, thought of all other peoples as mere barbarians living on the outer fringes of the great civilized world of which Rome or Mecca or Peking was the centre. So, while the Romans sincerely believed that they had established a single world government and universal peace, so too did the Emperors at Peking. Indeed, the latter persisted in their

[1]Article 1 of the Charter

illusion as late as 1793, when Chien Lung wrote to George III of England to tell him that, "My Capital is the hub and centre round which all the quarters of the earth revolve . . . Kings of all nations have sent their tribute by land and sea. . . . It is your duty to understand my feelings and reverently to obey my instructions."[1]

None of these attempts to establish a single world authority ever came near achieving their goal. But they were not entirely without effect in mitigating the ravages of war between the states which gave them allegiance. And they provide us with several valuable object lessons in the art of supernational government. Why did they fail ? Firstly, because they were all based on the idea of a privileged class or race, a *Herrenvolk*, just as the Nazi and Japanese imperialisms were ; and when circumstances altered, the subject peoples rose and overthrew their masters. Second, because they did not remain strong enough to control their vassal states. Third, because they could not handle the problem of nationalism. It is permissible, then, to argue that any successful world authority must at the very least be democratic in the broadest sense, that it must have, and retain, an overwhelming preponderance of military strength, and that it must somehow find a way of solving the nationalist problem. This last factor requires some examination.

Nationalism is unquestionably the most powerful force in modern politics. The wars of the last hundred years have been neither religious, dynastic, nor ideological ; they have been wars of nationalism, in which the driving force behind the attacking armies has been the urge to improve the position of a nation. Nationalism, born in Renaissance days and heavily tinged with the doctrines of Machiavelli, has during the past few centuries brought about the collapse of the old multi-national empires of such dynasties as the Ottomans and Habsburgs, and has erected on their ruins new national states such as Spain, Italy, Germany, Egypt, Poland and Yugoslavia. And during the last decades of the nineteenth century nationalism spread from Europe into both Near and Far East, where it is now almost as dominant as in the West.

Now there is of course nothing essentially evil about nationalism itself. The first nationalist movements were movements of liberation, directed against corrupt and tyrannical dynasties, and supported by all the liberal and progressive opinion of the world. But by the twentieth century nationalism was no longer associated with such names as Garibaldi or Bolivar, but rather with those of Hitler, Mussolini and Franco. Political groups whose intentions were anything but democratic were finding it convenient to cluster under the banner of nationalism, from which point of vantage they could accuse their liberal opponents of endangering their respective countries by pursuing pacific foreign policies. So, by the nineteen-thirties, the word " national " was being used by the right-wing

[1] From the letter returned with Lord Macartney's mission.

parties of nearly every country in Europe, particularly by those which tended towards a one-party system and fascism. Nationalism had come to mean not so much the liberation of a nation as an aggressive attitude towards other nations. Its appeal was no longer used for liberal objectives, but against them.

At an early stage it became clear that, bloody as the dynastic and religious wars of the past had been, nationalist wars were going to be even more harmful to the world as a whole. For in those earlier wars the great masses of the peoples were seldom drawn into the actual fighting, which was done by small professional armies ; and when, as frequently happened, the warring monarchs wearied of the conflict, or were replaced by less belligerent successors, the peoples merely gave thanks that they would no longer be robbed by the soldiery of both parties, and went to work to repair the ravages of war. But nationalist conflicts are based on the *levée en masse*, on the strength of a whole people fully mobilized for war ; and in order to rouse a whole people to take up arms it is necessary to use all the forces of modern propaganda. This propaganda must aim at evoking fear, jealousy or hatred of the neighbour nation which it is proposed to attack ; and fear, jealousy and hatred, once implanted in the collective mentality of a people, are very hard to root out. Nationalism is the easiest of all creeds to propagate, for it satisfies the powerful herd instinct common to us all, and can easily be made to satisfy man's latent vanities and passions. So in recent years we have seen on all sides the devising of national flags and adopting of national anthems, the exploitation of folklore and folk culture, and the fabrication of myths and mysteries, all designed to strengthen the nationalist sentiment of the masses. And once militant nationalism has got a grip on the mind of a people, bringing with it all the hatreds and fears without which it cannot live, it is almost impossible to shake it off. This is the strength and the menace of nationalism.

During the nineteenth century, when the nationalist tide was rising fast in Europe, there were several attempts to recreate some sort of international unity. The "Congress System" set up by the victorious alliance which had defeated Napoleon was intended to keep the peace of Europe by holding regular international conferences ; but it was speedily corrupted by legitimists such as Metternich into a device for maintaining the supremacy of the more reactionary Powers, and the risings of 1848 swept it away and Metternich with it. Then, where the governments had failed, the forces of social revolution tried to rebuild the lost unity of the West, but got little further. The International Labour Association founded by Karl Marx, better known as the First International, met in London in 1864, but expired twelve years later. The Second International did not begin to function until 1889, when Marx was already dead. It survived long enough to indulge in a good deal of bickering with the Third International, or Comintern, when the latter was founded in the next century, but it was never more than a congress of national delegations without any real supernational aims.

By the end of the nineteenth century the destructive power of modern war had been demonstrated in a number of short campaigns, and the international situation was steadily deteriorating. In 1899 an attempt was made to stave off the approaching cataclysm. Tsar Nicholas II invited representatives of the principal sovereign states of Europe and America to a World Peace Conference at the Hague. A second Hague Conference, at which President Theodore Roosevelt was co-sponsor, was held in 1907. At these conferences a Convention for the Pacific Settlement of International Disputes was agreed upon, but its only concrete effect was to set up a panel of judges known as the Permanent Court of Arbitration, from which the parties to an international dispute could, if they so wished, choose arbitrators for their particular case. This court, better known as the Hague Tribunal, did in fact dispose of several minor disputes, but it was obvious from the outset that if there were any really serious differences between nations, they would not be submitted to it. At the second Hague Conference a draft constitution for a court with wider authority, to be called the Court of Arbitral Justice, was produced, but the Powers were unable to agree on the method of selection of judges, and the draft never took effect. The delegates to the 1907 conference agreed to meet again at the Hague at intervals, but the war of 1914–18 supervened, and the next major international gathering was the Peace Conference at Paris in 1919.

THE LEAGUE OF NATIONS

Casualties on the battlefields of the First World War amounted to over eight million dead, and the famine, disease and suffering which followed in the wake of the fighting killed millions more. When the war ended there was a universal clamour for a lasting peace.

As early as January 1918, President Woodrow Wilson had published a list of " Fourteen Points " on which he hoped to see the peace treaties based. The Fourteenth Point was the creation of a League of Nations, a permanent organization which would effectively prevent the outbreak of any further wars.[1] Other voices were raised in support of the same idea ; a British official committee headed by Lord Phillimore was appointed to work out a draft plan for consideration at the Paris peace conference ; important suggestions were also contributed by General Smuts.

During the peace conference there were numerous sessions of a special " Commission on the League of Nations," on which the principal Allied and Associated Powers were represented, together with two or three smaller nations. It was this commission which drew up the Covenant of

[1]The actual wording of the Fourteenth Point was :
" A general association of nations should be formed on the basis of covenants designed to create mutual guarantees of the political independence and territorial integrity of states, large and small equally."

the League on the basis of Wilson's and other drafts. Naturally the influence of the Great Powers was stronger in this small body than it would have been in a world conference such as that which, at San Francisco in 1945, drew up the Charter of the United Nations. In fact, the commission was dominated by President Wilson, Lord Cecil and the French representatives.

By a very shrewd stroke, Wilson had the Covenant of the League inserted at the head of the Treaty of Versailles and the other treaties of peace. This meant that every signatory to the treaties automatically subscribed to the Covenant. The mere fact that Wilson found this device necessary is evidence of the unwillingness of the Allied governments in general to accept the obligations which membership of the League would involve. In point of fact, while the people of every nation longed for peace, no government was willing to accept any really substantial limitation to its own absolute sovereignty. When we pass judgment upon the League, we must not blame its creators for the fact that, as things were in 1919, a stronger Covenant would simply have meant a League without members.

The Covenant came into force on January 10, 1920. 27 signatories to the peace treaties were listed as original members of the League, and 13 neutral states were invited to accede. The number of members mounted during the years that followed as ex-enemy states and new nations created by the peace treaties were admitted, and at one time or another the League included 16 states which are not at present members of the United Nations.[1] But from the very beginning there were two notable absentees.

Soviet Russia was of course only in its infancy when the Covenant was drafted, and it is of interest that in the Smuts proposals and certain other documents the suggestion was made that Russia should be included in the League ; but hostility to the new state was so strong among the leading members of the League that there was an almost complete severance of diplomatic relations with Russia, and it was not until 1934 that representatives of the Soviet Government took their places at Geneva. Even then they were obliged to withdraw again five years later as a result of the Russo-Finnish war. Naturally the absence of Russia weakened the League's standing as a world organization, and gave rise to a widely held belief that it was little more than an anti-Soviet combination. But the League might still have overcome a single deficiency even of this magnitude. Its chances of becoming an effective instrument for the preservation of universal peace were, however, practically eliminated from the start when it became clear that the United States was not going to join.

President Wilson had been fully aware of the strength of isolationist opinion in America when he launched his plan for the League, and he

---

[1]Afghanistan, Eire, Portugal, Spain, Sweden, Switzerland ; Albania, Bulgaria, Finland, Germany, Austria, Hungary, Italy, Japan, Rumania and Siam.

made every possible concession to his own people's instinctive reluctance to become involved in the affairs of Europe[1].

Even so, and in spite of the fact that to reject the League meant rejection of all the peace treaties, and the conclusion of a whole set of separate treaties, the United States Senate refused to ratify the Covenant[2] ; and at no time during the League's subsequent twenty-six years of life was there any sign of American willingness to accept the responsibilities of membership.

Without America or Russia, without Germany except for the seven years from 1926 to 1933, the League came inevitably to resemble a heterogeneous alliance headed by France and Britain, with Italy and Japan in the second rank. There are some who say that there is no need to look further for the cause of the League's failure.

The organs set up by the Covenant in 1920 were all forerunners of similar organs now established under the United Nations Charter, but there were substantial differences in their respective powers. The League had an Assembly, in which each member state had three representatives but only one vote. It had a Council on which only a few states were represented, and which was therefore better equipped to handle urgent business than the Assembly. It had a Permanent Court of International Justice ; it had a commission on mandates, which covered much the same ground as the United Nations Trusteeship Council, but occupied a much less important position ; and it had a Secretary-General and an international secretariat. There was no body corresponding to the Economic and Social Council now set up by the United Nations ; but in separate sections of the peace treaties which embodied the Covenant there was set out a charter for a semi-independent International Labour Organization.[3]

The objectives of the ILO were far more limited than those of the Economic and Social Council, but in certain respects it achieved an importance of its own. Its membership eventually came to include the United States, as well as several nations which had withdrawn from the League ; and it survived the winding-up of its parent organization in 1946.

The Assembly of the League, like that of the United Nations, was a deliberative and advisory, rather than an executive body. It was

[1]The most astonishing of these concessions was the inclusion in the very first article of the Covenant of a clause permitting any member state to withdraw by simply giving notice. When other members of the drafting commission pointed out that this gave the impression that even the authors of the Covenant did not expect the League to survive, Wilson replied that unless withdrawal was specifically envisaged in the Covenant, it would be impossible for the United States to join. The Charter of the United Nations does not even mention the idea of any member state withdrawing.

[2]To be strictly accurate, the Senate offered to ratify the Covenant subject to the " Lodge reservations," which were too crippling for even the conciliatory President to accept.

[3]The ILO is discussed at greater length in Chapter 8.

authorized in general terms to "deal at its meetings with any matter within the sphere of action of the League or affecting the peace of the world."[1] ; but it was given no substantial powers with which to ensure that its decisions were carried out. Meeting regularly every September, and authorized to meet in extraordinary session whenever a majority of member states agreed to attend, it could discuss any circumstance brought to its notice by a member state which " threatened to disturb international peace or the good understanding between nations on which peace depends."[2] Disputes between member states were normally a matter for the Council, but either party to a dispute could insist upon the Council referring the case to the Assembly, providing this was done within 14 days after submission of the dispute to the Council. When this happened, the Assembly possessed the same powers as the Council would have in similar circumstances. It could investigate the whole situation and try to bring about a settlement ; and, if this attempt failed, it could announce its recommendations. If these recommendations had the approval of all the members of the Council and of a majority of the other members of the Assembly, excluding in each case the parties to the dispute, then, under Article 15 of the Covenant, member states were bound " not to go to war with any party to the dispute which complies with the recommendations." It will be seen that this, the Assembly's only specific means of making its decisions effective, was a somewhat shadowy authority.

Under Article 19 of the Covenant the Assembly was given the right to advise member states on the revision of treaties ; under Article 26 it possessed a share in the process of amending the Covenant ; and Article 4 empowered it to elect a proportion of the members of the Council. But in general the Assembly was no more than a forum in which representatives of the nations could air their views ; and if there was anywhere in the League structure an organ capable of actively maintaining peace, it was not the Assembly but the Council.

The Council of the League was originally designed to consist of five permanent and four non-permanent members. The permanent seats were to be held by the " Principal Allied and Associated Powers," that is to say the United States, the British Empire, France, Italy and Japan. The other four members of the Council were to be " selected by the Assembly from time to time in its discretion."[3]

This composition was subject to frequent changes. In the first place, the United States never occupied the seat allotted to her, thereby reducing the initial membership of the Council to eight. Two additional non-permanent seats were created in 1922, and three more in 1926 ; in the latter year Germany was granted a permanent seat, and the Council thus

[1]Article 3 of the Covenant.
[2]Article 11 of the Covenant.
[3]Article 4 of the Covenant.

came to comprise five permanent and nine elected members.[1] In 1933 a tenth non-permanent seat was created, and Germany and Japan—both permanent members of the Council—gave notice of withdrawal from the League ; and in 1934 the Soviet Union joined the League and was given a permanent seat. In 1936 a further non-permanent seat was added, making the membership of the Council fifteen (four permanent and eleven elected). The subsequent elimination of both Italy and the Soviet Union left Britain and France the only permanent members in a Council of thirteen.[2]

The term of office of non-permanent members of the Council was fixed at three years by rules of procedure adopted in 1926, and in making the elections the Assembly followed the principle that the Council should always be approximately representative of the various regions, races, and civilizations of the world.[3]

The Council met, on an average, five or six times a year, usually at the League Headquarters in Geneva, but occasionally in other cities. Like the Assembly, it was authorized to deal with " any matter within the sphere of action of the League or affecting the peace of the world." But the Covenant also gave it several specific powers which, although the looseness of the language in which they were phrased has been much criticized, were yet far more precise than any that the Assembly possessed.

Firstly, in the event of any act or threat of aggression, the Council was authorized to advise member states upon the means by which they should fulfil their undertaking in the Covenant to preserve the territorial integrity and political independence of all other members.[4]

Secondly, should any member of the League resort to war in defiance of its covenants, it would be deemed to have committed an act of war against all other members, and these would then be obliged to impose " sanctions," in other words, to sever economic relations with it. In such an event it was the duty of the Council " to recommend to the several

[1]In the same year Brazil demanded the creation of an additional permanent seat for herself, and, when this was refused, withdrew from the League.
[2]All these fluctuations were made possible by the fact that the Covenant empowered the Council to create additional seats, subject to the approval of the Assembly. There is no such provision in the Charter of the United Nations.
[3]For example, in 1930 and 1938 the elected members of the Council were :

	1930	1938
(Northern Europe)	Finland	Sweden and Latvia
(Western Europe)	Spain	Belgium
(Eastern Europe)	Yugoslavia and Poland	Yugoslavia and Greece
(Middle East)	Iran	Iran
(Far East)	—	China
(Pacific)	—	New Zealand
(North America)	Canada	—
(Central America)	Cuba	Dominican Republic
(South America)	Venezuela and Peru	Bolivia and Peru

[4]Article 10 of the Covenant.

governments concerned what effective military, naval or air force the Members of the League shall severally contribute to the armed forces to be used to protect the covenants of the League."[1] There was nothing in the Covenant to indicate how these forces would be employed.

Thirdly, the Covenant made it obligatory for member states to refer to the Council any dispute which they had not submitted to arbitration or judicial decision ; and, moreover, to accept and " carry out in full good faith any award or decision that may be rendered." In the event of any failure to carry out such an award or decision, the Council was empowered to " propose what steps should be taken to give effect thereto."[2]

Fourthly, the Council could expel from the League any member state which had violated the Covenant.[3]

The Council's other functions included the formulating of plans for the reduction of national armaments and the regulation of private manufacture of arms,[4] and the general supervision, through the Permanent Commission, of the system of mandates established by the Covenant.[5]

Now it will be seen that the way in which the first three of the Council's powers were framed made it quite clear that the real responsibility for action to defend peace lay with member states, and not with the Council, whose role was limited to making recommendations. The only really substantial authority given to the Council was the fourth, the power to expel any offending member state ; and there was nothing very terrible about expulsion when so many major powers were already outside the League.

There was a further provision in the Covenant which limited the effectiveness of both Assembly and Council. This was the unanimity rule, by which all important decisions in either body required the agreement of all member states present and voting. There were certain exceptions to this principle, the most important of which provided that in reaching unanimity on a report concerning a dispute between member states, neither Assembly nor Council need reckon the votes of the parties to the dispute.[6] There was, however, no such provision in cases where it was proposed to take economic or military measures against an aggressor ; and it was therefore possible for any member state to veto the application of any such measures against itself.[7]

[1]Article 16 of the Covenant.
[2]Articles 13 and 15 of the Covenant.
[3]Article 16 of the Covenant.
[4]Article 8 of the Covenant.
[5]Article 22 of the Covenant.
[6]Article 15 of the Covenant.
[7]In 1938 the Assembly received a British proposal to exclude the votes of any parties involved when decisions were being taken on the action necessary to deal with a threat of war under Article 11 of the Covenant. 29 votes were cast for this proposal and 2 against ; under the unanimity rule it was, therefore, not carried.

From this necessarily brief survey of the structure of the League it is clear that that structure was by no means perfect. There is still a great deal of argument as to the real cause of the League's failure. Some argue that the system could have been worked if only the member states had fulfilled their obligations. Others maintain that the defects inherent in the Covenant itself were enough to enable any aggressive minority group to sabotage the whole organization. There is no room here to set out in full the arguments of the two contending schools. But in justice to Wilson and his fellow pioneers, it must be said that their Covenant represents an advance in the development of world organization so huge and so unprecedented that it will inevitably take its place as a turning-point in human history. No subsequent organization aiming at the preservation of world peace could afford to ignore the example of the League ; in fact, no subsequent organization could avoid taking a form approximately similar to that of the League. The League may have been based on a Covenant full of loopholes ; it may have failed from the very beginning to achieve the universality which was essential to its success ; it may have become an instrument in the hands of a faction ; it may have been betrayed by its members in its hour of crisis. Certainly it has failed. But the League idea has not failed. Reformed and revitalized, it is the idea behind the Uinted Nations.

Speaking in London in October 1941, before the world had even heard the name of the " United Nations," Mr. Attlee said, " The principle that there must be in the world force to support the rule of Law has been reaffirmed in the Atlantic Charter. . . . The only way to preserve peace is to bind together all the peace-loving peoples and endow them with a force sufficient to prevent aggression. It may be that the old League of Nations will not be recreated, but I am certain that its principles must be applied if we are to have a peaceful and ordered world."

THE YEARS BETWEEN THE WARS

From the moment of its birth the League had to fight for its life against two equally dangerous attitudes of mind, the cynical indifference of those who thought the whole League idea a waste of time, and the vapid optimism of those who believed that once the League was established, war would automatically be banished from the earth. It must not be thought that Geneva itself was permeated with complacency. On the contrary, it was the apathy of the wider public which vitiated the efforts made by the more far-sighted of the Allied statesmen to strengthen the arm of peace.

Some of these efforts took the form of proposals to amend the Covenant ; others were framed in wholly separate conventions. As early as 1921, amendments which freed the application of sanctions from some of the restrictions imposed by Article 16 of the Covenant were passed by the Assembly ; but these amendments were never ratified by a sufficient number of governments to take effect. In 1923 a draft " Treaty of Mutual Assistance " was submitted to the Assembly as a proposed supplement to the Covenant. It specified formulæ for determining which party to a conflict was the aggressor, defined obligations in the matter of mutual assistance, and provided for regional agreements. The fifth Assembly of the League was unable to reach unanimity on this draft, and it was abandoned ; but next year the Assembly adopted a second supplementary proposal, generally known as the Geneva Protocol. This protocol included a general prohibition of war ; it defined the aggressor in any given conflict as that state which refused to accept either arbitration or the decision of the Council ; it made it obligatory for all states to impose sanctions once an aggressor had been identified, and it provided that all international disputes must be submitted either to the Council, or to a board of arbitration, or to the Permanent Court of International Justice, and that in either case the decision of the reviewing body would be binding. The Geneva Protocol was accepted by 14 nations, but by 1925 it became clear that it would not be accepted by several major Powers, and it was dropped. The opposition to the Protocol was chiefly directed against the idea of compulsory acceptance of judicial or arbitral decisions, and against the possibility, implicit in the new formula, of heavy economic burdens in the matter of sanctions. In more simple language, the members of the League were less concerned with fulfilling the spirit of the Covenant than with interpreting its letter so as to dodge as much responsibility as possible.

In 1928 the Assembly adopted, and threw open to accession by all states, a " General Act of Arbitration for the Pacific Settlement of International Disputes." This General Act provided procedures of conciliation, judicial settlement, and arbitration, intended to increase the security of member states and so to facilitate the long-delayed process of disarmament. By 1938 it had received 23 accessions, including those of the United Kingdom, France and Italy. But the General Act was overshadowed by a far more optimistic agreement which was also drawn up in 1928. This was the Pact of Paris, often called the Kellogg-Briand Pact. By 1939 this pact had been accepted by 63 states, including nine non-members of the League ; there were, in fact, only five countries in the whole world where it was not binding.[1] The signatories to the Pact " solemnly declare in the names of their respective peoples that they condemn recourse to war for the solution of international controversies, and renounce it as an instrument of national policy in their relations with one another. . . . The High Contracting Parties agree that the settlement or solution of all disputes or conflicts, of whatever nature or of whatever origin they may be, which may arise between them, shall never be sought except by pacific means."

[1] Argentina, Bolivia, Salvador, Uruguay and the Yemen.

In specifically prohibiting any resort to war as an instrument of policy, the Kellogg-Briand Pact went considerably further than the Covenant of the League ; and, unlike the Covenant, it was accepted by the United States of America. But the fact that within a few years of its signature over fifty of its signatories were already at war is convincing proof of the futility of pacific protestations unsupported by machinery capable of enforcing their provisions.

Another approach to the problem of international security that was continually under discussion during the years between the wars was disarmament. In 1920 the first Assembly of the League had set up a commission to examine the whole question of disarmament in relation to collective security. This commission remained in being until 1924, but achieved no constructive results. In 1925 the League set up a second commission to prepare a draft convention for discussion at a general international conference on the reduction and limitation of armaments ; and finally, in 1932, the Disarmament Conference assembled at Geneva. 65 nations, including the United States and four other non-members of the League, were represented. But although a general measure of agreement was achieved, the prospects of unanimous agreement on a Disarmament Convention were completely destroyed when the Nazis came to power in Germany in 1933 and thereupon withdrew that country from both the Conference and the League. The remaining governments represented at the Conference continued to exchange views on disarmament until 1937, but nothing emerged from the exchanges.

Meanwhile the League had succeeded, during the first ten years of its life, in handling a number of petty international disputes without departing from the principles of the Covenant. It was not until 1931 that it encountered its first major failure. In that year China appealed to the League to settle the question of Manchuria, which was being occupied by the Japanese. The League Council sent out a Commission of Enquiry headed by Lord Lytton, and in 1933 the Assembly adopted the Commission's report and unanimously condemned Japan's aggressive action. Japan thereupon announced her intention of withdrawing from the League, and rejected the Assembly's recommendations for settlement of the Manchurian problem. It was perfectly clear that Japan had violated the Covenant, and that all member states of the League were legally bound, under Article 10, to defend the territorial integrity of China ; but there was not a government in the whole world which was prepared to honour this bond. There was not even an attempt to apply sanctions ; and Japan remained in undisputed and undisturbed possession of Manchuria.

The position of the League was, however, strengthened in 1934 by the adherence of the Soviet Union. Soviet hostility to the Powers represented on the League Council was now less strong than the feeling that only through the League could peace be preserved.[1] But even with Russian support, the League was doomed to undergo a second major defeat in the ensuing year. In January 1935, the Ethiopian government pointed out to the Council that Italian actions on the Ethiopian frontier constituted a threat to peace as defined in Article 11 of the Covenant. Throughout the spring and summer the Council used every means at its disposal to arrange a settlement of the Italo–Ethiopian problem ; but in October Italian troops crossed the Ethiopian frontier in force, and the Council promptly declared that Italy was deemed, under Article 16, to have committed an act of war against all other members of the League. Even so, there was no suggestion that member states should fully implement their obligations to defend the territorial integrity of Ethiopia. Sanctions were imposed in a half-hearted manner which barely affected Italy's military potential. She was deprived of certain useful imports, but there was no attempt to limit supplies of oil, the most essential of all her wartime needs, and the Suez Canal remained open for the passage of her armies. Mussolini took the attitude that if any really crippling sanctions were imposed, Italy would be forced to fight the nations responsible, and the members of the League were not prepared to run the risk of war. Sanctions were finally lifted in July 1936, two months after Italy had formally annexed Ethiopia. Italy remained a member both of the League and of its Council.

The Manchurian and Ethiopian catastrophes effectively destroyed the League's position as a world security organization. Although the Council and the Assembly received several subsequent appeals, particularly from Spain and China, the world had ceased to have any faith in the possibility of preventing aggression through the machinery of Geneva. The 1936 Assembly set up a committee of representatives of 28 states to examine the question of more effective application of the spirit of the Covenant. Discussions on the reform of the League were still in progress when the next wave of aggression swept across Europe, engulfing in turn Austria, Czechoslovakia, Albania and Poland, and precipitating the general holocaust from which the world has just emerged.

The League of Nations is now dead. It survived the war, the diminished secretariat at Geneva occupying itself with statistical and other similar duties ; and in April 1946 the Assembly met for the last time to liquidate the organization and dispose of the assets. The Permanent Court of International Justice was closed, but its successor resembles it so closely as to be practically indistinguishable. The International Labour Organization was successfully amputated from its parent body, and survives as a

---

[1]In December 1933, Stalin said that, "notwithstanding the withdrawal of Germany and Japan, or perhaps just because of this, the League may become something of a brake to retard the beginning of military operations, or to hinder them." In September 1934, *Izvestia* said in an editorial that the Soviet Union was entering the League " in order to support those Powers which will struggle for the preservation and the consolidation of peace."

living link with the past. The territories held by various states under League mandates are being transferred to the care of the trusteeship system set up by the United Nations.

In a report to the League Assembly made in 1945, the acting secretary-general, Mr. Sean Lester, wrote :

" The first ' great experiment ' in international co-operation for peace and human progress has been made. Its lessons must now contribute to the success of the second experiment. The powers of destruction which would be let loose in a new conflict do not permit the envisaging of a possible failure."

THE CRISIS WE FACE

The fantasies of yesterday are the realities of today. It is only a few years since Mr. H. G. Wells outlined with vigorous inventiveness his vision of a war which would utterly destroy civilization as we know it. Now we already live under the shadow of such a war. The fantasy has become sober reality.

It is not the first time that mankind has faced a threat of this nature. Earlier civilizations have been overwhelmed by such disasters as pestilence, climatic change, or barbarian invasion. But no civilization has ever before perished, as ours may perish, by its own hand.

What new factors have created this unprecedented crisis in human affairs ? How has it come about that we of the twentieth century, who see more clearly than our ancestors how futile and inglorious war is, who know how easily our delicate and complex economy can be disrupted, should live in fear of a disaster which can only be precipitated by our own stupidity ?

There is nothing new about man's propensity to war. War has been part of the history of our species since that history began. Indeed, some philosophers have concluded in despair that it is an ineradicable element in the nature of humanity itself. The two hideous conflicts through which the world has passed in recent years were on a scale so vast as to dwarf, for us, all the wars that ever were before them. But in fact there have been several previous tragedies, such as the Thirty Years War or the invasions of Genghis Khan, which loomed just as large and as terrible on the smaller horizons of their own times. And we must remember that minor conflicts, sporadic in some parts of the world, almost uninterrupted in others, have been responsible in the long run for an amount of bloodshed and suffering fully comparable to that caused by the greater wars.

Modern man is in fact no more warlike than his ancestors ; on the contrary, having with much labour surrounded himself with more material comfort than earlier generations ever knew, he is naturally all the more reluctant to get involved in any sort of violence. But he has been unfortunate enough to develop his purely technical powers without a corresponding increase in his political capabilities. On the one hand, he has worked out techniques for the mobilization of the whole strength of a nation and has produced, in the long-range bomber, the rocket, and the atomic bomb, weapons powerful enough to destroy cities and their populations. On the other, he has failed to find any practical method of preventing war.

The crisis of our time is, quite simply, the impact of twentieth-century destructive power upon the age-old chaos which we are polite enough to call " the international situation." It is the impact of invention upon confusion. Invention cannot be undone ; our only hope of saving civilization lies, therefore, in finding a means of ending the confusion.

We must find it quickly. The war of 1939–45, in which rocket projectiles were only used towards the end and only two atomic bombs fell at all, was yet sufficiently destructive to set human progress back by several generations. In Europe alone over twenty million people perished ; and over vast areas of the earth's surface those who survived the war are now living the life of troglodytes on a near-starvation diet. But it is already clear that the arrival of the " atomic age " has brought in its train the possibility of outbursts of destruction on an incomparably greater scale. However badly the world needed an organization capable of ensuring peace before 1945, its need is far greater today. The plain fact is that just one more major war could easily destroy our civilization. That is why we need the United Nations ; that is why this " second experiment " must not fail.

CHAPTER II

HOW DID THE UNITED NATIONS BEGIN ?

THE NAME AND ITS APPLICATIONS

THE term " United Nations " was first used by President Roosevelt and Mr. Churchill shortly after Pearl Harbour. At that time it meant no more than a fighting alliance ; but from the very first it was hoped that by substituting " United Nations " for the purely military term " allies," the governments engaged in fighting the Axis would be enabled to go ahead more rapidly with plans for continued co-operation after the war. Long-term arrangements as regards food, relief, finance and other urgent problems were in fact made in the name of the United Nations long before the principal organization itself was set up.

As a result of the consistent use of the term " United Nations " in all the international projects of the allied countries since 1942, the following organizations are now associated with the name :—

a. The United Nations (commonly, but not officially, called the United Nations Organization, and abbreviated to UNO). The General Assembly, Security Council, Economic and Social Council, Trustee-ship Council and International Court of Justice are component organs of the United Nations.

b. The United Nations Relief and Rehabilitation Administration (UNRRA).

c. The United Nations Educational, Scientific and Cultural Organiza-tion (UNESCO).

d. The Food and Agriculture Organization of the United Nations (FAO).

e. The International Monetary Fund and the International Bank for Reconstruction and Development, whose creation was agreed upon by the United Nations Monetary and Financial Conference at Bretton Woods.

The list of member states varies for each organization, but provision is made in each case for the admission at a later date not only of allied countries which were not founding members, but also of other countries which are acceptable to the general body of members.

The Charter of the United Nations directs that " the various specialized agencies established by international agreement . . . shall be brought into relationship with the United Nations."[1] The last four of the above five organizations will then become integral parts of the first.

[1] Articles 57 and 63.

Throughout the chapters which follow, the term " United Nations " standing by itself, refers always to the Organization set up by the San Francisco Charter. The international agencies which do not derive their powers from that Charter are discussed in Chapter 8. It must be remembered that although the Charter anticipates that they will eventually become parts of that Organization, this has not yet taken place.

Much doubt has been expressed whether the phrase " United Nations " should take a singular or a plural verb. Logically, when the United Nations were merely fighting allies, they were plural ; but now that the Charter has specifically created " an organization to be known as the United Nations," this organization, being singular, takes a singular verb, as can be seen from Article 8 of the Charter.

CONCEPTION : WASHINGTON AND MOSCOW

The first official appearance of the words " United Nations " in an international agreement was in Washington on January 1, 1942. The " Joint Declaration by United Nations " signed on that date by representatives of 26 Allied countries[1] was in itself no more than a pledge of wholehearted co-operation against the Axis. But it included the significant statement that the signatory governments " subscribed to a common declaration of purposes and principles embodied in the joint declaration of the President of the United States and the Prime Minister of Great Britain and Northern Ireland, dated August 14, 1941, known as the Atlantic Charter."

The Washington Declaration may therefore be said to have embodied some small part of the ideas ultimately realized in the creation of the United Nations as an organization. For in the Atlantic Charter we find the following principles stated :

" . . . They (the United States and the United Kingdom) believe that all of the nations of the world, for realistic as well as spiritual reasons, must come to the abandonment of the use of force. . . ."

" . . . They believe, *pending the establishment of a wider and permanent system of general security*, that the disarmament of . . . nations which threaten aggression outside of their frontiers . . . is essential."

" They desire to bring about the fullest collaboration between all nations in the economic field, with the object of securing for all improved labour standards, economic advancement, and social security."

Neither the Atlantic Charter nor the Washington Declaration made any definite proposals for the " establishment of a wider and permanent system of general security." But during the months that followed, opinion in the

[1]China, Soviet Union, United Kingdom, United States ; Canada, Australia, South Africa, New Zealand, India ; Belgium, the Netherlands, Czechoslovakia, Greece, Luxembourg, Norway, Poland, Yugoslavia; Costa Rica, Cuba, the Dominican Republic, Salvador, Guatemala, Haiti, Honduras, Nicaragua and Panama.

allied countries became more and more convinced of the need for such a
system. Mr. Sumner Welles, United States Under-Secretary of State,
said in May 1942, " I believe the voices of the men who will make our
victory possible will demand . . . that the United Nations become the
nucleus of a world organization." A month later, Mr. T. V. Soong, foreign
minister of China, told a Yale University audience that, " . . . past failures
have not dimmed our hopes that an effective world instrument to dispense
and enforce justice will arise from the sufferings and sacrifices of this war,
and for such an international government, China, with all other liberty-
loving nations, will gladly cede such of its sovereign powers as may be
required." In December Mr. Eden told the House of Commons that
" our general object is to form a world system for ensuring the peaceful
development of all peoples." In February 1943 Mr. Herbert Morrison
spoke in the Guildhall of " a genuinely representative world political
association." In March Mr. Churchill spoke of " the future world
organization " in a broadcast to the British people. And in June the
Foreign Affairs Committee of the American House of Representatives unanimously adopted a resolution " that the Congress expresses itself as
favouring the creation of appropriate international machinery with power
adequate to establish and maintain a just and lasting peace among the
nations of the world, and as favouring participation therein by the United
States."

But the machinery which ultimately created the United Nations Organization in its present form was not set in motion until the conference of
foreign ministers met in Moscow in October 1943.

The Moscow Declaration, signed on October 30 by the foreign ministers
of the Soviet Union, the United States and the United Kingdom, and by
the Chinese Ambassador in Moscow, declared in its fourth article that,
" . . . the four Powers recognize the necessity of establishing at the
earliest practicable date a general international organization, based on the
principle of the sovereign equality of all peace-loving states, large and small,
for the maintenance of international peace and security."

In December 1943, at the two conferences held at Cairo and Teheran,
personal discussions took place between President Roosevelt, Mr.
Churchill, Marshal Stalin and Marshal Chiang Kai-Shek, and a general
measure of agreement on the establishment of an international organization
was reached between the four Great Powers.

Meanwhile, although no legal government of France now existed, the
leaders of Free France had indicated their agreement with the principles
of the Washington Declaration, as had also the Danish Minister in the
United States. Other new adherents to the Declaration were Mexico,
the Philippine Commonwealth, Ethiopia, Iraq, Brazil, Bolivia, Iran and
Colombia. The United Nations team was shaping up.

SPADEWORK : DUMBARTON OAKS, 1944

From August 21 to October 7, 1944, representatives of the four Great Powers, assembled at the Dumbarton Oaks estate near Washington, worked on a detailed plan as a basis for discussion of the new organization.

Inevitably, the Dumbarton Oaks plan owed much to the Covenant of the League of Nations. For example, it proposed to create a large Assembly in which all nations would be represented, and a small, manageable Council. Naturally a great experiment in internationalism like the League, however obvious its failings appear in the perspective of time, was still a source from which many practical techniques for international co-operation could be lifted.

But there were a number of important points at which the Dumbarton Oaks planners broke away from League precedent. It is generally agreed today that one of the League's principal weaknesses was its lack of armed force. The 1944 plan took as one of its basic premises the idea that, to be effective in maintaining peace, the new organization must have substantial forces ready under its hand.

There has been much discussion in recent years about the creation of an " international police force " which would prevent aggression anywhere in the world. Obviously there would be great advantages in providing an international organization with a single force in which men from every country, recruited without discrimination, and owing loyalty not to any particular government but only to the United Nations, served side by side. But the planners at Dumbarton Oaks had to face the hard fact that every trained soldier, sailor and airman alive today has taken an oath of allegiance to one country or another. So the only immediately practicable method of providing the United Nations with armed forces was for the member nations to undertake to maintain specified contingents on which the United Nations could call at short notice.

The Dumbarton Oaks plan proposed that a small Security Council should be set up as one of the principal organs of the new organization, so that any serious threat to peace could be dealt with expeditiously. This Council was to be charged with the primary responsibility of maintaining peace and security, and empowered to call upon the member states for the national contingents which they would have to undertake to provide.

It was also agreed at Dumbarton Oaks that since the nations which at present possess the strongest armed forces would shoulder most of the responsibility for the maintenance of peace, they should be represented on the Security Council more strongly than the smaller nations. This was to be affected by making the Great Powers permanent members of the Council, while all other countries were to be eligible for election to the non-permanent seats. On the other hand, it was recognized that in the General Assembly all nations, large and small alike, should be on an equal footing and should each control one vote only, regardless of population. The same principle was to be followed in the proposed Economic and Social Council, whose members would all be elected by the General Assembly.

On one point the conference at Dumbarton Oaks failed to reach agreement. This concerned the procedure for voting within the Security Council, which was later to be the subject of the fiercest debates of the whole San Francisco conference. But a working formula to cover this point was reached between President Roosevelt, Mr. Churchill and Marshal Stalin at the Yalta conference in February 1945. It was also agreed at this conference that representatives of all the United Nations[1] should be invited to discuss the Dumbarton Oaks plan at a conference to be held at San Francisco on April 25, 1945.

CONSTITUTION : SAN FRANCISCO, 1945

The sponsoring Powers invited to San Francisco all nations which were at war with one or more of the Axis Powers, and which had adhered to the Washington Declaration of January 1, 1942. 46 national delegations were present when the conference opened.

During the conference, four more nations were admitted to membership of the organization, and their representatives accordingly took their places in the conference rooms. Two of these were the Ukrainian and Byelorussian Soviet Socialist Republics, whose claims had been pressed by the Soviet Union at the Yalta meeting. The third was Denmark, and the fourth Argentina, whose application, supported by the United States, was strongly opposed by the Soviet delegation. The total number of delegations at San Francisco thus became 50.

The official number of originating members of the United Nations is, however, 51, the fifty-first being Poland. When issuing invitations to the San Francisco conference, the sponsoring Powers had not been able to agree to recognize a properly constituted government of Poland, and there were therefore no Polish representatives at the conference. But towards the end of the session, as progress was being made in the formation of a Polish government which could be recognized by the sponsoring powers, it was agreed that Poland should rank as an originating member. Space was accordingly left on the Charter for the signatures of her representatives, which were duly added at a later date ; and Article 3 of the Charter provided that the original members of the United Nations should be those states which had either attended the San Francisco Conference or signed the Washington Declaration of 1942. Poland qualified as an original member under the latter proviso.

[1]Between the Moscow Declaration and the San Francisco Conferences the following nations signified their adherence to the Washington Declaration and so joined the ranks of the United Nations : Liberia, Chile, Ecuador, Paraguay, Peru, Venezuela, Uruguay, Turkey, Egypt, Saudi Arabia, Syria and Lebanon.

The San Francisco Conference, officially known as the United Nations Conference on International Organization (UNCIO), lasted a little over two months. When the delegates met they had before them not only the Dumbarton Oaks plan as agreed to by the four sponsoring Powers, but also a mass of proposed amendments sent in by the other nations represented. These amendments totalled an estimated 12,000 items, although this figure includes many proposals, tabled independently by different nations, which overlapped or were substantially similar. The sponsoring Powers themselves contributed a further list of 24 joint proposals, developing and elaborating their original ideas.

The most important of the new proposals concerned trusteeship. The Dumbarton Oaks plan had made no provision for the administration of non-self-governing territories. This subject was raised in the amendments sent in by several governments, and a comprehensive draft plan was jointly presented by the United States and the United Kingdom.

In order to get through the details of the Dumbarton Oaks plan and the amendments within a reasonable time,[1] the Conference agreed to divide the plan into four sections, under the headings of General Provisions, General Assembly, Security Council, and Judicial Organization. Four commissions were then organized to examine the four sections and the amendments proposed for each section. Each nation was represented on each commission, and the posts of chairmen and *rapporteurs* were equitably distributed between all the nations present. The commissions in turn set up smaller sub-committees to examine particular parts of their respective sections. After the opening plenary sessions of the Conference, in which the chairman of the various delegations expressed their countries' attitudes to the general purposes of the United Nations, the commissions and sub-committees got down to a solid six weeks of hard work, arguing their way through the whole plan sentence by sentence. To be included in the Charter, every article or amendment had to receive the support of two-thirds of the members present and voting in each commission. The reports of the four commissions were laid before a co-ordination committee which ironed out inconsistencies and presented a final draft of the Charter to the ninth plenary session of the Conference. This draft was adopted by acclamation, and on June 26 the final text of the Charter, prepared in English, French, Russian, Chinese and Spanish, was duly signed by all the delegations.

The fact that the Dumbarton Oaks plan, the basis for the Charter, was drawn up by four Great Powers, and that most of the amendments to it proposed at San Francisco came from smaller countries, sometimes gave the conference the appearance of a struggle between large nations and small in which now one side and now the other seemed to be winning. Actually

[1] The surrender of Germany only a few days after the Conference had assembled undoubtedly heightened the atmosphere of urgency at San Francisco.

the debates were mostly many-sided, both small nations and Great Powers often arguing vigorously among themselves. But the smaller nations succeeded in making important alterations to the Dumbarton Oaks plan in three matters, concerning respectively the General Assembly, the Economic and Social Council, and the Security Council.

The powers of the General Assembly had been very restricted in the Dumbarton Oaks proposals. At San Francisco, owing to the pressure of the smaller nations, the Assembly was given much broader powers. It was authorized to receive and consider reports from the Security Council on all its actions intended to safeguard peace, and from the other organs of the United Nations ; and in other ways its status vis-a-vis the Security Council and the other organs was improved.

The status of the Economic and Social Council was also considerably raised during the San Francisco Conference. Several different nations contributed proposals which were incorporated in the Charter and whose effect was to expand the Council's authority. Among points successfully urged by smaller nations were the inclusion of health and education among the responsibilities of this Council, and the substitution of " full employment " for the more limited objective of " high and stable employment."

As was somewhat natural, the smaller nations were concerned more with the limitation than with the extension of the powers of the Security Council. The Dumbarton Oaks plan empowered the Security Council to call into use the military contingents of nations not represented on the Council. This was amended at San Francisco so that if the Council found it necessary to call upon the military contingents of a nation which was not represented on the Council at that time, that nation would have the right to participate in Council meetings which decided the disposition of the contingents concerned.

The most hotly contested point in the whole Charter concerned the voting procedure of the Security Council. As finally signed the Charter provides that, on all matters other than procedure, the Council must approve decisions by at least seven out of eleven votes, including the concurring votes of the five permanent members.[1] This gives to any one of the five the power to veto decisions agreed upon by all the other nations.

This " Great Power veto " was strongly opposed by many delegations, but it was eventually embodied in the Charter. It was agreed, however, that when one of the five Powers was a party to a dispute before the Council it must refrain from voting on that dispute.

In the Dumbarton Oaks draft there was nothing comparable to the Preamble which now stands at the head of the Charter. Representatives of smaller nations took the lead in the drafting of this Preamble, in securing it its present place of honour, and in ensuring that its terms would be

[1]China, France, Soviet Union, United Kingdom, United States.

considered as binding as those in the numbered Articles which follow it. In this task an outstanding part was played by Field-Marshal Smuts, who thus repeated, after an interval of twenty-six years, the distinguished role he had played during the drafting of the Covenant of the League.

Another difficult issue discussed at San Francisco was whether the Charter should provide machinery for the revision of treaties. In the Covenant of the League of Nations provisions had been made for the reconsideration of treaties on the grounds that they were no longer suitable. While it was generally agreed by the Conference that treaties between states must sometimes be altered to suit changed conditions, it was also appreciated that the mere mention of treaty revision in the League Covenant had led to heated " revisionist " propaganda with regard to the 1919 treaties. The consensus of opinion at San Francisco was that it would be better to omit any specific reference to treaty revision from the Charter.

Other controversies which engaged the attention of the Conference for some time concerned regionalism, non-self-governing territories and the International Court. It was finally agreed that regional agreements would be accepted as part of the new world organization provided that the acts of the regional groups were consistent with the principles of the United Nations. As regards non-self-governing territories, it was agreed that the United Nations should supervise their administration through a trustee-ship system, but there was disagreement on the exact aims of trusteeship. Some nations urged that the territories concerned should be helped to become " independent," others preferred the term " self-governing," as implying that small territories could, if they chose, profit by remaining parts of larger aggregations of territories. It was eventually decided that the trusteeship system should promote " development towards self-govern-ment or independence, as may be appropriate to the particular circum-stances of each territory and its peoples."[1]

The difficulty that arose over the International Court was that, if to sign the Charter meant to accept without question the jurisdiction of the Court on all legal disputes, several countries would probably refuse to accept the Charter at all. The Statute of the International Court had to be accepted by all signatories as an integral part of the Charter, but in its ultimate form it left each member state free to decide whether it would unreservedly accept the jurisdiction of the Court.

Finally, there was the question of future amendments to the Charter itself. After considerable discussion, during which the sponsoring Powers brought in several different proposals, it was agreed that amendments could be effected if two-thirds of the General Assembly voted for them, and provided they were then ratified by the governments of two-thirds of the United Nations, including the five permanent members of the Security Council.

[1]Article 76.

B

Naturally, the fact that the Charter was unanimously adopted by all the 50 nations present does not imply that it was perfectly satisfactory to all the signatories. Perfection would have been impossible, for the simple reason that governments, like individuals, have different points of view, and on some important matters are practically irreconcilable. But the fact that delegates representing some eighteen hundred million people, more than 80 per cent of the whole population of the world, were able to sink their differences and find enough common ground to enable them all to sign the Charter, was an event without precedent in the history of mankind.

IN RUNNING ORDER : LONDON, 1946

The signing of the Charter did not by any means complete the complicated task of creating the United Nations as an organization. First, the governments represented at San Francisco had to ratify the Charter. Different governments have different constitutional processes for the ratification of treaties ; in Britain Parliament, in the United States the Senate (but not the House of Representatives), is the ratifying body. The Charter provided that it should come into effect as soon as ratifications had been received from the five permanent members of the Security Council and from a majority of the other originating states.[1]

It was agreed in San Francisco that a Preparatory Commission should at once be set up to arrange for the first sessions of the General Assembly and Security Council, and to make recommendations for the approval of the Assembly about the Secretariat, the procedure of the various organs, the site for the permanent headquarters of the organization, and other matters. The Preparatory Commission consisted of one representative of each member state. It held one session in San Francisco immediately after the signing of the Charter, and then dispersed, delegating its powers to an executive committee of representatives of 14 nations.[2] The executive committee was instructed to examine the problems concerned in detail, and to make recommendations to the full Preparatory Commission, which would reassemble as soon as the Charter had been ratified by enough nations to take effect.

The executive committee began its regular sessions on August 16, 1945, in London. The Charter took effect on October 24, just under four months after it had been signed, and accordingly the Preparatory Commission reassembled in London on November 24. The executive committee had already concluded its work and presented its report ; and the Preparatory Commission, finding very little that needed amending in the Committee's report adjourned on December 24, having made arrangements

[1] Article 110.
[2] China, France, Soviet Union, United Kingdom, United States ; Brazil, Mexico, Chile, the Netherlands, Czechoslovakia, Yugoslavia, Iran, Australia and Canada.

for the General Assembly and Security Council to meet in London in January 1946.

This Preparatory Commission ceased to exist as soon as the Secretary-General was appointed, but during its brief life it had set up an interim committee to select a site for the permanent headquarters, and, when the General Assembly first met, a delegation from this committee was still in the United States, inspecting possible sites.

The General Assembly has a part to play in the creation of each of the other organs ; and these latter could not therefore meet until the Assembly had completed the elections to each of them. The Assembly began its first plenary sessions on January 10. It at once proceeded to the election, first of its own President and Vice-President, then of the non-permanent members of the Security Council, and finally, of the Economic and Social Council. The Security Council met on January 18, and the Economic and Social Council on January 23. Then the Assembly and the Security Council, voting simultaneously as prescribed by the Statute, jointly elected the judges of the International Court. The Security Council's Military Staff Committee held its first meeting on February 4. The formation of the Trusteeship Council was postponed until the Assembly should have received and approved the trusteeship agreements which the nations holding League of Nations mandates have undertaken to put forward.

Hitherto the Secretariat had been operating on a temporary basis, under the direction of an executive secretary. On January 29 the Security Council agreed to recommend the name of Mr. Trygve Lie, Foreign Minister of Norway, for appointment by the Assembly as Secretary-General of the United Nations. The Assembly approved this nomination, and Mr. Lie then took over the Secretariat and began to select his principal officials.

It could now be said that the organization was in running order. It remained to be seen whether mankind was capable of working the machinery which had been so laboriously created.

CHAPTER III

THE CHARTER

THE Charter of the United Nations is the most important document in existence today. The sad fate of the Covenant of the League has made most people justly sceptical of the value of any " scrap of paper," however imposing its language may be. It is true that the strength of the United Nations lies not in the wording of the Charter but in the will of the member states. But it is also true that in any agreement between men or nations the terms used can either invite backslidings or seek to prevent them. So long as the United Nations retains its moral leadership among the nations of the world, those nations will always be reluctant to take any action which is flagrantly contrary to the Charter. Any weakness in the wording of the Charter would constitute a weakness in the whole organization.

In order to avoid leaving loopholes, the framers of the Charter were compelled to go into considerable detail on each point of substance. This makes the Charter itself somewhat heavy reading ; and in this chapter an attempt has been made to reduce the contents of the Charter to more manageable proportions without omitting any of the essential provisions. The full text of the Charter will be found at the end of the book.

The Charter begins with a Preamble couched in such fine language that it must be reproduced in full :—

WE THE PEOPLES OF THE UNITED NATIONS
DETERMINED

> to save succeeding generations from the scourge of war, which twice in our lifetime has brought untold sorrow to mankind, and
> to reaffirm faith in fundamental human rights, in the dignity and worth of the human person, in the equal rights of men and women and of nations large and small, and
> to establish conditions under which justice and respect for the obligations arising from treaties and other sources of international law can be maintained, and to promote social progress and better standards of life in larger freedom,

AND FOR THESE ENDS

> to practice tolerance and live together in peace with one another as good neighbours, and
> to unite our strength, to maintain international peace and security, and
> to ensure, by the acceptance of principles and the institution of methods, that armed force shall not be used, save in the common interest, and

to employ international machinery for the promotion of the economic and social advancement of all peoples,

HAVE RESOLVED TO COMBINE OUR EFFORTS TO ACCOMPLISH THESE AIMS.

Accordingly, our respective Governments, through representatives assembled in the city of San Francisco, who have exhibited their full powers found to be in good and due form, have agreed to the present Charter of the United Nations and do hereby establish an international organization to be known as the United Nations.

PURPOSES AND PRINCIPLES
(Chap. 1, Articles 1 and 2)

The Purposes of the United Nations are then stated to be : the maintenance of peace and security by the prevention of all threats to, or breaches of, the peace and by the peaceful settlement of disputes ; the development of friendly international relations on the basis of self-determination of peoples ; and co-operation in solving economic and social problems and in encouraging respect for human rights and fundamental freedom for all.

In pursuit of these Purposes, the Organization and its members are to act on the following Principles : the sovereign equality of all members ; the fulfilment in good faith of the obligations assumed by members under the Charter ; the peaceful settlement of disputes ; undertakings by members not to use force or the threat of force against the territorial integrity or independence of any other state, to assist the United Nations in its operations and not to assist any state against which the Organization is taking enforcement action ; and non-intervention by the Organization in the domestic affairs of any state. It is provided that the Organization shall ensure that non-member states too shall conform to these Principles as far as the maintenance of peace and security require them to.

MEMBERSHIP
(Chap. 2, Articles 3–6)

The 50 states represented at the San Francisco Conference, and any other states which had signed the Declaration by United Nations of January 1, 1942, are original members of the United Nations. Membership is open to any other state whose admission is recommended by the Security Council and approved by the General Assembly.

The Security Council can recommend to the Assembly the suspension of any member state against which the Council has had to take preventive or enforcement measures. The Council can restore such a state to membership ; but it also has the power to recommend the Assembly to expel any state which has persistently violated the principles of the Charter.

THE GENERAL ASSEMBLY
(Chap. 4, Articles 9–22)

Each member state can send up to five representatives to the General Assembly, but can only have one vote. On all important questions a decision of the Assembly requires a two-thirds majority of members present and voting. Other questions may be settled by a simple majority. A member state which is two years or more in arrears with its contribution to the Organization forfeits its vote unless the Assembly decides that the non-payment is not the member state's own fault.

The Assembly is to meet annually, but special sessions may also be convoked at the request of either the Security Council or a majority of member states.

The Assembly may discuss any question relating to the maintenance of peace and security brought before it by a member state or by the Security Council. It may also consider any international dispute brought to its attention by a non-member state, provided that the non-member state accepts the obligations laid down elsewhere in the Charter for the pacific settlement of the dispute. The Assembly may call the Council's attention to any situation likely to endanger peace and security; it may also make recommendations for the settlement of any such situation; but if the Council has already begun to consider a particular situation, the Assembly may not make any recommendations concerning it unless requested to do so by the Council.

The Assembly may consider the general principles of co-operation in the maintenance of peace, the question of disarmament and the regulation of armaments, and any other matters within the scope of the Charter. It shall recommend measures to promote co-operation in international law and politics, in economic, social, cultural, educational and health matters, and in the realization of human rights and fundamental freedoms for all. It shall control the work of the Economic and Social Council and the Trusteeship Council. It shall receive annual and special reports from the Security Council and the other organs of the United Nations. It shall consider and approve the budget of the Organization, and shall apportion the expenses between the member states.

THE SECURITY COUNCIL
(Chap. 5, Articles 23–32)

The Security Council shall consist of only eleven member states. Five of these shall be permanent members: China, France, the Soviet Union, the United Kingdom and the United States. The other six shall be elected by the General Assembly for two-year terms, three retiring every year; retiring members may not be re-elected immediately. Each member state shall have only one representative and only one vote on the Council.

On procedural matters, the Council can make decisions by an affirmative vote of seven out of its eleven members ; but on all other matters, these seven votes must include the concurring votes of the five permanent members, provided that a party to a dispute shall abstain from voting in decisions concerning that dispute.

The Council may invite other member states to take part in its discussions on matters which particularly affect those members' interests ; and it must invite the participation of any state which is a party to a dispute under discussion, whether that state belongs to the United Nations or not. In neither case have the invited states any right to vote.

In order that the Council may function continuously, each of its members will always be represented at the seat of the Organization. The Council may, however, meet at any other place if it wishes to.

The United Nations confer on the Security Council primary responsibility for the maintenance of peace and security, and member states undertake to accept and carry out the Council's decisions in accordance with the Charter.

DISPUTES
(Chap. 6, Articles 33–38)

Any member state may call the Security Council's attention to the existence of a dispute, or a situation which might lead to international friction or cause a dispute, and the Council may then investigate any such situation or dispute in order to determine whether it is likely to endanger the maintenance of peace and security.

The Council may call upon the parties to a dispute to settle it locally by negotiation, arbitration, judicial settlement or other peaceful means of their own choice. As a general rule, it should recommend that legal disputes be referred to the International Court. If the parties fail to settle their dispute by the methods of their own choice, they must refer it to the Council, which may then recommend terms of settlement. In any case, even if the case is not referred to the Council, the latter may recommend methods of adjustment.

THREATS TO THE PEACE
(Chap. 7, Articles 39–51)

The Council shall determine the existence of any threat to the peace, breach of the peace or act of aggression, and shall take action or make recommendations as necessary to maintain peace and security. Before doing so, it may call upon the parties concerned to comply with whatever provisional measures it considers necessary to prevent the situation becoming aggravated.

The Council may call upon the member states of the United Nations to sever economic and diplomatic relations with any state whose actions constitute a threat to the peace. If the Council considers that economic measures have proved or would prove inadequate, it may take such action by armed forces as may be necessary to maintain or restore peace and security. Such action may include demonstration, blockade or other operations by air, sea or land forces.

All member states agree to make available to the Council armed forces, assistance, and facilities including rights of passage for armed forces. Agreements shall be concluded as soon as possible between the Council and member states (or groups of members) governing the numbers, types, location and degree of readiness of these armed forces, and the nature of the assistance and facilities to be provided. In order to enable the United Nations to take urgent military measures, members shall hold air force contingents immediately available.

If the Council decides to use the armed forces of any member state not represented on the Council, it shall first invite that member to take part in its decisions on the employment of that member's forces.

A Military Staff Committee, consisting of representatives of the chiefs of staff of the permanent members of the Security Council, shall advise the Council on all questions relating to the Council's military requirements, including the regulation of armaments. The Committee shall make plans for the application of force, and shall direct the operations of the armed forces placed at the Council's disposal.

The Council shall decide whether it requires all or only some of the member states to take action to maintain peace in any given situation. In taking such action, member states shall afford one another mutual assistance. If any state, whether a member of the United Nations or not, finds itself faced with serious economic difficulties owing to the preventive or enforcement measures taken by the United Nations against another state, it can consult the Security Council with regard to a solution for these difficulties.

Any member state which is attacked by another state may take any necessary measures in self-defence until the Council has succeeded in restoring peace, but it must report such measures to the Council as soon as they are taken.

REGIONAL ARRANGEMENTS
(Chap. 8, Articles 52–54)

Any regional arrangements made between member states for the maintenance of peace and security must be consistent with the principles and purposes of the United Nations. The Security Council shall encourage the settlement of disputes through such regional arrangements, and shall, wherever appropriate, use regional arrangements for enforcement action. Regional agencies shall inform the Council of all activities they may undertake to maintain peace and security.

INTERNATIONAL ECONOMIC AND SOCIAL CO-OPERATION
(Chaps. 9 and 10, Articles 55–72)

As conditions of stability and well-being are necessary for peaceful relations between nations, the United Nations shall promote higher standards of living, full employment, international co-operation in economic, social, health, cultural, and educational matters, and universal respect for human rights and fundamental freedoms. All members pledge themselves to take both joint and separate action for the achievement of these purposes.

An Economic and Social Council, consisting of single representatives of 18 member states, each with one vote, shall be elected by the Assembly. Six members will be elected every year to serve for three years. Retiring members may be re-elected immediately. Decisions in the Council will be taken by a simple majority of members present and voting. The Council shall meet as required and shall be convened on the request of a majority of its members.

The Economic and Social Council is responsible, under the authority of the Assembly, for all the economic, social, cultural, educational, health and related activities of the United Nations. It shall study and report on all such matters, and may make recommendations and submit draft conventions either to the Assembly or to member states. It may call international conferences. It may also perform services requested by member states, subject always to the Assembly's approval.

The Council will make agreements, which must be approved by the Assembly, with the various agencies[1] already established by international conventions for economic and social purposes, so that they may be brought into relationship with, and be co-ordinated by, the United Nations. The Council may arrange for the participation in its discussions of representatives either of these specialized agencies or of member states not represented on the Council.

NON-SELF-GOVERNING TERRITORIES AND TRUSTEESHIP
(Chaps. 11, 12 and 13, Articles 73–91)

Member states responsible for administering non-self-governing territories recognize that the interests of the inhabitants of those territories are paramount, and pledge themselves to promote their well-being to the utmost, to ensure their political and social advancement, to develop self-government, to apply the Good Neighbour principle, and to supply the Organization with full information about economic and social conditions in such territories.

A Trusteeship Council, operating under the authority of the Assembly, shall supervise the administration of such Trust Territories as may be

[1]These include UNRRA, UNESCO, FAO, ILO and others.

B*

placed under trusteeship by subsequent agreements. Such Trust Territories may be former League of Nations mandates, or territories detached from enemy states as a result of the Second World War, or other territories voluntarily placed under trusteeship by the states administering them.

If, in the agreements placing territories under trusteeship, part or the whole of any trust territory is designated as a " strategic area," the Security Council shall exercise all the functions of the Organization as regards that area, including the approval of the terms of the agreement. The Security Council shall avail itself of the assistance of the Trusteeship Council, but without prejudice to security considerations.

The objectives of the Trusteeship system shall be : to further international peace and security ; to promote the political, economic and social advancement of the inhabitants of trust territories, and their progressive development towards either self-government or independence, as may be appropriate to each territory ; to encourage respect for human rights and fundamental freedoms for all ; and to ensure equal treatment in economic matters for all member states and equal justice for all their nationals.

The Trusteeship Council shall consist of the five permanent members of the Security Council, any other states which may be administering trust territories, and sufficient other states to ensure that the Council is equally divided between states administering trust territories and states which are not. The last category of members shall be elected by the Assembly for three-year terms. Each member of the Council will have one vote, and decisions will be made by a simple majority of members present and voting. The Council shall meet as required, and must be convened if a majority of its members so request.

Trust territories may be administered by single states, or by groups of states, or by the Organization itself. The administering authority of each trust territory must submit an annual report, on lines laid out by the Trusteeship Council, for the Assembly's consideration. The Assembly and the Trusteeship Council may arrange for periodic visits of inspection to trust territories ; they may also receive petitions from these territories. The Trusteeship Council may make use of either the Economic and Social Council or of the specialized agencies wherever appropriate.

THE INTERNATIONAL COURT OF JUSTICE
(Chap. 14, Articles 92-96)

The Statute of the International Court of Justice is an integral part of the Charter, and all members of the United Nations are automatically parties to the Statute. Non-members may become parties to the Statute if their applications are approved by the Assembly on the recommendation of the Security Council.

Member states may submit disputes to other tribunals set up by other international agreements ; but if they submit a dispute to the International

Court, they must abide by its decisions, and if one party fails to carry out the Court's decision, the other may apply to the Security Council, which may then decide what measures should be taken to give effect to the Court's judgment.

The Assembly, the Security Council, and other organs of the United Nations may request the Court to give advisory opinions on legal questions.

THE SECRETARIAT
(Chap. 15, Articles 97–101)

A Secretary-General shall be appointed by the Assembly on the recommendation of the Security Council. He shall act as Secretary-General at all meetings of the Assembly, the Security Council, the Economic and Social Council and the Trusteeship Council, and shall make an annual report to the Assembly on the working of the Organization.

The Secretary-General may bring to the attention of the Security Council any matter which in his opinion may threaten the maintenance of international peace and security.

The Secretary-General shall appoint his staff in accordance with regulations established by the General Assembly. Due regard shall be paid to the importance of recruiting the staff on as wide a territorial basis as possible.

The Secretary-General and the Secretariat under him shall refrain from any action which might reflect upon their position as international officials, responsible only to the Organization. They shall neither seek nor receive instructions from any government or other authority outside the Organization. Member states undertake not to seek to influence the Secretary-General or his staff in the discharge of their responsibilities.

AMENDMENTS TO THE CHARTER
(Chap. 18, Articles 108 and 109)

Amendments must be adopted by a vote of two-thirds of the members of the General Assembly and ratified by two-thirds of the member states, including all the permanent members of the Security Council.

If two-thirds of the members of the Assembly and seven members of the Security Council so demand, a General Conference of the United Nations shall be convoked to review the Charter. Each member state shall have one vote in the General Conference. Amendments to the Charter may then be adopted by a two-thirds vote in the General Conference, and must, as before, be ratified by two-thirds of the member states, including all the permanent members of the Security Council. If no General Conference has been held before the tenth annual session of the Assembly, the Assembly may then decide to convoke a Conference by a simple majority vote confirmed by a vote of seven members in the Security Council.

OTHER PROVISIONS
(Chaps. 16, 17 and 19, Articles 102–107, 110 and 111)

Member states will register with the Secretariat all treaties and agreements concluded between them after the Charter comes into force. If the Charter conflicts with any obligations incurred by member states under some other agreement, the Charter shall prevail.

The Organization, its officials, and representatives of member states shall enjoy all necessary privileges and immunities in the territory of each member state.

Until the Security Council, through its military arrangements with member states, is able to begin to exercise its responsibilities for preventive or enforcement action against threats to the peace, China, France, the Soviet Union, the United Kingdom and the United States shall consult together, and if necessary with other nations, with a view to whatever joint action may be necessary to maintain peace and security.

The Charter shall come into force when ratified by China, France, the Soviet Union, the United Kingdom and the United States, and by a majority of the other signatory states. The Charter, of which the Chinese, French, Russian, English and Spanish texts are equally authentic, shall remain deposited in the archives of the United States Government, which shall transmit duly certified copies to the Governments of the other signatory states.

CHAPTER IV
THE GENERAL ASSEMBLY

THE General Assembly occupies a central position in the structure of the United Nations ; but it cannot be said to be the supreme authority. All the other organs—the Security Council, the Economic and Social Council, the Trusteeship Council, the Secretariat, the International Court of Justice, the Commission on Atomic Energy—are wholly or partly its creations ; and the Economic and Social and Trusteeship Councils are subordinate to its direction. But the Security Council, with its subsidiary the Commission on Atomic Energy, is in no way bound to accept the Assembly's recommendations, and indeed is exclusively granted the right of action in security matters, the Assembly being forbidden even to make recommendations about any case which is already in the Council's hands ; the Secretary-General is the servant of both Security Council and Assembly ; and the International Court, once elected, enjoys the usual independence of a judicial body.

What then can the Assembly do ?

Before examining its functions and powers, we must briefly survey its internal structure. The Assembly consists of representatives of all the member states of the United Nations, each member being allowed not more than five representatives. Each member state possesses one vote. On all important questions, the Assembly must make its decisions by a two-thirds majority of members present and voting. On minor points a simple majority is sufficient. Any member which is in arrears with its contributions to the Organization to the extent of two years' contributions forfeits its vote, unless the Assembly decides that the failure to pay is due to conditions beyond the member's control.

The Assembly is therefore the principal platform on which the minor members of the United Nations can be heard. Here it is pertinent to point out that of the 51 founder members of the Organization, 24 are at present not represented in any of the smaller organs, and that these 24 " back-benchers " can therefore only express themselves through the Assembly. In the Assembly the smaller nations' weight of numbers gives them proportionate voting power, whereas in the Security Council and the Trusteeship Council the Great Powers have a privileged position, reinforced in the former by their veto rights. If " the principle of sovereign equality " of members set forth in the second article of the Charter means anything, it means that the Assembly must be an effective instrument for the preservation of the rights of the smaller nations.

Now the League of Nations had an Assembly and a Council whose relative positions were somewhat similar to those of the General Assembly and the Security Council of the United Nations. And it was said of the Assembly of the League that it could do nothing without the consent of the Council, and that even if it had possessed the power to do so, it would have referred the matter to the Council. But it must be remembered that in the organs of the League no important action could be taken except with the unanimous consent of all the members present and voting. This meant that although the Great Powers could not compel the Assembly to act in accordance with their wishes, they could completely block any action which the smaller nations wished to take by interposing their veto. In the United Nations Assembly, it is perfectly possible for the smaller nations to combine to outvote the Great Powers, even when the latter are supported by certain of their " satellite states." In this respect, then, the smaller nations now have a more effective instrument under their hand than they possessed in the League Assembly.

But the Charter imposes strict limitations on the extent to which this instrument may be used. In effect, the Assembly's powers in the field of international security are limited to recommendation ; and while it is allotted a definite part in such important processes as the admission and expulsion of member states, by which political pressure can obviously be brought to bear upon recalcitrants, its powers are in all such matters subject to the agreement of the Security Council. In three matters only is the Assembly authorized to take definite action without the consent of the Security Council ; finance, trusteeship, and economic and social co-operation.

EXCLUSIVE POWERS OF THE ASSEMBLY

Article 17 of the Charter gives the General Assembly exclusive control over the finances of the Organization. It is empowered to consider and approve the budget, to apportion the total expenses between member states, and to consider and approve any financial arrangements that may be made with the " specialized agencies " such as UNESCO, the FAO and the ILO. It may also examine the administrative budgets of these agencies and make recommendations to them on financial matters.

The " power of the purse " is universally recognized as one of the most effective means by which an assembly can exercise control over an executive. Certainly this financial authority gives the General Assembly a considerable degree of negative control over the actions of the Security Council and the other organs. But it must be pointed out that the Assembly's concern is more likely to be directed towards urging the Security Council to take preventive or enforcement action than towards discouraging it. In the maintenance of peace and security a purely negative control of the executive can hardly be sufficient ; and the financial authority of the Assembly does not endow it with any positive power.

The second of the Assembly's exclusive powers is concerned with trusteeship, a subject which is more fully examined in a later chapter. The Trusteeship Council is a subordinate organ which operates under the Assembly's authority in supervising the administration of United Nations Trust Territories. Article 85 of the Charter declares that :

" The functions of the United Nations with regard to trusteeship agreements for all areas not designated as strategic, including the approval of the terms of the trusteeship agreements and of their alteration or amendment, shall be exercised by the General Assembly. . . . The Trusteeship Council, operating under the authority of the General Assembly, shall assist the General Assembly in carrying out these functions." The Assembly is also responsible for electing to the Trusteeship Council such members as are not automatically entitled to membership by virtue of trusteeship agreements or as permanent members of the Security Council. The Assembly is to receive annual reports from each trusteeship authority ; and it is empowered to accept petitions from the peoples of the trust territories, to arrange visits of inspection to these territories, and to authorize the Trusteeship Council to take similar action.

The third field in which the Assembly can operate without the consent of the Security Council is that of economic and social co-operation. Here again the Charter specifically states that the General Assembly is responsible for discharging the United Nations' economic and social responsibilities, and that the Economic and Social Council will operate under the Assembly's authority.[1] The Assembly elects the whole of the Economic and Social Council, in which there is therefore no position of privilege for the Great Powers. This Council is given the duty of preparing draft conventions which will be submitted to the General Assembly, to which it must also submit any agreements made with the " specialized agencies." These agreements, like trusteeship agreements, require the Assembly's approval. Finally, the Assembly is empowered to assign to the Council " other functions " in the field of social and economic co-operation than those specified in the Charter.[2]

In possessing exclusive control of the two fields of trusteeship and of economic and social work, the Assembly assumes vast responsibilities ; but it is clear from the Charter that it is not endowed with any very effective powers of enforcement with which to bring member states into line with its policies and objects. The second article of the Charter specifically forbids the Organization to " intervene in matters which are essentially within the domestic jurisdiction of any State " ; and, apart from the moral force of the Assembly's recommendations, the only means of enforcing the United Nations policies in the fields exclusively controlled by the Assembly would be by the threat of expulsion, which the Assembly cannot even initiate without a recommendation from the Security Council.

[1] Article 60 of the Charter.
[2] Article 66 of the Charter.

POWERS SHARED WITH THE SECURITY COUNCIL

The Assembly and the Security Council are both required to give their consent to all matters regarding the membership of the United Nations. On the recommendation of the Council, the Assembly may admit to membership any peace-loving state which accepts the obligations contained in the Charter and which is considered able and willing to carry them out. On the recommendation of the Council, the Assembly may suspend from the rights and privileges of membership any member state against which the Council has taken preventive or enforcement action ; and on the recommendation of the Council, the Assembly may expel any member which has persistently violated the principles of the Charter.

It is to be noted that in all these cases the Assembly must wait upon the recommendations of the Security Council. It has no power to initiate any action with regard to membership ; in effect, it can only act as a limitation to the Security Council's powers.

The Assembly and the Council share responsibility for the creation of two of the organs of the United Nations, the International Court of Justice and the Secretariat. In the case of the Court, the Assembly and Council are required to meet simultaneously but separately and to elect the judges of the Court from identical lists of candidates. To be elected, each judge must secure an absolute majority in the Assembly and a majority of seven votes in the Council. This procedure was followed in the League of Nations when elections to the old Permanent Court were being made, and, although it appears cumbrous, in practice it has been successfully operated.

In the case of the Secretariat, Article 97 of the Charter provides that the Secretary-General shall be appointed by the General Assembly on the recommendation of the Security Council. When the first Secretary-General was appointed it was noticeable that the Council was at some pains to agree upon a candidate, but that the Assembly's approval of the Council's choice was instant and unanimous. It is probable that the Council will always play the dominant role in the selection of the Secretary-General. Perhaps the Assembly may be thought to be compensated by its power, under Article 101, of establishing the regulations under which the Secretary-General is to appoint the Secretariat. Certainly the Assembly has taken this responsibility seriously, and has laid down in some detail the manner in which it wishes to see the staff of the Organization created.

The process of amending the Charter is a function which the Assembly shares not with the Security Council as such, but with its five permanent members (the Soviet Union, the United States, the United Kingdom, France and China). Amendments can be made in two ways. They may be adopted by the Assembly (by the usual two-thirds majority), and must then be ratified by the governments of all five permanent members of the

Security Council, and of enough other member states to make up two-thirds of the membership of the United Nations. Alternatively, if the Assembly and the Security Council agree to the holding of a " General Conference of the Members of the United Nations," such a Conference may, by a two-thirds vote, recommend alterations to the Charter which must be ratified in exactly the same way as amendments adopted by the Assembly. In the General Conference each member state will have one vote, and this body is therefore substantially the same as the General Assembly.

We have now reviewed the powers which the Assembly shares with the Security Council, and those which it possesses exclusively. In both categories there is a strong resemblance to the powers of the Assembly of the League of Nations. The General Assembly shares with the Security Council the appointment of the Secretary-General and of the International Court ; so did the League Assembly share these powers with the League Council. The General Assembly votes amendments to the Covenant, as did the Assembly of the League ; in the United Nations these amendments require ratification by two-thirds of the member states including the five permanent members of the Council, whereas in the League a simple majority of members including all members of the Council were required to ratify amendments. But whereas in the United Nations system the Assembly and the Council share the power of admission and expulsion, in the League it was the Assembly which admitted and the Council which expelled.

The League Assembly enjoyed the same exclusive control of finance as the present General Assembly ; but the League's mandated territories, which were roughly equivalent to the new trusteeship system, were the concern of the Council and not, as in the United Nations, of the Assembly. Economic and social matters were not allotted by the Covenant of the League to any specific organ (other than the ILO, which was confined to labour problems) ; but the later development of the League's economic and social work brought about the existence of what was known as " concurrent competence," by which both Assembly and Council could handle these matters. Steps were being taken in 1939 to relieve the Council of its responsibilities in economic and social matters, but this project never took effect.

In both League and United Nations there is the same provision by which the Assembly elects part of the Security Council. In the case of the League it was also possible for the Assembly, with the approval of the Council, to increase the number of either temporary or permanent members of the Council. There is no similar provision in the Charter of the United Nations.

THE ASSEMBLY AND SECURITY

The Assembly has no concrete authority whatsoever in the field of international peace and security, which is expressly reserved by the Charter to the Security Council. This abrupt division of function is justified by its supporters on the grounds that a large assembly can never be satisfactorily entrusted with so delicate and urgent a task as the prevention of war ; and this argument is supported by the indubitable fact that in the League of Nations, the Assembly showed itself capable of endless discussion on dangerous situations without ever appearing to reach a decision. It is also argued that much of the delay and indecisiveness noticeable in the League's attempts to maintain peace was due to the vagueness of the division of function between the Council and the Assembly. Articles 11 and 15 of the Covenant made it possible for the two bodies to deal with disputes and other circumstances which might endanger the peace either simultaneously or successively, and this was in fact frequently done. The result was a marked tendency to " pass the buck " from one body to another, which both wasted time and encouraged inaction.

The Dumbarton Oaks draft for the Charter accordingly reduced the Assembly's interest in security matters to almost invisible proportions ; and this was one of the most vigorously debated issues at the San Francisco Conference. The smaller nations, which were of course in a strong majority at the Conference, fought hard to give the Assembly a degree of control over the Council's actions, and a Committee of the Second Commission, which was examining the proposals for the Assembly, recommended that " the General Assembly should have the right to approve or disapprove the reports of the Security Council, to make observations and recommendations thereon, and submit recommendations to the Security Council with a view to ensuring complete observance of the duties of the Security Council inherent in its responsibility to maintain international peace and security." But it was objected that this clause would practically make the Security Council a subordinate organ like the other councils, and in any case would reintroduce the division of responsibility which had been so unfortunate in the League ; and the Assembly was eventually empowered merely to " receive and consider annual and special reports from the Security Council ; these reports shall include an account of the measures that the Security Council has decided upon or taken to maintain international peace and security."[1] The latter part of this clause was added to the Dumbarton Oaks draft in order to meet the demands of several smaller nations.

The Assembly is by no means debarred from discussion of any threat to international security ; the prohibition is upon action, not upon deliberation. The Charter empowers the Assembly to discuss any matter connected with the maintenance of peace brought before it by any nation, and to call the attention of the Security Council to situations which might endanger peace and security. It is even authorized to make recom-

[1] Article 15 of the Charter.

mendations for the peaceful adjustment of any such situation either to the Council or to the states concerned. But its role is limited to recommendation ; and even this right is limited by a provision that it must make no recommendation about any situation which is already in the hands of the Council.[1]

A point of some interest about the Assembly's power to recommend peaceful adjustment of dangerous situations is the complete absence from the Charter of any reference either to treaty revision or to " peaceful change." The nineteenth article of the Covenant of the League gave the League Assembly the right to recommend treaty revisions to member states when it considered that treaties had become inapplicable or that a continuation of existing conditions might endanger the peace of the world. At San Francisco many delegations demanded an explicit reference in the Charter to treaty revision, but this was opposed by a number of nations, including the Soviet Union and the United States, on the ground that all existing treaties would thereby be weakened, and that the weight of the Organization would be thrown too heavily on the side of revision. Eventually it was agreed that the text now found in Article 14 of the Charter would be sufficient to enable the Assembly to make a useful contribution to the process of " peaceful change."

THE DELIBERATIVE FUNCTION

It has been said that the General Assembly will be, and that the League Assembly before it was, no more than a " talking-shop," in other words, a purely deliberative body without any powers. We have, however, seen that it does possess certain restricted powers, some of them exclusively its own, some shared with the Security Council ; and that it also possesses a limited advisory function in the field of security, the effect of which will depend, as that of the League depended, on the moral influence wielded by the United Nations. The Assembly is not a mere talking-shop. But there is no doubt that a large proportion of its work is confined to pure deliberation, and it must not be assumed that this will be entirely valueless.

It is already being said that the nations which had already had experience of working in the League have shown themselves much more proficient in internationalism than those which have not had that experience. The mere assembling together in one place of delegates from many nations may not have much effect in overcoming serious differences of opinion ; but there is no doubt that international co-operation, like everything else, becomes a habit. In this sense the mere existence of the General Assembly has a slow but beneficial effect.

Critics of the Assembly's workings have already been busy attacking the amount of time spent in long and frequently flowery speeches at its first session. More detailed examination of those speeches shows that in each

[1] Article 12 of the Charter.

there was a great deal that provided valuable information about the intentions of the nation concerned towards the aims and activities of the United Nations.   The Assembly does in fact provide a magnificent platform from which the governments of all nations, small as well as great, can proclaim their objectives and call for the sympathy and support of other nations.   This freedom is only limited by the clause restricting the Assembly to discussion of " any questions or any matters within the scope of the Charter,"[1] and it is clear that almost any international problem can be discussed within these terms.   At its first session the Assembly held major debates and reached agreement on important resolutions concerning the food emergency, the fate of refugees and displaced persons, the control of atomic energy, the apprehension and trial of war criminals, and the requirements of UNRRA.   It is authorized by Article 11 of the Charter to discuss the "general principles of co-operation in the maintenance of international peace and security, including the principles governing disarmament and the regulation of armaments," and to make appropriate recommendations either to members or to the Security Council ; and its decision to create a Commission on Atomic Energy was clearly taken under this heading.

The Assembly is also responsible, under Article 13 of the Charter, for the initiation of studies and the framing of recommendations designed to encourage the progressive development of international law and its codification.

PROCEDURE

The Charter lays down that the General Assembly shall meet in regular annual sessions, and in such special sessions as occasion may require.[2] It has been decided that the regular sessions shall be held in September of each year, as were the Assemblies of the League.   Special sessions may be convoked by the Secretary-General at the request either of the Security Council or of a majority of the member nations.   The Assembly elects a different President for each session[3], and decides its own rules of procedure.

In order to avoid the anomaly of holding two separate sessions in one year, it was decided that the meeting in London in January and February, 1946, should be designated the First Part of the First Session of the Assembly, and that the September meeting, which will take place in New York, will be the Second Part of the First Session.   The London meeting was largely taken up with the work of constructing the United Nations machine by electing the members of the various other organs, with decisions about the internal organization of the new machine, and with

[1]Article 9 of the Charter.
[2]Article 20 of the Charter.
[3]The first President to be elected was Mr. P. H. Spaak, Foreign Minister of Belgium.

consultations about such initial matters as the site for a permanent head-quarters and the taking over of League of Nations properties and responsibilities.

THE COMMITTEES

Like most other large representative bodies, the Assembly has adopted the technique of referring the requests and proposals put before it to one or other of a set of committees. The committees dispose of much of the detailed discussion, and the Assembly's task is then reduced to approving or amending the recommendations of the committees. There are six Main Committees, a General Committee, and two or three temporary committees set up for special purposes such as the selection of a head-quarters site.

The General Committee is composed of fourteen members, and the Rules of Procedure lay down that no two of these may be nationals of the same state. The Committee comprises the President of the Assembly, the seven Vice-Presidents, and the chairman of the six Main Committees.[1]

Both Vice-Presidents and Chairmen of Committees are to be selected in such a manner as to ensure the representative character of the General Committee and equitable geographical distribution as well as on their personal qualifications.

The chief task of the General Committee is to consider the items put forward for discussion by the Assembly and to decide which of them shall be placed on the Assembly's agenda, and in which order. It is not intended that the General Committee shall exercise any political power, but it is obvious that to some extent it must decide political and other issues in selecting items for the Assembly's consideration. The General Committee may amend the form of any resolution adopted by the Assembly, but not the substance ; it must of course report any such amendment to the Assembly for its consideration. The Committee also gives general assistance to the President of the Assembly in carrying out his responsibilities.

The first of the six Main Committees is the Political and Security Committee. Each delegation may designate one member for this, as for the other five Main Committees. Main Committees choose their own Chairmen, Vice-Chairmen and *Rapporteurs*, and may set up sub-committees, which again choose their own officers. These Committees may only discuss the subjects referred to them. Thus the Political and Security Committee will be given the task of discussing any proposal or request put before the Assembly which deals with the admission, suspen-

[1] At the London meeting the General Committee was made up as follows :
President of the Assembly : Mr. Spaak,—Belgium.
Vice-Presidents : The Chief Delegates for—Soviet Union, United States, United Kingdom, France, China, Venezuela and South Africa.
Chairmen of Committees : Dr. Manuilsky, Ukraine ; Mr. Konderski, Poland ; Mr. Fraser, New Zealand ; Mr. MacEachen, Uruguay ; Mr. Al Khoury, Syria ; Dr. Jiminez, Panama.

sion or expulsion of member states, disarmament and the regulation of armaments, the promotion of political co-operation between nations, and the general problems of maintaining peace and security, including the peaceful adjustment of dangerous situations.

The second Main Committee is the Economic and Financial Committee. This would be allotted all proposals and questions dealing with economic co-operation between nations, the raising of standards of living, full employment, equilibrium and stabilization of prices, and economic and financial projects in general, including the work of the Economic and Social Council and of the specialized agencies.

The third Main Committee, the Social, Humanitarian and Cultural Committee, would handle all matters such as social, educational, cultural, health, and humanitarian projects, and international assistance in the realization of human rights and fundamental freedoms.

The fourth Main Committee is the Trusteeship Committee, which will, of course, deal with the trusteeship system and related subjects, and possibly with other matters concerning non-self-governing territories.

The fifth Main Committee, the Administrative and Budgetary Committee, will consider matters pertaining to the budget of the United Nations, the individual contributions to be made by member states, and the budgets of the specialized agencies. It will also consider the regulations concerning the Secretariat and other staff.

The sixth and last Main Committee is the Legal Committee, which will deal with the legal and constitutional aspects of amendments to the Charter and like matters, and with requests for advisory opinions from the international Court of Justice. It will also consider the development and codification of international law, and will handle legal problems referred to it from the other Committees.

Temporary committees hitherto created by the Assembly have dealt with such subjects as the choice of a site for the permanent headquarters of the Organization, the transfer to the United Nations of the assets and records of the League of Nations, and the immediate requirements of UNRRA. There have also been small *ad hoc* committees established to handle such purely internal matters as delegates' credentials.

The full workings of the committee system are clearly seen in the handling of a difficult case such as the application of the World Federation of Trade Unions for a seat in the Economic and Social Council. This case was put before the Assembly when it met in London in January 1946. The first stage was the consideration by the General Committee whether or not to place the item on the Assembly's agenda. After considerable discussion, during which various delegates argued that this was not the time to consider a single application from one non-governmental organization and that the case should not therefore go on the agenda, it was eventually allowed to come before the Assembly in plenary session. The

Assembly found itself in disagreement on the application, and after only a brief discussion decided, in accordance with the General Committee's recommendation, to pass the matter to the First Committee (Political and Security). The first Committee, in which of course the division of opinion of the Assembly is exactly reflected since all member states are represented in it, was also divided on the application, but as the Committees are empowered to make decisions on the basis of a simple majority, it was able to get enough agreement to produce a Committee recommendation for the Assembly. In the next plenary session of the Assembly this Committee's recommendation was presented ; there was a vigorous but brief debate in which the minority opinions were fully heard ; and the Assembly then got together the necessary two-thirds majority required to pass the Committee's recommendation. Naturally most issues are not as difficult as this, but it is evident from this one example that the Committee system has considerable advantages both in avoiding lengthy debates in plenary session and in enabling the Assembly to divine the " sense of the meeting " and act accordingly on an agreed formula.

CHAPTER V

THE SECURITY COUNCIL

WHAT HAS IT GOT TO DO?

THE aims of the United Nations are diverse, generous and ambitious. They range from the feeding of starving peoples to the development of self-government in backward territories. But the keystone of the whole structure is the maintenance of peace. Without peace, there can be no economic or social progress ; there can be no raising of the stature of mankind ; none of the noble purposes set out in the opening words of the Charter can possibly be achieved. Indeed, the two terrible wars through which we have lately passed not only obstructed humanity's natural progress, but set civilization back by many years ; and in any future war in which atomic weapons were used, civilization itself might easily go under. Peace, then, must be the first and most essential objective of the United Nations.

But we have known many years of so-called peace during which the whole world lived in fear. We have felt the effects of a " war of nerves." We have seen small nations swallowed up by their neighbours without any official hostilities. We know also that it is possible to " make a desert and call it peace." That is the peace of the graveyard. Tortured humanity demands something more than formal peace. It demands freedom from fear of aggression ; in other words, international security.

The principal organ established by the United Nations to preserve peace and security is the Security Council. It is a small body of only eleven men, perhaps the smallest single body in whose hands the world has ever agreed to place its fate. All the member nations have agreed to confer upon it " primary responsibility for the maintenance of international peace and security " ;[1] and they have also agreed to accept and carry out its decisions.[2] This is an unprecedented abrogation of national sovereignty. It may enable the Security Council, if it can be successfully operated, to outlaw war and initiate a new age of freedom from fear.

We have already learnt that to outlaw war it is not enough merely to bring the nations together into an organization whose professed aim is to maintain peace. The first such organization, the League of Nations. failed tragically to prevent the aggressions of the Axis powers. And if the League failed, how can the United Nations hope to succeed ?

Perhaps the answer may be that the United Nations have endowed their organization with three essentials which the League lacked ; speed, strength, and unity. Let us see how this has been done.

[1]Article 24 of the Charter.
[2]Article 25.

SPEED

Modern war comes swiftly. We learnt from Hitler how easily a peaceful state can be overrun. With armies and air forces massed secretly behind the frontiers, a petty incident can be trumped up overnight, an impossible ultimatum presented, and the victim is faced with the choice between surrender and the immediate devastation of open cities by bombing. We learnt from the Japanese how a crippling attack may be launched upon an unsuspecting victim when negotiations for the settlement of a dispute are actually in progress. Modern aggressor states have invariably tried to attain their objectives so swiftly that they could then present the world with a *fait accompli* which would be very difficult to undo. This would be an even easier process for any aggressor which possessed the secret of the new atomic bomb.

So if we are to preserve peace we must have machinery which can act swiftly, and before hostilities have actually broken out.

This the League of Nations did not possess. Any member of the League could draw the attention of the League Council to any situation which threatened to end in war ; but there was nothing in the Covenant which suggested that the Council itself or the Secretary-General should take the initiative in reviewing a dangerous situation. It was thus possible for situations in which peace was undoubtedly in danger to arise without ever being considered by the Council of the League.

Further, the Covenant drew a sharp distinction between actual outbreaks of war and the mere threat of such outbreaks. Once war had actually broken out, members of the League were bound to join in imposing sanctions on any aggressor state which had violated the Covenant ; but we know to our cost that modern wars cannot be dealt with by waiting until they break out. Faced with a situation in which war was slowly but in-exorably approaching, the League was practically powerless. Article 11 of the Covenant provided that any action should be taken " that may be deemed wise and effectual to safeguard the peace of nations." But there was no indication of what this action should be. To some extent the omission was rectified in 1927, when the League drew up a programme of possible deterrent actions very similar to those mentioned in Articles 41 and 42 of the United Nations Charter. But these actions were not obliga-tory upon the states which composed the League. In the event of a threat to the peace, the Council of the League had to obtain from each individual state, by agreement, whatever facilities or assistance it might think neces-ssary to safeguard peace in the particular circumstances of the moment. The possibilities for prevarication were obviously endless ; and, in fact, no military forces were ever called upon.

Even when war had actually broken out, the terms of the Covenant only made it obligatory to impose sanctions on a belligerent nation when it was either a member of the League acting in disregard of its obligations under the Covenant, or a non-member which had refused to accept similar obligations. Reasonably construed, this definition might be made to cover almost any aggression ; but it offered many terminological loopholes through which a reluctant nation could escape its obligations. It must be remembered that the Covenant did not include any renunciation of aggressive war as categorical in its terms as that of the Charter of the United Nations.[1] In practice, the effect of the Covenant's unfortunate wording was that even when the world was unmistakably faced with wanton aggression, the whole question of whether the Covenant had definitely been violated had still to be discussed and decided in the Council, the Assembly, and the national parliaments of all League members. By the time sanctions were applied, the aggressor could reasonably expect to have achieved most of his objectives ; and, faced with the obvious futility of action at such a late stage, the member nations were all the more inclined to avoid unpleasantness and shelve the whole business.

The machinery now set up by the United Nations and controlled by the Security Council is very different from that of the League. In the first place, the Security Council is not allowed to wait until somebody else points out a menacing situation to it. By Article 24 of the Charter, the member nations specifically confer upon it " the primary responsibility for the maintenance of international peace and security." It can, at any time, decide to consider a threat to the peace at the request of one of its members, or of any other state, or of the General Assembly, or of the Secretary-General ; but it is clearly the intention of the Charter that the Council itself must always be on the watch for signs of trouble, and it is presumably for this reason that the Secretary-General, who as an international official should be free from the natural reluctance of any one nation to involve itself or others in unpleasantness, is empowered to draw the Council's attention to " any matter which in his opinion may threaten the maintenance of international peace and security."[2]

The Charter states that every nation which is a member of the Security Council must be permanently represented at the seat of the Organization, and that the Council " shall be so organized as to be able to function continuously."[3] The Security Council has now decided that its President must call a meeting if any one member of the Council, or any member state, or the Secretary-General, or the General Assembly, so requests,

---

[1] Article 2 of the Charter obliges the member states " to settle international disputes by peaceful means in such a manner that peace, security and justice are not endangered . . . to refrain, in international relations, from the threat or use of force against the territorial integrity or political independence of any State, or in any other manner inconsistent with the Purposes of the United Nations."

By contrast, the Covenant specifically forbade member states to go to war until three months after their dispute had been pronounced upon by the Council ; the implication being that after that time they were free to go to war at will.

[2] Article 99 of the Charter.

[3] Article 28 of the Charter.

and that in any case the interval between meetings must never exceed fourteen days[1]. So the Council can always meet without more than a few hours delay.

In the second place, the Council's authority is not circumscribed by the kind of limitation which hampered the League Council. Where the machinery of the League made it necessary for decisions to be taken by the Assembly and Council of the League and by the member nations before any action in defence of peace could begin, the United Nations Charter places all the authority firmly in the hands of the Security Council. The Council has complete discretion in determining whether peace is threatened. It does not have to decide whether the Charter is being violated, which could involve all sorts of quibblings over the interpretation of the text. It has only to decide the simple question : does a threat to, or breach of, the peace exist ? Its power of investigation is practically unlimited. It can investigate " any situation which might lead to international friction or give rise to a dispute."[2] And having decided that a dangerous situation does exist, the Council has at its disposal a full range of alternative powers, any or all of which it can use at its own discretion and without reference to the Assembly or to any other authority in the world.

It may decide first of all to call upon the nations concerned in the trouble to settle their dispute by arbitration, judicial settlement in the International Court, or other peaceful means.[3] If this fails to bring about a satisfactory solution, the Council may itself recommend terms of settlement.[4] Under Article 25 of the Charter, member states of the United Nations are bound to accept the Council's recommendations.

So any nation which thinks of using the threat of force against another will find that the Security Council is capable of giving a rapid and uncompromising verdict against it. But it may happen that a determined nation will not be so easily baulked of its prey, and that the Council's verdict, although swifter and more decisive than that of the League, will not be enough to prevent further trouble. The Charter accordingly gives the Council further powers to deal with situations in which it appears that there is a threat to the peace.

The Council may consider that the situation is already becoming worse, and that it is imperative to check this deterioration before taking any further action. It can therefore " call upon the parties concerned to comply with such provisional measures as it deems necessary or desirable " to prevent the situation being aggravated ; and it shall " duly take account of failure to comply " with such measures.[5]

But it is entirely in the hands of the Council to decide whether to give

[1] Rules of Procedure 1,2 and 3, adopted on April 9, 1946.
[2] Article 34.
[3] Article 33.
[4] Articles 37 and 38.
[5] Article 40.

he offending parties notice of any action it may take against them. It may prefer at once to use its powers under Article 41, and call upon all or any member states to apply all forms of pressure short of armed force ; or, if it thinks this will be inadequate, it can make use of Article 42, and " take such action by air, sea or land forces as may be necessary to maintain or restore international peace or security."

In other words, the Security Council can go into action against a nation which threatens to disturb the peace with a minimum of delay. It need not consult any other authority. It need not decide difficult textual questions such as whether the Charter is being violated. It need not wait until the crisis has become acute. In fact, it possesses all the speed which the League lacked.

We must now consider another essential requirement : has it the necessary strength ?

STRENGTH

One of the most marked characteristics of the League of Nations was its faith in disarmament. The warring nations had for years borne a tremendous economic burden in order to feed the insatiable battlefields of Europe ; and it was natural for them to seek a way to peace which would at the same time enable them to cut down their armies and munition dumps to a minimum. But this universal war-weariness had an unfortunate effect on the constitution of the League. As we have seen, it was only after discussion in both national and international assemblies that the member states could be persuaded to take any decisive action against aggression. Member states were under no obligation to carry out unified plans made for them by the League. The Council could only recommend to certain members that they should use their armed forces against the aggressor. There was a Military Commission which was intended to advise the Council of the League ; but its powers were in no way comparable to those of the Military Staff Committee of the United Nations. The League had, in fact. no machinery capable of producing an effective military answer to aggression.

When the Charter of the United Nations was first under discussion, it was generally agreed that this time the world must establish " a league with teeth." The " teeth " of the new organization are to be found in Articles 41 to 49 of the Charter. These articles not only empower the Security Council to use effective force in the event of a threat to the peace ; they also give it every facility for making its preparations, so that the force will be ready at an instant's notice if an emergency arises.

We have already seen that the overriding authority of the Security Council is the most striking feature of the new security system. This is nowhere more evident than in the articles concerning armed force. The Council is empowered to proceed at once to negotiate with all member nations agreements setting out the precise nature and size of the armed forces which the nations will then place at its disposal. These agreements will in many cases involve an undertaking that a contingent of the member nation's air forces will always be instantly ready to respond to any call from the Council. Nations on whom the Council calls for armed forces are entitled to be represented at the meetings of the Council which decide the disposition of their forces ; but they have no voice in deciding *whether* their forces shall be used ; and in deciding *how* they shall be used, the Council has the last word. Further, all nations, whether their forces have been called upon or not, must accept the Council's decisions as to how, by applying economic pressure, or providing transit facilities or supplies, they can be of most use in the general plan.

It is, in fact, possible under the Charter for really unified action to be taken against aggression. To provide the Council with expert advice for this complicated task, a Military Staff Committee is established. The Committee consists of representatives of the Chiefs of Staff of China, France, the Soviet Union, the United Kingdom and the United States. It must invite the presence of representatives of any other member nation " when the efficient discharge of the Committee's responsibilities requires the participation of that member in its work."

The Military Staff Committee met for the first time in London on February 4, 1946. It was directed by the Security Council to proceed at once to the preparation of the military agreements which will be concluded between the Council and member states. These agreements have not yet materialized, but the Committee is still at work in New York, and appears to have reached certain tentative conclusions. It is probable that the forces called for by the agreements will remain in their respective countries and under national command until actually required by the Council for preventive action. Once they have been called upon by the Council, they will be subject to the Committee's overall strategic direction, which will be transmitted through a supreme international commander and down through national subordinate commanders. The supreme commander is likely to be an airman.

The Committee will probably organize its strategic plan on a regional basis, so that national forces will normally be used only in their own continent or strategic region ; but this would naturally depend on the size of the emergency.

The Military Staff Committee is also responsible for advising the Security Council on the regulation of armaments, and disarmament in general. It is empowered by the Charter to establish local sub-committees where necessary ; this will require the co-operation of the " regional security agencies " which are described on a later page.

Articles 50 and 51 of the Charter provide safeguards intended to compensate the member states for the loss of independence involved in the conferring of these tremendous powers upon the Council. Article 50 states that any nation, whether or not a member of the United Nations, may consult the Security Council if it finds that the economic preventive action taken against another state is adversely affecting its own economy. Article 51 makes it clear that the " inherent right of individual or collective self-defence " is not impaired by the Charter. But there are limitations to this right. Measures taken in self-defence must be immediately reported to the Council, and must cease once the Council has taken the necessary steps to restore international security.

REGIONAL SECURITY AGENCIES

During the lifetime of the League of Nations, many of its member states urged that some sort of regional arrangement could be made, within the framework of the Covenant, by which member states would be primarily responsible only for the maintenance of peace in their own continents or strategic regions. Other states opposed this suggestion on the grounds that it would weaken the whole idea of the Covenant, and merely serve to create large regional blocs or alliances which might in the long run be more dangerous than the individual dissensions of their component states. But it is an incontrovertible fact that most nations are less willing to become involved in the troubles of the other side of the world than in those which occur right on their own doorsteps. And at the San Francisco Conference the framers of the Charter decided to make use of, rather than ignore, the regional defensive groupings which already existed.

The most obvious of these groupings was the Pan-American. By an agreement known as the Act of Chapultepec, signed in Mexico City in March 1945, the American states bound themselves together by " a regional arrangement for dealing with such matters relating to the maintenance of international peace and security as are appropriate for regional action in this Hemisphere." The agreement set up an Inter-American Defence Board, and reaffirmed the policy outlined by the 1940 meeting of American Foreign Ministers, which had declared that " any attempt on the part of a non-American state against the integrity or inviolability of the territory, the sovereignty or the political independence of an American state, shall be considered an act of aggression against all the American states."

A less clearly defined regional grouping is that of the European nations which have bound themselves, by a set of parallel treaties, to co-operate in the task of preventing further Axis aggressions. A third is the League of Arab States established by the Cairo Pact of March 1945. By this pact the seven Arab nations of Egypt, Iraq, Transjordan, Saudi Arabia, Yemen, Syria and Lebanon bound themselves together for mutual protection and for the maintenance of peace and security in the Middle East.

Article 52 of the Charter declares that the Charter does not preclude the existence of such regional arrangements or agencies " provided that their activities are consistent with the Purposes and Principles of the United Nations " ; and it expressly urges all members of the Organization to " make every effort to achieve pacific settlements of local disputes through such regional arrangements or agencies before referring them to the Security Council." The Council itself is directed both to encourage the settlement of disputes through the regional agencies, and, where appropriate, to refer disputes to them. The Council may also use regional agencies for enforcement action. The Charter forbids regional agencies to take any enforcement action without authorization from the Council ; but Article 53 specifically excepts action taken " against renewal of aggressive policy on the part of . . . any state which during the Second World War has been an enemy of any signatory of the present Charter." Regional agencies must provide the Security Council with full information about the activities which they have undertaken and those which they contemplate.

STRATEGIC AREAS

Articles 82 and 83 of the Charter provide that certain areas in the " trust territories " which may be placed under the authority of the United Nations Trusteeship Council may be designated as " strategic areas." These areas will then come under the control of the Security Council, and the Trusteeship Council will exercise no functions with regard to them, unless the Security Council requests its assistance. Strategic areas may include the whole or any part of a trust territory. A more detailed discussion of the Security Council's responsibilities towards them will be found in Chapter VII.

UNITY

We have seen that the Charter provides the Security Council with powers which enable it to act with unprecedented speed and to bring into play forces never before controlled by an international organization. It has, in fact, successfully surmounted two of the obstacles which proved fatal to the League's hopes of maintaining peace.

But the third obstacle is the most difficult of all. To overcome this, the Security Council must achieve the unity which eluded the League. Without unity of control, the most efficient machinery cannot be worked.

But unity itself cannot be ensured by machinery. There is a limit to the extent to which any given body of men can be compelled to agree. The most that can be done is to create a framework within which co-operation is easy, and disunity difficult, and, by bringing the nations together within it, to break down their mutual mistrust by making them collaborate for common ends. This is what the Security Council sets out to do.

At San Francisco, many governments which signed the Charter were by no means wholehearted in their agreement with some of its clauses. They accepted those clauses rather than be left out of the brotherhood of the United Nations. But it is obvious that the new Organization will have to tackle many problems on which its members will hold very different views ; and indeed it is already clear that the Security Council is seriously divided on several issues. Now the Council must be able to act swiftly and firmly to maintain peace. Therefore it must be able to act on a majority vote, like all other workable representative bodies. Insistence on unanimity would tie its hands from the very start. But if there is a minority whose views are overruled on an issue of such importance as peace and war, there is always the danger of complete secession ; and the secession of a powerful nation or group of nations might imperil the whole structure.

It has often been said of the League of Nations that it was doomed to failure from the moment when the United States refused to ratify the Covenant. And at no time did the League command the allegiance of as large a proportion of mankind as does the United Nations today. But at one time or another it included among its members Soviet Russia, Italy, Germany and Japan, and it always had the faithful support of Britain and France. Was there ever a chance that the League, by adopting a more suitable constitution, might have kept all these nations together ?

In the League, as in the United Nations, there were originally five " principal powers " which were to be permanent members of the Council.[1] There were to be only four elected members of the Council, so that the principal powers would be in a majority. The smaller nations protested vigorously against this.[2] President Wilson replied that if the Great Powers guaranteed in the Covenant the integrity of all the small nations, the latter need have no fears that any injustice would be done to them[3] ; and other representatives of the Big Five said, more realistically, that " of course the control of the League must in reality be with the Great Powers."[4] Of the five principal powers, America never joined the League, Japan and Italy were among the first aggressor states with which the League had to deal, and so France and Britain were eventually left as the only permanent members of the Council. The smaller nations then had a majority. But in any case, the Covenant provided that decisions of the Council, as of the Assembly, must be unanimous to be valid. This made it impossible for the smaller nations, even after they had obtained a majority in the Council, to get any action taken against the will of the surviving Great Powers. In any case, the unanimity requirement practically hamstrung the League from the beginning.

[1]France, Italy, Japan, the United States and the British Empire.
[2]The original draft only allowed the smaller nations two seats.
[3]Minutes of the 3rd Meeting of the Commission on the League of Nations, February 5, 1919.
[4]" Comments and Suggestions on Wilson's Second Draft," dated January 10, 1919.

The sad experience of the League was extremely valuable to the creators of the United Nations. It was obvious that the principle of unanimity had to be jettisoned. It was equally obvious that the new organization would not survive its first and most dangerous years without the united support of the major powers ; and there was the additional certainty that those powers would not join an organization in which the smaller nations, by outvoting them, could take over control of their armed forces. The compromise on which agreement was finally reached satisfied the major powers but gave the smaller nations a great deal more than they had obtained in the League Covenant.

In the Assembly, where all nations are on an equal footing, decisions can be made by a two-thirds majority, and it is therefore possible for a combination of smaller nations to override the unanimous opposition of all the major powers. But the Assembly cannot make any decision affecting peace and security without the consent of the Security Council. In the Council the balance between great powers and small is delicately adjusted. Of the eleven seats, six are filled by election from the General Assembly, while five are reserved for China, France, the Soviet Union, the United Kingdom and the United States. The small nations, therefore, possess a clear majority. But this is balanced by the inclusion in the voting provisions of the much debated " Great Power veto."

The six non-permanent members of the Council are elected for a two-year term, three retiring every year. Retiring members are not eligible for immediate re-election. There is thus a constant change in the composition of the Council. The Charter provides that in these elections due regard must be paid to the candidates' respective contributions to the maintenance of peace and the other objects of the United Nations, and to equitable geographical distribution.

In the first elections these conditions would appear to have been satisfactorily fulfilled. If we divide the member states into six geographical groups we find that one seat in the Council has been given to each group, as follows :

North and Central America (12 members) : Mexico.[1]
South America (10 members) : Brazil.
Western Europe (7 members) : The Netherlands.[1]
Eastern Europe (7 members) : Poland.
Africa and Middle East (10 members) : Egypt.[1]
Pacific and Far East (5 members) : Australia.

All six of these are states whose contributions to the work of the United Nations have been or are likely to be considerable. If the non-permanent seats are distributed with equal success in future elections, the Council will be as representative of the United Nations as any body of eleven men could be.

[1]Retiring after one year.

C

The five permanent members of the Security Council are endowed by the Charter with several specific powers. They are automatically members of the Trusteeship Council, and their chiefs of staff constitute the Military Staff Committee.[1] The Charter itself, and any amendment to it, must be ratified by all of them in order to take effect.[2] But their most important and most debated power is their right of veto in the Security Council itself.

THE GREAT-POWER VETO

Article 27 of the Charter provides that, while each member of the Council shall have only one vote, decisions on all except procedural matters " shall be made by an affirmative vote of seven members including the concurring vote of the permanent members ; provided that, in decisions under Chapter 6 and paragraph 3 of Article 52, a party to a dispute shall abstain from voting."

Procedural questions may be decided by an affirmative vote of any seven members of the Council.

On any point of substance a permanent member of the Security Council can, therefore, block a decision which is distasteful to him. This " veto power " has been fiercely criticized ever since it was agreed upon by President Roosevelt, Marshal Stalin, and Mr. Churchill at the Yalta Conference in February, 1945. It was attacked at San Francisco, during the General Assembly's London session, and in some of the first meetings of the Security Council itself. To justify it, some of the creators of the United Nations point out that the five Great Powers will in any case have to play the main parts in preventing any future aggression, and their armed forces will be the Security Council's real weapon ; that these Powers would not adhere to the United Nations if they were thereby liable to lose control of their armed forces ; and that it is essential to the very existence of the Organization that the Great Powers should not leave it as they left the League. Their opponents reply that the veto gives the Powers an implicit right to violate the Charter when they please, and protects them from the consequences.

In fact the veto is a concession to reality, a concession to the supreme importance of unity in the Council, a concession at the expense of equality. At San Francisco the opposition of the smaller nations to the whole idea of the veto led them to submit a *questionnaire* to the five sponsoring Powers, and the reply, while of course not of the same authenticity as the Charter itself, can be taken as an accurate indication of the real significance of the veto.

The five-Power reply begins by stating the voting rules contained in the quotation from the Charter at the head of this chapter. It continues : " No one member of the Council could prevent consideration and dis-

[1] Articles 47 and 86 of the Charter.
[2] Articles 108, 109 and 110 of the Charter.

cussion of a dispute threatening world peace. . . . a hearing on that dispute in the Council, or a decision of the Council to remind a State of its obligations under the Charter. Beyond these points, actions of the Council may have major political consequences and require enforcement measures. Consequently the unanimity of the five permanent members would be required on decisions to make an investigation, to call upon States to settle their differences or to make recommendations. A permanent member party to a dispute would refrain from voting. . . . Withdrawing from a situation after launching an enquiry or making a recommendation would be at the risk of the Council's failing to discharge its responsibilities. . . . The Yalta formula permitting action on a majority of seven would make the Council less subject to obstruction than was the League Council under the unanimity rule. . . . Under the Yalta formula . . . any five of the non-permanent members could block a Council action. . . . Since the permanent members have primary responsibility for maintaining peace, they could not be expected, in the present condition of the world, to take enforcement action in which they had not concurred. If the Council is to work in practice, the five permanent members and at least two non-permanent members must agree."

The five-Power statement also stated that in the view of the permanent members, the veto could be applied in deciding whether or not any particular decision was procedural or substantial.

Since the Council began its actual handling of important issues, there has been much controversy about the exact limits of the veto power. In the first place, of course, there is the question of which decisions are procedural, and therefore not subject to the veto. A committee of experts set up by the Council to straighten out doubtful points such as this failed to reach agreement after numerous sessions. The Soviet member of this committee submitted a document which stated that in his view " a decision whether a question . . . is of a procedural nature, and also whether a question is a dispute or a situation . . . shall be accepted if it is voted for by seven members including the concurring votes of all the permanent members." The effect of this application of the veto power to the question of whether the veto power can be applied in any particular case would be to remove entirely the limitations imposed on the veto by Article 27. In fact the new Soviet proposal goes further than the five-power statement issued in San Francisco, for the latter declared that the veto could not be used to prevent the bringing of a dispute before the Council, while the new Soviet suggestion would in effect enable any Great Power to prevent a small nation bringing a complaint against it. As no decision has yet been reached as to which questions are procedural and which are disputes, there is still likely to be a long and apparently futile discussion of terms every time the Council is asked to deal with a case which is distasteful to a Great Power.

There is the further question as to precisely how the veto can be applied. The Soviet thesis is that it can be applied either by a direct vote against the motion before the Council, or by abstention from voting, or by the non-attendance of a permanent member. It is incontestable that when a Great Power votes against a motion, that motion is lost. But when the permanent member merely abstains from voting, the effect is by no means clear. On April 29, 1946, the Soviet representative on the Council abstained from voting on an important issue before the Council, but announced that " this does not in any sense constitute a precedent on the question of abstinence from voting by a permanent member of the Security Council." Other members of the Council then stated that since it had never been decided whether the particular issue under discussion was procedural or substantial, they would not consider the Soviet members action to constitute a precedent ; and the incident was closed. It is obvious that if the matter had been formally declared to be one of substance, then the Soviet abstention would either have blocked the Council's motion, or would have been tantamount to an admission that more abstention from voting does not amount to an exercise of the veto power ; and in the latter case, it would appear that a veto could only be exercised by a direct negative vote.

The non-attendance at Council meetings of a permanent member is also claimed by Soviet representatives to be an effective method of exercising the veto. After absenting himself from several Council meetings during March and April 1946, Mr. Gromyko, the Soviet representative, declared that he held the decisions taken in his absence to be illegal and void. This attitude was sharply criticized by the Australian member who argued that by absenting himself from Council meetings a member would " abandon the powers that accrue to him as a member, and have no powers greater than those of any member of the United Nations." It was the Australian representative's opinion that if a member stayed away from meetings he was failing in his duty towards all the member states which are not directly represented on the Council, and that it would be most dangerous for the Council to entertain the idea that any member could, by absenting himself, bring into question the ability of the Council to function and take action. This view appeared to have the support of all the other members attending the meeting at which it was expressed.

But however much discussion there may be about its limitations, the veto power still remains. It is really just as simple for a permanent member to attend Council meetings and vote against motions as to stay away ; and the first of these alternatives is clearly a legal exercise of the veto power. Whether the United Nations will eventually find it possible to do away with the veto is a matter for speculation. For the present, it is there, and the machinery must be worked with due regard to it. It is important in this connection to notice that the veto right is, of course, extended to all the powers which the Council shares with the General Assembly. Something must now be said about these powers.

THE COUNCIL AND THE ASSEMBLY

The question of the relative status of the Security Council and the General Assembly is discussed at some length in Chapter IV. Here it is only necessary to state briefly the points of contact between the two organs. First, there are several important powers which can only be exercised by the two acting in agreement. These include all questions relating to the membership of the United Nations. Member states may be admitted to the Organization, suspended from membership, and finally expelled, by the Assembly acting on the Council's recommendations. It will be noted that this implies that the Council alone can initiate such actions. Recently the Australian member of the Council has raised the whole question of the Assembly's share in these processes, and has emphasized that it must not come about that the Assembly be forced to play the part of a rubber stamp. As a concession to this feeling, the Council has now decided to consider applications for membership in August of each year, so that it may then pass its recommendations directly to the General Assembly, which will meet each September.

The Security Council shares with the Assembly the duty of electing judges to the International Court, and it also shares the right to request the Court for advisory opinions on any legal matter. The Council is responsible for recommending candidates for the post of Secretary-General to the Assembly; and it is likely that the Assembly will generally accept the Council's nominations without much question.

In the general field of security, the Council is, of course, supreme; but it must allow the Assembly certain privileges. The Assembly may discuss any question relating to international peace and security brought before it by a member or non-member state; it may call the Council's attention to such a question; and it may make recommendations either to the states concerned or to the Security Council itself. But the Assembly must refer any such questions to the Council either before or after discussing them; and it is expressly forbidden to make any recommendations in connection with a dispute or dangerous situation which the Council is already considering unless the Council asks it to do so. Finally, the Council is directed by the Charter to make annual reports to the Assembly on all its activities connected with the maintenance of peace and security; special reports may also be made if necessary.

HOW THE COUNCIL WORKS

Each nation which is a member of the Security Council can only appoint one representative. There are, therefore, only eleven men with voting powers seated round the Council table. The Secretary-General, or his deputy, attends Council meetings, prepares the agenda and arranges for a verbatim record of all meetings except private ones to be kept. Under the agreed rules of procedure, meetings will normally be public, but certain questions, such as the appointment of a Secretary-General, will be discussed in private.

Under Article 31, the Council may permit representatives of nations whose interests are affected by particular questions to take part in discussions on those questions, but these representatives have no votes.[1] Under Article 32, the Council is obliged to invite the presence and participation of any nation which is a party to a dispute under discussion, but again, participation does not include the right to vote.

The Charter gives the Council considerable freedom to arrange its own procedure. It provides that in addition to the ordinary meetings there shall be " periodic " meetings ; these will apparently be held every six months, and attended by foreign ministers or representatives of equivalent rank. Less important meetings will be attended by the permanent representatives which member nations must maintain at the official seat of the United Nations. Although normally the Council will meet at the official headquarters (which will be near New York) it may at any time decide to meet elsewhere, if another location is more suitable for its particular purpose.

The Council was also permitted by the Charter to decide for itself how to choose its President. It has decided that each member shall hold the Presidency for one calendar month, the order followed being the alphabetical order of the English names of the members. Thus Australia provided the first President, and Brazil, China, Egypt and France followed in that order. The President has the difficult double task of controlling the Council and representing his own country. At the first sessions, the first two or three Presidents faced the additional difficulty that procedure had not yet been clarified, and disputing members naturally tried to stretch procedural points as far as possible in their own favour. A good many questions of procedure have yet to be decided ; and even when finally approved, they are liable to be altered by a simple decision of seven members of the Council.

The Council is empowered to set up sub-committees of any number of members. These sub-committees frequently, but not invariably, sit in private session. They are normally only appointed to carry out a specific task and to report to the Council on its completion ; but a standing committee to consider applications for membership of the United Nations is being considered. This, like some of the other sub-committees, will consist of one representative of each state represented on the Council.

[1] At the first meetings of the Council, Persia, the Ukraine, Greece, Syria and Lebanon attended under this article.

ATOMIC ENERGY

The Charter of the United Nations was drawn up before the first atomic bomb in history fell upon Hiroshima. It therefore contains no reference to this terrifying innovation in warfare. But naturally the possibility of an outbreak of atomic warfare has already become the worst nightmare of all who are concerned with the peace of the world ; and, while there is something to be said for the argument that war has at last become too terrible for any nation to contemplate, the responsibility of the Security Council towards the maintenance of peace has become all the heavier. It was generally agreed among the Powers, shortly after the end of the Japanese war, that the control of atomic energy should be placed in the hands of the United Nations ; and at the Moscow Conference held in December 1945, the foreign ministers of the Soviet Union, the United States and the United Kingdom drew up a draft resolution for submission to the General Assembly. On January 24, 1946 the Assembly passed this resolution. It establishes an Atomic Energy Commission empowered, in general terms, to " deal with the problems raised by the discovery of atomic energy and other related matters."

The Commission is composed of one representative of each member of the Security Council, together with Canada when that nation is not a member of the Council. Canada's special position is, of course, due to her partnership with the United States and Britain in the pioneer work on atomic energy carried out during the war. Each member state has one representative on the Commission. The Commission will not infringe upon the responsibilities of the Security Council, the General Assembly or any other United Nations organ, but will make recommendations for those organs to consider in the performance of the tasks allotted to each by the Charter. In all matters affecting security, the Security Council shall issue directions to the Commission, and the Commission will be responsible to the Council for its work on such matters. The Commission's reports will be first submitted to the Security Council, which will decide whether or not the interests of peace and security permit that they be made public. If it thinks fit, the Council will transmit the reports to the Assembly, the member states, and the other organs of the United Nations. It is clear from these provisos that the Atomic Energy Commission, although the creation of the Assembly, will in fact be a subordinate organ of the Security Council. This point was brought up in the Assembly debate by the Philippines delegate, who argued that to ask the Assembly to create the Commission and then to take away from it all power to control its offspring was a grave blow to the status of the Assembly in the eyes of the world.

The work of the Commission is to proceed, according to its terms of reference, by separate stages ; it is hoped that the successful completion of each stage will develop the necessary confidence throughout the world which will enable the next stage to be undertaken.

The Commission is authorized to enquire into all phases of the atomic energy problem, and in particular " to make specific proposals :

" (a) for extending between all nations the exchange of basic scientific information for peaceful ends ;

" (b) for control of atomic energy to the extent necessary to ensure its use only for peaceful purposes ;

" (c) for the elimination from national armaments of atomic weapons and of all other major weapons adaptable to mass destruction ; and

" (d) for effective safeguards by way of inspection and other means to protect complying States against the hazards of violations and evasions."

The member states had all nominated their representatives[1] to the Atomic Energy Commission by May 1946, and the Commission met for the first time on June 14 in New York.

Meanwhile a board of consultants appointed by the United States Government has issued a report outlining a " basis for discussion " for the Commission's consideration. This report, published in March 1946, declares that for the time being it is comparatively safe to assume that atomic energy can only be released if uranium and thorium are available as raw materials. Uranium and thorium are only found in certain geological conditions ; and it is therefore suggested by the board of consultants that the United Nations atomic authority should at once proceed to bring under its direct control all world supplies of these two materials. The atomic authority must, of course, conduct intensive and continuous surveys to discover new deposits of uranium and thorium, and must explore new methods of extracting them from media in which they are found in small quantities. Similar safeguards could later be extended to other materials which proved to have a value for atomic purposes.

The American report emphasizes that such measures would not provide absolute security against the possibility of illicit operations. But it is argued that a scheme such as the above would be far better than reversion to an international anarchy in which each nation would attempt to outstrip its rivals in equipping itself with atomic weapons, and also considerably better than the creation of a mere police-like agency with only negative powers of supervision.

[1] The representatives are :
Mr. Paul Hasluck, Australia ; Capt. da Motta Silva, Brazil ; Dr. Quo Tai-chi, China ; Hafez Afifi Pasha, Egypt ; M. Henri Bonnet, France ; Senor M. S. Vallarta, Mexico ; Dr. van Kleffens, Netherlands ; Prof. Pienkowski, Poland ; Mr. A. A. Gromyko, Soviet Union ; Sir Alexander Cadogan, United Kingdom ; Mr. Bernard Baruch, United States ; Gen. MacNaughton, Canada.

CHAPTER VI

THE INTERNATIONAL COURT OF JUSTICE

ORIGINS

THE International Court of Justice is an integral part of the United Nations organization. But the idea of a world court has developed separately from the idea of a league or union of nations, and the structure of the new Court cannot be explained without a brief reference to its predecessors. The idea of settling international disputes by arbitration or adjudication is, of course, very old. The states of mediæval Europe sometimes submitted their differences to the Papacy, sometimes to a disinterested neighbour. The first modern treaty of arbitration was that of 1794 between Britain and the United States ; and during the nineteenth century *ad hoc* tribunals were constituted to deal with several disputes between nations. Finally, the two Hague Conferences of 1899 and 1907, at which the principal sovereign states of Europe and America were represented, agreed upon the creation of a Permanent Court of Arbitration.

THE HAGUE TRIBUNAL

The Permanent Court of Arbitration, often called the Hague Tribunal, still exists, although it has recently been quiescent. It consists simply of a panel of judges from whom states may select an *ad hoc* court to arbitrate on a particular question. Each state which was a party to the " Convention for the Pacific Settlement of International Disputes " adopted by the Hague Conferences is entitled to nominate up to four members to this panel. The members nominated by each state form a " national group," and these national groups play an important part in the machinery for creating the new International Court of Justice. The Charter of the United Nations also implicitly recognizes the continued validity of the Hague Tribunal by specifically stating that member states may submit their disputes to tribunals other than the new Court.[1]

The 1907 Conference produced a draft for a second world court, to be known as the Court of Arbitral Justice. This was to be a unified body of judges, not a panel from which contesting nations could select suitable members. There was so much difference of opinion about the method of electing judges to the proposed Court that the draft never took effect ; but when in 1919 the League of Nations decided to set up a new world

---

[1]Article 95 of the Charter provides that " nothing in the present Charter shall prevent members of the United Nations from entrusting the solution of their differences to other tribunals by virtue of agreements already in existence or which may be concluded in the future."

C*

court, the committee of jurists appointed to prepare a draft Statute made considerable use of the 1907 draft, and some of its provisions have survived in the Statute approved at San Francisco.

THE LEAGUE AND ITS COURT

Article 14 of the Covenant of the League of Nations provided that the Council of the League should submit to the member states plans for the establishment of a Permanent Court of International Justice. The Statute creating this Court was adopted by the League Assembly in 1920, and came into force in 1921.[1] The Permanent Court began its sessions at the Hague in 1922, and by 1938 had dealt with 79 cases, of which 28 were requests from the League Council for advisory opinions. Its prestige was inevitably affected by the decline of the whole League ; but it retained the confidence and respect of the nations to a greater degree than its parent organization. The United Nations have decided to supersede the Permanent Court, but this is clearly only intended to be a change in form, and a convenient means of shedding the League's unhappy associations and some of its unhappier member states.[2] The Statute of the Permanent Court is reproduced almost verbatim in the Statute of the new Court ; indeed, such changes as have been made have been described as " disappointingly few."[3] Further proof that the United Nations appreciate the past services of the Permanent Court and intend to preserve an organic continuity between it and the new Court can be found in the explicit recognition of the Permanent Court in both the Charter and the new Statute.[4] No other organ of the League of Nations receives any such recognition.

As early as 1943 a committee of United Nations judicial experts was set up in England to discuss the revision of the Statute of the Permanent Court. This committee recommended several substantial changes in the Statute, such as the extension of the Court's powers of compulsory jurisdiction. But at San Francisco the commission on judicial organization preferred to retain the old Statute almost without amendment. In the summary of the new Statute given in this chapter, attention is drawn to the points at which the two texts differ.

[1]The only substantial amendments were those made by the Protocol of 1936.
[2]Spain is still (in 1946) a party to the Statute of the Permanent Court.
[3]Professor Norman Bentwich, in " The United Nations Charter : A Commentary."
[4]Article 92 of the Charter states that " the annexed Statute is based upon the Statute of the Permanent Court of International Justice." Article 37 of the new Statute provides that " whenever a treaty or convention in force provides for the reference of a matter to the Permanent Court of International Justice, the matter shall, as between the parties to the present Statute, be referred to the International Court of Justice."

THE NEW COURT

The International Court of Justice derives its powers directly from the Charter of the United Nations, which declares that " the International Court of Justice shall be the principal judicial organ of the United Nations. It shall function in accordance with the annexed Statute, which . . . forms an integral part of the present Charter."[1]

The Court is the only organ of the United Nations whose " members " are not States but individuals holding their seats in their own right. Article 2 of the Statute provides that they shall be " independent judges, elected regardless of their nationality from among persons of high moral character, who possess the qualifications required in their respective countries for appointment to the highest judicial offices, or are jurisconsults of recognized competence in international law."[2]

In addition to these individual qualifications, the Court as a whole must ensure adequate representation of " the main forms of civilization and the principal legal systems of the world."[3] This would presumably include at least the Latin, Anglo-American, Russian, Chinese and Islamic systems.

ELECTION OF MEMBERS

The Court shall consist of 15 members, no two of whom may be nationals of the same state.[4] The method of election is complicated. First we must recall the Permanent Court of Arbitration (the Hague Tribunal) established by the conventions of 1899 and 1907. The states which were parties to those conventions each nominated a " national group " of not more than four judicial experts. The Statute provides that member states which were not parties to the Hague Conventions shall now appoint similar national groups, and that the national groups of all the United Nations shall then proceed to nominate candidates for membership of the Court.[5] No national group may nominate more than four candidates, not more than two of whom shall be of their own nationality.[6] The Secretary-General shall then draw up a list of candidates

[1]Article 92. This definition is confirmed by Article 1 of the Statute : " The International Court of Justice established by the Charter of the United Nations as the principal judicial organ of the United Nations shall be constituted and shall function in accordance with the provisions of the present Statute."

[2]The inclusion of these two alternative qualifications has its origins in the 1907 draft for the Court of Arbitral Justice. Generally speaking, British and American legal opinion considers practical experience of the courts to be a more important qualification for an international judge than the specialized, but often academic, knowledge of the expert in international law. European jurists tend to take the opposite view.

[3]Article 9 of the Statute.

[4]Article 3 of the Statute. This article also provides that a member " shall be deemed to be a national of the state in which he ordinarily exercises civil and political rights."

[5]Article 4 of the Statute.

[6]Article 5 of the Statute.

nominated and present it to both the Security Council and the General Assembly, and these two bodies, meeting simultaneously but independently of one another, shall elect the members of the Court[1]. Candidates obtaining an absolute majority in the Assembly and a majority of 7 in the Council shall be considered elected.[2] If any seats then remain to be filled, further meetings of the Assembly and the Council shall be held ; but if, after three such meetings, there are still vacancies, the Assembly and the Council may, instead of taking further votes, each send three representatives to a joint conference which may decide by a simple majority to submit for the approval of the Assembly and the Council a single name for each vacant seat.[3] Finally, if the joint conference can find no candidate who can secure election, the Security Council shall fix a period during which the judges who have already been elected may, by a simple majority vote, fill the vacant seat or seats from among those candidates who have already received votes in either the Assembly or the Council. If, even in this last resort, there is an equality of votes between the judges, the eldest judge is to have a casting vote.

All this sounds very cumbersome. But it worked reasonably well in the Permanent Court, and it has been decided to retain it because it satisfied several difficult requirements. The nomination of candidates by national groups instead of by governments is meant to bring into the Court true jurists instead of mere political lawyers. The proviso that groups may only nominate two candidates of their own nationality is an ingenious device which compels the groups to consider seriously the claims of candidates of other nationalities. The division of the elections between the Assembly and the Council gives the Great Powers a substantial, but not overwhelming, share in determining the composition of the Court.[4] And the detailed provisions for completing the Court in the event of deadlock in either Assembly or Council ensure that neither body can indefinitely delay the creation or renewal of the Court.

In practice, the first elections to the Court were completed in one day. 13 judges were elected at the first ballot, one at the third and one at the fourth.

The term of office is nine years ; retiring judges may be re-elected.

[1] Article 8 of the Statute.
[2] Article 10 of the Statute. If, however, more than one national of the same state should obtain the necessary majorities, only the eldest of these shall be considered elected.
[3] Article 12 of the Statute. The joint conference may propose a candidate who was not included in the original list, but only if the conference agrees to support his nomination unanimously.
[4] In the original Covenant of the League, the Great Powers had a majority on the Council, and it was thought that the dual election of the Court would ensure that each Great Power got a judge on the Court. But although the smaller nations soon achieved a majority in the League Council and now have one in the Security Council, there is no sign of any tendency to exclude the candidates of Great Powers. Each of the Big Five has a judge in the present court.

Five of the 15 judges are to retire every three years.[1] Judges continue to discharge their duties until replaced, and they will remain to finish any cases begun before their replacement.[2] A member elected to replace another member whose term has not expired shall only hold office for the remainder of his predecessor's term.[3]

SAFEGUARDS OF JUDICIAL INDEPENDENCE

On assuming their duties, members of the Court are to make a solemn declaration in open court that they will exercise their powers impartially and conscientiously.[4] During their terms of office, they may exercise no political or administrative function ; they may not engage in any other professional occupation ; they may not participate in the decision of any case in which they have previously taken part as agent, counsel or advocate, or as a member of another court or of a commission of enquiry, or in any other capacity.[5]

The salaries of members of the Court are fixed by the General Assembly. During a judge's term of office, his salary and allowances cannot be diminished.[6] Members of the Court engaged on the Court's business are entitled to normal diplomatic privileges and immunities.[7]

No member of the Court may be dismissed unless in the unanimous opinion of the other members, he has ceased to fulfil the conditions required of a judge of the Court.[8]

MACHINERY OF THE COURT

The Court shall elect its own President and Vice-President every three years ; both are eligible for immediate re-election. The Court shall also appoint a Registrar and such other officials as may be necessary.[9]

The seat of the Court shall be at the Hague, where the President and Registrar must reside ; but the Court may sit elsewhere if it thinks fit.

---

[1]This is one of the few points in which the new Statute differs from that of the Permanent Court.

The following table shows the members of the present Court and the number of years each will serve :

Prof. Basdevant (France) 9 ; Dr. Guerrero (El Salvador) 9 ; Sir A. D. McNair (U.K.) 9 ; Dr. Alvarez (Chile) 9 ; Dr. Azevedo (Brazil) 9 ; Dr. de Visscher (Belgium) 6 ; Prof. Krylov (U.S.S.R.) 6 ; Mr. F. Alfaro (Mexico) 6 ; Hon. G. H. Hackworth (U.S.A.) 6 ; Dr. Klaestad (Norway) 6 ; Dr. Hsu Mo (China) 3 ; H. E. Badawi Pasha (Egypt) 3 ; Mr. J. E. Read (Canada) 3 ; Dr. Zoricic (Yugoslavia) 3 ; Mr. Winiarski (Poland) 3.

[2]Article 13 of the Statute.
[3]Article 15 of the Statute.
[4]Article 20 of the Statute.
[5]Article 17 of the Statute.
[6]Article 32 of the Statute.
[7]Article 19 of the Statute.
[8]Article 18 of the Statute.
[9]Article 21 of the Statute.

The Court shall remain permanently in session except during judicial vacations, whose duration it shall itself decide.[1]

The full Court shall sit except where the Statute expressly provides otherwise ; but periodic leave will be granted to judges, and up to four judges may be dispensed from sitting at any one time. A quorum of nine judges shall suffice to constitute the Court.[2]

The Statute empowers the Court to delegate its authority to "chambers" consisting of groups of its members. Judgments given by these chambers shall be considered as rendered by the Court.[3] When a chamber is formed to deal with a particular case, the number of judges shall be decided by the Court in agreement with the parties concerned. Standing chambers of at least three judges may be formed to deal with particular categories of cases (e.g., labour cases, cases relating to international communications, etc). The Statute also directs the Court to appoint annually a chamber of five judges to deal with cases by summary procedure where this is accepted by the parties to the case.[4]

PROVISIONS FOR IMPARTIALITY

Any judge who considers that he should not sit in a particular case shall so inform the President ; similarly, if the President considers that a particular judge should not sit in a particular case, he shall give him notice accordingly. If in any such case the President and the judge concerned do not agree, the Court shall decide the point.[5]

But no judge shall be disqualified from sitting in a case simply because his own nation is involved in it ; and, as this might be thought to give an unfair advantage to those nations whose nationals are already members of the Court, the Statute provides that extra " national judges " shall be appointed to the Court whenever a nation which is not represented on the Court is a party to a case before it. Even when neither party to a case is represented on the Court, both have the right to nominate extra judges.[6] Experience in the Permanent Court showed that these " national judges " regularly gave minority opinions favouring their own nations ; but it is

[1]Articles 22 and 23 of the Statute. The original Statute of the Permanent Court did not provide for permanent session, but this was introduced by the Protocol of 1936.
[2]Article 25 of the Statute.
[3]Article 27 of the Statute.
[4]Article 29 of the Statute. The Permanent Court made very little use of chambers and none at all of those intended to deal with special categories of cases. Proposals were made at San Francisco that " branch courts " should be set up in different parts of the world, but this idea was rejected.
[5]Article 24 of the Statute.
[6]When several parties are contending in the same interest, they may only choose one extra judge between them. If the case is to be heard by a chamber, the President shall request one or if necessary two of the members of the chamber to give place either to the members of the Court who are of the required nationality or to the extra judges chosen by the parties to the case.

evidently thought better that both parties should always be represented, and automatically counterbalance each other, than that there should be any room for accusations of partiality on the part of the Court.[1]

THE COURT'S JURISDICTION

Only states may be parties in cases before the Court.[2] The Court shall be open to all states which are parties to the present Statute,[3] and to other states subject to conditions to be laid down by the Security Council. When a state which is not a member of the United Nations is a party to a case before it, the Court shall decide the amount which that state, if not already sharing the expenses of the Court, shall contribute towards the costs of the case.[4]

No State can be compelled to submit its case to the Court. Article 93 of the Charter states that "all members of the United Nations are *ipso facto* parties to the Statute of the International Court of Justice;" but to be a party to the Statute by no means implies acceptance of the Court's jurisdiction. The Court has in fact jurisdiction only over such cases as are voluntarily referred to it by both the parties involved. There is, however, an "optional clause" in the Statute, under which states may at any time declare that, in relation to any other state accepting the same obligations, they accept the jurisdiction of the Court in all legal disputes concerning the interpretation of treaties, international law, the existence of a breach of international obligations, or the reparation to be made for such a breach. This declaration may be made unconditionally, or on condition of reciprocity on the part of other specified states, or for a limited time.[5]

Through the "optional clause" in the Statute of the Permanent Court, 49 states had by 1939 accepted compulsory jurisdiction, but many of these

---

[1]Article 31 of the Statute.

[2]Article 34 of the Statute. The San Francisco conference rejected proposals that international organizations and private individuals should be allowed to institute proceedings before the Court. But a State may, of course, take up the cause of one of its nationals and present it to the Court.

[3]Article 93 of the Charter provides that states which are not members of the United Nations may become parties to the Statute under conditions to be laid down by the General Assembly on the recommendation of the Security Council.

[4]Article 35 of the Statute.

[5]At San Francisco 16 nations voted in favour of compulsory jurisdiction, 26 against. Delegates of the USSR and USA said that their Governments would find it difficult to accept the Statute of the Court if jurisdiction was made compulsory from the first, but that they might be able to accept compulsory jurisdiction later. Eventually the committee concerned agreed to retain the League Statute's provisions for optional acceptance, at the same time unanimously adopting a resolution proposed by Iran recommending all member states to accept compulsory jurisdiction as soon as possible.

In April 1946 the U.S. State Department announced that it favoured acceptance by the United States of the Court's compulsory jurisdiction, and appropriate bills were submitted for the approval of Congress.

had made reservations.[1] The new Statute provides that where such acceptances are still in force they shall now be deemed to be acceptances of the compulsory jurisdiction of the new Court.

The jurisdiction of the Court comprises not only all cases referred to it by the parties concerned and all matters referred to it by the Charter and other treaties, but also all matters which would previously have been referred under the terms of various treaties, to the Permanent Court of International Justice.[2]

Finally, if there is any dispute as to whether the Court has jurisdiction in any particular case, the Court itself shall decide.[3]

THE LAW TO BE APPLIED

In deciding the cases submitted to it, the Court is to apply :—

(a) International conventions, whether general or particular, establishing rules expressly recognized by the contesting states.

(b) International custom, as evidence of a general practice accepted as law.

(c) The general principles of law recognized by civilized nations.

(d) Judicial decisions and the teachings of the most highly qualified publicists of the various nations, as subsidiary means for the determination of rules of law.[1]

Provided the parties concerned agree, the Court may also decide a case *ex aequo et bono*, i.e., on the basis of general equity. This gives the Court a certain power of arbitration as distinct from adjudication. In practice, the experience of the Permanent Court showed that there was never any very great difficulty in finding a suitable law to apply.

In directing the Court to apply " judicial decisions and the teachings of publicists," the Statute draws attention to the fact that its own previous decisions are not binding precedents.[2]

PROCEDURE

The Court shall use either the French or the English language, or both, by agreement with the parties to each case. The Court may also authorize any party to use any other language it prefers.[6] The Court shall provide each party with certified copies of all documents submitted by other parties. Cases shall be decided on both documentary and oral evidence, and unless

---

[1]The United Kingdom, for example, had stipulated that the Court's jurisdiction should not cover disputes with other members of the British Commonwealth, disputes falling within British domestic jurisdiction, and certain other categories. When renewing acceptance in 1940 for a further period of five years, the U.K. made additional reservations.

[2]Article 37 of the Statute.

[3]Article 36 of the Statute.

[4]Article 38 of the Statute.

[5]Article 59 of the Statute.

[6]Article 39 of the Statute.

the Court or the parties concerned object, hearings shall be in public.[1] The Statute gives the Court considerable freedom to decide for itself the actual conduct of cases. If one party fails to appear before the Court, the other may ask for a decision in its favour.[2]

The Court shall deliberate in secret, and its deliberations shall remain secret. All questions shall be decided by a simple majority of judges present. If there is an equality of votes, the President of the Court or the judge presiding in his place shall have a casting vote. Any dissenting judge may deliver a minority opinion. The judgments of the Court are final and without appeal ; but the Court itself may revise them if fresh facts of a decisive nature are discovered after judgment has been given.[3]

Decisions of the Court have no binding force except between the parties immediately concerned and in the particular case under decision. International law is not, therefore, case law in the English sense, and a previous decision of the Court cannot be quoted as a binding precedent in support of a later case. But the Court will inevitably be influenced by its own previous decisions and by those of other international and national courts ; and it is clearly intended that its work should ultimately create a generally accepted body of international law.

ADVISORY OPINIONS

Under Article 96 of the Charter, the Security Council, the General Assembly and such other organs of the United Nations as may be so authorized by the Assembly have the right to request the Court to give an advisory opinion on legal questions arising within the scope of their activities. This is confirmed in Article 65 of the Statute.[4]

States whose interests are likely to be affected either by advisory opinions or by other decisions of the Court may represent their particular cases to the Court.[5]

AMENDMENTS TO THE STATUTE

The Court may itself propose amendments to the Statute by communicating with the Secretary-General. Amendments shall be affected by the same procedure as that for amending the Charter, subject to any provisions which the General Assembly may adopt on the recommendation of the Security Council concerning the participation in the work of amendment of states which are parties to the Statute but not members of the United Nations.

[1] Article 46 of the Statute. The Permanent Court's hearings were invariably in public.
[2] Article 53 of the Statute.
[3] Article 61 of the Statute. No application for revision was ever made to the Permanent Court.
[4] The Council of the League was the only body which ever requested an advisory opinion from the Permanent Court.
[5] Articles 62, 63, 66 and 67 of the Statute.

THE COURT COMES TO LIFE

Although the Statute was accepted by all the nations represented at San Francisco and duly signed on June 26, 1945, it was not possible to constitute the Court until both the General Assembly and the Security Council were ready for the simultaneous elections of the fifteen judges. These elections were completed on February 9, 1946. The Permanent Court of International Justice was wound up in April, and a few days later the new Court met for the first time at the Hague. The essential continuity between the two Courts was marked by the election as first President of Dr. Guerrero of El Salvador, who had been the last President of the Permanent Court.

CHAPTER VII

THE TRUSTEESHIP SYSTEM

NON-SELF-GOVERNING PEOPLES

HUNDREDS of millions of the inhabitants of this planet do not at present possess the right of self-government. That is universally acknowledged ; but there is room for considerable difference of opinion as to exactly which peoples can be classed as " non-self-governing," and this uncertainty has been the basis of much of the argument in United Nations debates on trusteeship. For the Charter provides that "Members of the United Nations which have or assume responsibilities for the administration of non-self-governing territories . . . accept as a sacred trust the obligation . . . to take due account of the political aspirations of their peoples, and to assist them in the progressive development of their free political institutions."

Now there are many territories, principally in Africa, whose peoples possess very little self-government, and there is general agreement that these territories come under the heading of " non-self-governing." But when we turn to consider territories which already enjoy a high degree of self-government, it is not so easy to make the distinction. If, for example, the British Government grants Burma full authority over her domestic affairs, but retains control over her foreign relationships and her defence, would Burma be " non-self-governing ? " Are the autonomous republics of Soviet Asia, whose defence and foreign affairs are the responsibility of the All-Union Government in Moscow, self-governing ?

Obviously it is possible to stretch the term " non-self-governing " to its logical maximum, and so to include all the small units of territory, such as Wales, Corsica, and Tasmania, which have become almost completely merged into larger states ; but in general the peoples of these territories would describe themselves as citizens of sovereign states, with rights as full as those of their neighbours in England, France and Australia, including representation in the parliaments at London, Paris and Canberra. On the other hand, it must be remembered that the French Government has granted to several African territories the right to elect members of the French Assembly. Does this automatically transfer French Cameroons, for example, to the same status as that of Scotland ?

It may be argued that when a large state absorbs a small territory adjacent to it (as Britain has absorbed Wales, or France Brittany) and when there is a general unity of political thought and culture common to both, the absorbed territory does not become " non-self-governing " ; whereas when a metropolitan state such as France acquires territories overseas, the mere grant of representation in a central assembly does not amount to a grant of self-government. It might be possible to define a " non-self-governing " territory as one which was part of a large political unit, but clearly did not wish to be ; but this is a dangerous definition, which might even to be extended to cover any territory, such as the Southern States during the American Civil War, which felt itself bound to oppose by force a particular policy of the central government.

How then can we define the non-self-governing territories of the world ? It seems that the only test left to us is that of general opinion. Most people would agree that, with the exceptions of Egypt, Ethiopia, Liberia, and the South African Union, the whole continent of Africa is non-self-governing ; there are various degrees of local autonomy, but in general the ultimate authority in each territory is wielded by a government whose seat is elsewhere. In South-East Asia, although here there has been more progress towards self-government, it cannot yet be said that it has been fully attained in Burma, Indo-China, Malaya, the East Indies, and many smaller Pacific islands. In the Caribbean area there is a third group of non-self-governing territories ; and in Central Asia there is a large area whose status is not very clearly defined, but the peoples of which are all dependent in some degree upon external authorities.

It is, then, to these territories that the eleventh chapter of the United Nations Charter refers. This chapter marks an entirely new stage in the relationship of the " colonial powers " to their dependent peoples. There is nothing corresponding to it in the Covenant of the League, which merely provides for " just treatment of the native inhabitants " of territories under the control of member states. In the Charter, on the other hand, the member states make a series of far-reaching undertakings with regard to all their dependent territories. First, they recognize the principle that the interests of the inhabitants of these territories shall be paramount. Second, they promise to ensure their political advancement, to develop self-government, to take due account of the inhabitants' political aspirations and to assist them in the progressive development of their free political institutions, " according to the particular circumstances of each territory and its peoples, and their varying stages of advancement." Third, they undertake to promote constructive measures of development, to encourage research, and to ensure the general economic advancement of the peoples concerned. Fourth, they will also ensure the just treatment and protection against abuses of these peoples, and their social advancement, with due respect for their culture. Fifth, they will base their policy in respect of these territories upon the good-neighbour principle, and take due account of the economic and commercial interests of other countries. Sixth, they will transmit to the Secretary-General statistical and other information about economic, social and educational conditions in their dependent territories.

Read together with the chapter of the Charter on Economic and Social

Co-operation,[1] the above undertakings constitute an important international convention on colonial administration, and their consequences may be far-reaching. On the other hand, no effective machinery is provided for the realization of these aims ; the only pressure which can be brought to bear upon a colonial power which is reluctant to carry out its " sacred trust " is that of world opinion. It is therefore all the more heartening that British proposals should have been so prominent in the drafting of this part of the Charter, for Britain, as the most important colonial power, must by her example exercise considerable influence on all the others, whether or not they are members of the United Nations.[2]

The Dumbarton Oaks plan made no provision at all for a convention on non-self-governing territories ; nor did it touch upon the future either of League Mandates or of territories taken from enemy countries during the Second World War. However, a set of supplementary proposals were agreed upon by the five Powers sponsoring the San Francisco conference, and these proposals, with certain amendments, are now embodied in Chapters 11, 12 and 13 (Articles 73 to 91) of the Charter. The first of these chapters contains the declaration on non-self-governing territories generally which is set out above. The other two are concerned with the creation of a Trusteeship System. It is important to make it quite clear here that, while the Charter recognizes the principle of trusteeship for all non-self-governing territories, the actual trusteeship system which it creates is solely concerned with a small category of " trust territories," and that the Trusteeship Council has no responsibility for, or authority over, colonial areas in general.

THE MANDATE SYSTEM

The principle of trusteeship for all colonies and other dependent territories is new ; but the trusteeship system itself is merely a strengthened version of the League's system of Mandates. The Mandate idea was originally conceived by Field-Marshal Smuts, and was incorporated in the Covenant of the League as Article 22. This article provides that, where the people of any territory taken from a defeated country are not able to stand by themselves, more advanced nations shall, as members of the League, accept their tutelage as a sacred trust. It does not make any comprehensive declaration about the future of all such territories, but instead divides the mandates into three classes, which have since become officially known as A, B, and C.

[1] Chapter 9 of the Charter pledges the United Nations to promote " higher standards of living, conditions of economic and social progress . . . and universal respect for, and observance of, human rights and fundamental freedoms for all without distinction as to race, sex, language or religion."
[2] Of the nations generally recognized as " colonial powers," Britain, France, Belgium and Holland are members of the Organization, Spain and Portugal are not.

Class " A " covered former Turkish territories whose peoples had reached " a stage of development where their existence as independent nations can be provisionally recognized, subject to the rendering of administrative advice and assistance by a Mandatory until such time as they are able to stand alone." It was laid down that " the wishes of these communities must be a principal consideration in the selection of a Mandatory."

Five Class " A " Mandates were created : Syria and Lebanon under French mandate, Iraq, Transjordan and Palestine under British. Iraq was recognized as a sovereign state in 1932, and became a member of the League of Nations. Syria and Lebanon were granted independence in 1941, and are now members of the United Nations, as is Iraq. Transjordan remained under British mandate until January 1946, when the British Government recognized it as a sovereign state and announced that it would sponsor its adherence to the United Nations. Palestine is still being administered by the United Kingdom under the terms of the League Mandate ; the bitter antipathy between its two communities has hitherto defeated all efforts to create autonomous political institutions.

The Class " B " Mandates were all in tropical Africa. Of them the Covenant said that " the Mandatory must be responsible for the administration of the territory under conditions which will guarantee freedom of conscience and religion, subject only to the maintenance of public order and morals, the prohibition of abuses such as the slave trade, the arms traffic and the liquor traffic, and the prevention of the establishment of fortifications or military and naval bases and of military training of the natives for other than police purposes and the defence of territory, and will also secure equal opportunities for the trade and commerce of other Members of the League." There was no mention of the development of self-government, or of free political institutions, far less of independence.

The three former German colonies in tropical Africa, Togoland, Cameroons and Tanganyika, were all placed under " B " Mandate, the first two being divided between France and Britain, while Tanganyika was placed under British authority with the exception of the small but populous region of Ruanda-Urundi, which became a Belgian responsibility. All these territories still retain their status as League mandates, pending the application of the new trusteeship system.

" C " Mandates were defined as " territories which, owing to the sparseness of their population, or their small size, or their remoteness from the centres of civilization, or their geographical contiguity to the territory of the Mandatory, and other circumstances, can best be administered under the laws of the Mandatory as integral portions of its territory, subject to the safeguards above mentioned (those referring to Class " B ") in the interests of the indigenous population."

There were five " C " Mandates. South-West Africa, a former German colony, was entrusted to the Union of South Africa, while of the German possessions in the Pacific, the Mariana, Caroline and Marshall Islands were given to Japan, Western Samoa to New Zealand, and North-Eastern New Guinea, with New Britain, New Ireland, the Solomons and other adjacent islands went to Australia. Australia was also charged with the actual operation of the mandate for Nauru, which was in law a joint mandate held by the United Kingdom, Australia and New Zealand.

The future of the Japanese mandate is now, of course, in the hands of the peacemakers for the second time ; it is likely to become a United States trust territory, but there has been no definite pronouncement to that effect. The remaining " C " Mandates are at present still being administered under the terms of the Covenant by the three Dominions concerned.

It will be noticed that, with the exception of Nauru, all the League's mandates were entrusted to single member states ; and in the case of the Nauru mandate the actual administration was in the hands of one state only. Indeed, the Covenant is so worded that it would have been difficult within its framework to create any joint responsibility for a mandate which could be exercised by all the members of the League, or by any group of them other than the British Dominions.

The League controlled its mandates with a very slack rein, the only provision for supervision in the Covenant being a requirement that all mandatories should make annual reports to the Council. A Permanent Commission on Mandates was set up to examine these reports and generally to advise the Council on mandates ; it consisted not of representatives of governments but of individuals appointed for their specialist qualifications, and possessed little tangible authority. But in general there is reason to believe that the mandate system was adequately carried out, and that the mandatory Powers, under the critical eye of world opinion, fulfilled the limited aims set out in the Covenant.

THE TRUST TERRITORIES

The United Nations plan for a trusteeship system is wider in its scope than the League's was, but at the same time it can only be effective if a number of rather difficult conditions are fulfilled. In fact, at the time of writing the Trusteeship Council is the only major organ of the United Nations which has not yet begun to operate.

The new system will only be in working order when three requirements, all of them matters of some delicacy, have been successfully implemented. First, it has to be decided which territories are to come under trusteeship. Second, individual trusteeship agreements must be made for each " trust territory." Third, the Trusteeship Council must be constituted.

At the present moment seven former mandates have been offered for trusteeship,[1] and it is probable that there will be little difficulty in securing three more.[2] The only remaining mandate, Palestine, presents certain difficulties. It is at present administered by the United Kingdom, and the Anglo-American Committee of Enquiry which presented its recommendations for the future of the country in April 1946 suggested that it should continue under British mandate until a trusteeship agreement had been made. The Committee did not make any recommendations as to the terms of the agreement beyond a comment to the effect that this particular trusteeship was " a very heavy burden for any single Government . . . which would be lightened . . . if the trustee had the support of other members of the United Nations."

Article 77 of the Charter provides that the new " trust territories " may be either former mandates, or territories taken from enemy states during the Second World War, or any other territories voluntarily placed under the trusteeship system by the states administering them. As we have seen, sufficient former mandates are already available to give the system a fairly solid basis. But the future of the territories taken from Italy and Japan is still completely undecided, and there are at least six potential " trust territories " in this category, three being the Italian colonies in Somaliland, Eritrea and Libya, and the others, former Japanese possessions.

There are at the moment several alternative proposals for the future of the Italian colonies. The United States favours a single trusteeship covering all three, with the United Nations Organization itself as the responsible authority, exercising its control through a board composed of representatives of the United States, the United Kingdom, France, Italy and the Arab States. France has suggested that Italy herself be made trustee for all her former colonies. The Soviet Government, which had originally proposed that Libya be divided into its two provinces of Tripolitania and Cyrenaica, and that each should constitute a separate trust territory, the first with a Soviet and the second with a British or American administrator, seems now to have accepted the French suggestion. The United Kingdom at first proposed that Libya be granted early independence as a sovereign state, but has since agreed to an Italian trusteeship for Tripolitania, provided that Cyrenaica is simultaneously entrusted to Britain. As regards Eritrea and Italian Somaliland, the British Government have suggested that a new trust territory, to be called " Somalia," should be formed by uniting Italian and British Somaliland with the Ogaden district of Ethiopia, and that this should be placed under British trusteeship ; Ethiopia might under this plan be compensated for the loss of Ogaden by the satisfaction of her claims on Eritrea.

[1] At the General Assembly session in January 1946, the British, Australian, New Zealand and Belgium governments announced that they would negotiate agreements as soon as possible in respect of Tanganyika, Western Togoland, Northern Cameroons, New Guinea, Nauru, Western Samoa and Ruanda-Urundi.

[2] France and South Africa have begun consultations on the subject of trusteeship agreements for Eastern Togoland, Southern Cameroons and South-West Africa.

Of the Japanese possessions in the Pacific area the areas most likely to become trust territories are two island groups. The first, which embraces the Marianas, Carolines and Marshalls, was, of course, entrusted to Japanese mandate after the First World War (a mandate which Japan flagrantly violated). These islands have been recaptured by American forces, and if they are to come under trusteeship the United States will require terms of agreement which will permit her to fortify them. The second island group taken from the Japanese is the Kuriles, at present in Russian hands. The Soviet Government has not yet secured the assent of the other Powers to outright annexation of this group, but in view of its strategic importance to the Soviet Union it is doubtful whether a trusteeship arrangement could be satisfactorily concluded on the basis of the Charter.

A third Pacific territory which may come under the United Nations trusteeship system is Korea. The report of the Moscow Conference held in December 1945 stated that the Soviet Union, the United States, the United Kingdom and China would consider an agreement establishing a four-Power trusteeship for Korea for a period of up to five years, while steps were being taken to develop democratic self-government and to establish Korean independence. There was, however, no reference in this report to the United Nations trusteeship system.

The category of " territories voluntarily placed under trusteeship " introduces a completely new idea, to which the Covenant did not even refer. While there are at present no territories which answer the description given, the " Somalia " scheme would involve two voluntary transfers, one by the Ethiopian Government and one by the British.

We have then a list of nineteen potential trust territories[1], of which eleven are former mandates, six former enemy territories, and two voluntary transfers. The second stage in the creation of the trusteeship system, the making of individual agreements, has already begun in the case of ten of the nineteen. But there are difficulties inherent in the wording of the Charter on this point. Under Article 79, the terms of trusteeship must be agreed upon between " the states directly concerned." The Trusteeship Committee of the General Assembly devoted several debates during the January session to attempting to determine which states would be those directly concerned, and eventually agreed that this point would have to be left to the discretion of the states which were offering trusteeship agreements. The General Assembly passed a resolution on February 9 urging all states holding League mandates to conclude negotiations with other " states directly concerned " in time to submit trusteeship agreements to the Assembly at its September session ; but it was, of course, unable to make any definite recommendations about former enemy territories or voluntary transfers.

[1] See list at end of this chapter.

Under Article 85 of the Charter, trusteeship agreements must be approved by the General Assembly, which must also approve any alteration proposed by the trustee state.[1] Other articles provide that the terms of the agreement " shall in each case . . . designate the authority which will exercise the administration of the trust territory. . . . Such authority hereinafter called the administering authority, may be one or more states or the Organization itself." It may be noted that this possibility of direct United Nations control of trust territories is a new conception which is not paralleled in the Mandate System.

THE TRUSTEESHIP COUNCIL

The Trusteeship Council has not yet been constituted, and it is now clear that it will not be in operation before the next Assembly session. This is due to the manner in which, under Article 86 of the Charter, it has to be selected. There are three classes of member states represented on the Council. First, the five permanent members of the Security Council. Second, members who are administering trust territories. Third, " as many other members elected for three-year terms by the General Assembly as may be necessary to ensure that the total number of members of the Trusteeship Council is equally divided between those members of the United Nations which administer trust territories and those which do not." It is obvious that the second class of members cannot be defined until at least a minimum number of agreements have been concluded, and that the third can only be called into being at the next session of the Assembly held after the agreements have been concluded. It is even possible that these conditions may not be fulfilled in September, but it is much to be hoped that there will be no further hitch, as a marked feature of the London session of the Assembly was a tendency for delegates to attribute the delay in forming the Council to each other.

It is possible even now to forecast part of the membership of the Council, as follows :

United States
Soviet Union
United Kingdom } Permanent members of the Security Council
France
China

Belgium
Australia } States which have undertaken to conclude trutsee-
New Zealand   ship agreements
South Africa

If we assume that only the holders of former mandates will have made

[1]This, however, does not apply to " strategic areas," which are discussed in a later section.

trusteeship agreements by the time the Council is set up, there will then be six trustee states (the four last, France and the United Kingdom) already on the Council, as against three others (China, the United States and the Soviet Union) and it will only be necessary to elect three temporary members to make an evenly divided Council of twelve. If, on the other hand, the United States and the Soviet Union have become parties to trusteeship agreements for Libya, Palestine, Korea or the Pacific Islands, there will be eight trustee states on the Council, and seven temporary members must be elected by the Assembly, forming, with China, a Council of sixteen.

Article 86 of the Charter also lays down that each member state shall designate one specially qualified person to represent it thereon.

The Trusteeship Council, like the Economic and Social Council, is a subordinate organ which operates under the authority of the General Assembly. It is unable to take any important action without reference to the Assembly, and it is presumably for this reason that the Charter empowers it to make decisions by a simple majority vote, since these decisions are always subject to review by the superior body. The Council is free, under the Charter, to meet as required, although a meeting must be convened if a majority of the members so demand. In practice it will probably hold regular meetings every six months, normally at the headquarters of the United Nations. It will select its own President, who will have no casting vote; if there is an equal division, the motion at issue will be considered lost.

It will be seen that the Council is a far stronger body than the League's Permanent Commission on Mandates. Also, although in both cases supreme authority is in the hands of another organ, it is significant that in the League this was the Council, while in the United Nations it is the Assembly. Inevitably an Assembly in which small nations, predominantly non-European, have a substantial majority, is more likely to judge fairly between ruler and ruled than a Council in which Great Powers hold a key position. And whereas in the League machine any colonial Power which disliked the intervention of the League in its relations with its mandates could block a critical motion by using the unanimity rule, this will not be possible in either the Trusteeship Council or the Assembly of the United Nations.

The powers of direct supervision exercised by the United Nations are also stronger than those entrusted to the League. There are four principal methods of supervising the trustee states in their work. First, approval of the terms of the original agreement, and of any alteration or amendment to it. Second, periodic visits to the trust territory; these, under Article 87 of the Charter, must be at times agreed upon with the administering authority. Third, the Trusteeship Council and the Assembly are empowered to accept petitions from the peoples under the trusteeship and to examine them in consultation with the administering authority. Fourth, the administering authority must make an annual report to the Assembly on the basis of a *questionnaire* on the political, economic, social and educational advancement of the people of the territory which will be drawn up by the Council. The Charter does not provide for the termination of a trusteeship agreement by the Assembly ; but it would be possible for the Assembly, provided the Security Council concurred, to expel from the United Nations any member state which failed to fulfil its obligations under the Charter (Articles 2 and 6) ; and this would automatically terminate the expelled member's rights in any trust territory under its care.

STRATEGIC AREAS

It has already been pointed out that the states now in occupation of certain potential trust territories will not be likely to conclude agreements placing them under trusteeship unless they are satisfied that the terms will satisfy their needs for military and naval bases. Now whereas the Covenant strictly forbade " the establishment of fortifications or military and naval bases, and military training of natives for other than police purposes and the defence of territory," the Charter makes no such conditions. Indeed, in Article 84 it declares that it is the duty of each administering authority to ensure that its trust territories shall play their part in the maintenance of international peace and security, and that " to this end the administering authority may make use of volunteer forces, facilities, and assistance from the trust territory in carrying out the obligations towards the Security Council undertaken in this regard by the administering authority, as well as for local defence and the maintenance of law and order within the local territory." This contrast sums up an essential difference of spirit, which shows itself elsewhere, but in less obvious forms, between the Covenant and the Charter ; the former was based on the idea of peace by disarmament, the latter on the maintenance of peace by united force.

But there is an additional reservation, and an important one, to the general principle of control of trust territories by the General Assembly. Several nations, particularly those with Pacific interests, urged at San Francisco that even the rights granted under Article 84 were not enough to enable a trustee Power to make full use of the strategic value of its trust territories. It was therefore decided to create a special category of territories, termed " strategic areas." Article 82 of the Charter states that " there may be designated in any trusteeship agreement a strategic area or areas, which may include part or all of the trust territory." In all matters concerning strategic areas, including the approval and amendment of the original trusteeship agreement, it is the Security Council, and not the Assembly and the Trusteeship Council, which exercises the functions of the United Nations. The Security Council may make use of the Trusteeship Council to carry out its political, economic, social and educational functions in the strategic areas ; but it retains complete control, and need pay no attention to the wishes of the General Assembly. During the Assembly meetings of January and February nothing was said about the choice of strategic areas ; but it is generally believed that at least part of the former Japanese mandate covering the Marianas, Carolines and Marshalls will be made a strategic area, and other obvious possibilities are the Kuriles, South-West Africa, and part of Korea.

If any trust territory is designated wholly as a strategic area, it will not of course be necessary for the Security Council to wait until the Trusteeship Council is constituted before it can exercise its own authority. It is therefore quite possible that the strategic areas will be the first trust territories to be brought under United Nations supervision.

THE BASIC OBJECTIVES

Under Article 76 and 83, the same basic objectives will apply to all trust territories, whether or not they are strategic areas. These objectives require somewhat careful study. They are of course very different from those set out in the covenant of the League, although the Covenant was the original inspiration of the whole present system. They are also different, in several interesting particulars, from the objectives listed in Article 73 as applicable to non-self-governing territories generally.

The first objective is, quite simply, to further international peace and security. This is found, phrased with equal simplicity, in the declaration on non-self-governing territories. There is no equivalent objective in the Covenant.

The second objective is the promotion of " the political, social, economic and educational advancement of the inhabitants." This too is identically phrased in the article on non-self-governing peoples, and is implicit in the Covenant's statement that " the well-being and development of such peoples form a sacred trust of civilization."

The third objective for Trust Territories is " their progressive development towards self-government or independence, as may be appropriate to the particular circumstances of each territory." There was considerable argument at San Francisco as to whether " independence " or " self-government " should be the goal, and it was eventually decided to include both, with the qualifying phrase about " the particular circumstances of each territory " expanded by the words : " and the freely expressed wishes of the people concerned." The equivalent part of the general declaration on non-self-governing peoples does not mention independence ; it reads : " to develop self-government, to take due account of the political aspirations of the peoples, and to assist them in the progressive development of their free political institutions, according to the particular circumstances of each territory and its peoples and their varying stages of advancement." In the Covenant, as we have seen, there is no mention of political develop-

ment of any except the Class " A " Mandates, for which early independence
was clearly envisaged.

Fourth among the objectives of the trusteeship system is " to encourage
respect for human rights and for fundamental freedoms for all without
distinction as to race, sex, language or religion," and " to encourage recognition of the inter-dependence of the peoples of the world." The language
of the statement on non-self-governing peoples in general is much more
modest on this point. It merely lays down an obligation " to ensure, with
due respect for the culture of the peoples concerned . . . their just treatment
and their protection against abuses." Indeed, it is here very similar to the
terms of the Covenant, which binds member states " to secure just treatment for the native inhabitants of territories under their control."

Fifth, the trustee states are " to ensure equal treatment . . . for all
Members of the United Nations and their nationals " in social, economic
and commercial matters and in the administration of justice. In other
non-self-governing territories the responsible Power agrees to base its
policy on " the general principle of good-neighbourliness, due account
being taken of the interest and well-being of the rest of the world in social,
economic and commercial matters." The Covenant was in this matter
more sweeping in its language than either of the two United Nations texts ;
it directed all " B " and " C " Mandatories " to secure equal opportunities
for the trade and commerce of other members of the League."

Clearly the successful operation of the trusteeship principle will have an
important bearing on the world's chances of peace and security in the long
perspective of the future. As the chief Chinese delegate pointed out
during the debate on trusteeship in the London Assembly, " millions of
dependent peoples are looking to the United Nations for a new future," ;
and, in the words of an American delegate, it is an urgent necessity that the
dependent peoples should realize that the Charter provides orderly processes for the attainment of their aspirations, and that the administering
nations should quickly give concrete evidence of their intention to vitalize
those processes. Given these two conditions, the trusteeship idea can be
a tremendous positive contribution both to the welfare and to the peace
of the world.

TERRITORIES WHICH MAY BE BROUGHT INTO THE UNITED NATIONS TRUSTEE-
SHIP SYSTEM

Territory and Estimated Population	Former Status	Proposed Administering Authority
AFRICA :		
1. Togoland (west) (350,000)	British " B " Mandate	United Kingdom
2. Togoland (east) (800,000	French " B " Mandate	France

TERRITORIES WHICH MAY BE BROUGHT INTO THE UNITED NATIONS TRUSTEE-
SHIP SYSTEM. (*cont.*)

Territory and Estimated Population	Former Status	Proposed Administering Authority
3. Cameroons (north) (850,000)	British " B " Mandate	United Kingdom
4. Cameroons (south) (2,500,000)	French " B " Mandate	France.
5. Tanganyika (5,200,000)	British " B " Mandate	United Kingdom.
6. Ruanda-Urundi (3,700,000)	Belgian "B " Mandate	Belgium.
7. South-West Africa (300,000)	South African " C " Mandate	South Africa.
8. Libya (1,000,000)	Italian colony	Alternative proposals : (1) Italian trusteeship ; (2) United Nations authority exercised through board representing U.S.A., U.S.S.R., U.K., France, Italy and Arab States ; (3) Division into the two provinces of Tripolitania and Cyrenaica, the first administered either by the Soviet Union (with a mixed advisory council) or by Italy, the second either by the United States or the United Kingdom.
9. Eritrea (640,000)	Italian colony	Alternative proposals : (1) Italian trusteeship ; (2) United Nations authority exercised through board representing U.S.A., U.S.S.R., U.K., France, Italy, and Arab States ; (3) Transfer wholly or in part to Ethiopia.
10. Italian Somaliland (1,000,000)	Italian colony	Alternative proposals : (1) Italian trusteeship ; (2) United Nations authority exercised through board representing U.S.A., U.S.S.R, U.K. France, Italy, and Arab States ; (3) Incorporation into new territory of " Somalia," probably under British trusteeship.

TERRITORIES WHICH MAY BE BROUGHT INTO THE UNITED NATIONS TRUSTEE-
SHIP SYSTEM. (*cont.*)

Territory and Estimated Population	Former Status	Proposed Administering Authority
11. British Somaliland (350,000)	British colony	Incorporation into new trust territory to be called " Somalia," probably under British Trusteeship. Italian Somaliland would also become part of " Somalia."
12. Ogaden (no estimate)	Province of Ethiopia	
MIDDLE EAST :		
13. Palestine (1,500,000)	British " A " Mandate	Alternatives : (1) United Nations ; (2) United Kingdom ; (3) joint trusteeship by a group of major powers.
FAR EAST :		
14. North-East New Guinea, the Solomon Islands, New Britain and New Ireland (600,000)	Australian " C " Mandate	Australia.
15. Nauru (3,000)	British Empire " C " Mandate, operated by Australia	Australian authority, with U.K. and New Zealand agreement.
16. Western Samoa (60,000)	New Zealand " C " Mandate	New Zealand.
17. Mariana, Caroline and Marshall Is. (100,000)	Japanese " C " Mandate	United States ; probably to be designated as a " strategic area."
18. Kurile Is. (5,000)	Japanese territory	Soviet Union (unless incorporated as Soviet territory).
19. Korea (22,000,000)	Japanese territory	Joint trusteeship by U.S.A., U.S.S.R., United Kingdom and China for not more than five years ; then independence.

NOTE:—

(The following former Mandates in the Middle East have been acknowledged as sovereign states since 1919:

Iraq (3,600,000)	British " A " Mandate	Independent since 1932.
Syria (1,700,000)	French " A " Mandate	Independent since 1941.
Lebanan (900,000)	French " A " Mandate	Independent since 1941.
Transjordan (300,000)	British " A " Mandate	Independent since March 1946.

CHAPTER VIII

THE ECONOMIC AND SOCIAL AGENCIES

THE United Nations do not seek merely to set up a security organization which will prevent the outbreak of war. The Charter provides also for a determined attempt to remove the roots from which war springs. The ninth chapter sets out the following aims :

" With a view to the creation of conditions of stability and well-being which are necessary for peaceful and friendly relations among nations, based on respect for the principle of equal rights and self-determination of peoples, the United Nations shall promote :

" (a) Higher standards of living, full employment, and conditions of economic and social progress and development.

" (b) Solutions of international economic, social, health and related problems ; and international and cultural educational co-operation.

" (c) Universal respect for, and observance of, human rights and fundamental freedoms for all without distinction as to race, sex, language or religion."

Never before has such a vast undertaking in international sociology and economics been made by a world organization. The League of Nations Covenant merely bound member states to " endeavour to secure and maintain fair and humane conditions of labour for men, women and children," and for that purpose to " establish and maintain the necessary international organization." This clause in the Covenant led to the creation of the International Labour Organization, which did admirable work in the years between the wars, but in a limited field. Meanwhile the fluctuations of currency values, capital investments, commodity prices and other uncontrolled factors rushed the world through a series of booms and slumps which resulted in unprecedented unemployment and prodigious social unrest. In 1939 the Assembly of the League discussed a report from its " Special Committee for the Development of International Co-operation in Economic and Social Affairs." This report, generally known as the Bruce Committee Report, proposed the creation of a Central Committee to unify all the economic and social work of the League. This Central Committee was due to meet at the Hague in the summer of 1940, but the German invasion of the Netherlands interfered with this plan, and subsequent events prevented the League from implementing its new projects. But the idea behind the Central Committee has been developed by the United Nations into the present Economic and Social Council, which, under the authority of the General Assembly, is now responsible for all the economic and social functions of the new Organization.

The Council is not the only body concerned with economic and social

D

work in the United Nations structure. Such organizations as UNESCO, the FAO, UNRRA, and the International Bank, which have been set up by United Nations agreements other than the San Francisco Charter, are also at work in this field. There are also several international organizations, such as the International Labour Office, the International Co-operative Alliance, the International Chamber of Commerce and the International Institute of Agriculture which were operating, in their own specialized spheres, before the United Nations began to shape their new system. Finally, there are international bodies such as the World Federation of Trade Unions, which, although constituted at the same time as the United Nations Organization and looking towards it for supreme authority, are none the less independent of the Charter. It will be part of the task of the Economic and Social Council to draw together the contributions which all these organizations can make towards the aims set out in the ninth chapter of the Charter and quoted at the head of this chapter. Meanwhile, all members of the United Nations are bound by Article 56 of the Charter " to take joint and separate action in co-operation with the Organization for the achievement " of these aims.

THE ECONOMIC AND SOCIAL COUNCIL

The Council consists of eighteen members of the United Nations, elected by the General Assembly. Six will normally be elected every year to serve a three year term. Retiring members are eligible for immediate re-election. At the first elections, which were held on January 12 and 14, 1946, six members were elected for a one-year term, six for two years, and six for three. The Council was thus composed as follows :

Elected for three years : China, France, Chile, Canada, Belgium, Peru.

Elected for two years : Soviet Union, United Kingdom, India, Norway, Cuba, Czechoslovakia.

Elected for one year : United States, Ukraine, Greece, Lebanon, Colombia, Yugoslavia.[1]

Each member of the Council has only one representative and only one vote. The Council makes its decisions by a simple majority of members present and voting.

The Council operates under the authority of the General Assembly, and must accept the Assembly's instructions. It may make recommendations either to the Assembly, or to the member nations, or to the specialized international agencies, with respect to economic, social, cultural, educational, health and related matters, or for the purpose of promoting respect for and observance of human rights and fundamental freedoms for all. It may prepare draft conventions for submission to

[1] New Zealand, which had received approximately the same number of votes as Yugoslavia in several ballots, withdrew when it became clear that neither would receive a clear two-thirds majority if both continued to compete.

the Assembly on all these subjects. It may call international conferences on economic and social matters.

Subject to the approval of the Assembly, the Council may make agreements with the various economic and social " specialized agencies " defining the terms on which these agencies shall be brought into relationship with the United Nations, and may co-ordinate the activities of these agencies.

Such agencies will obviously include the Food and Agriculture Organization of the United Nations (FAO), the United Nations Relief and Rehabilitation Administration (UNRRA), the United Nations Educational, Scientific and Cultural Organization (UNESCO) and the two financial agencies created by the Bretton Woods conference, the International Monetary Fund and the International Bank for Reconstruction and Development. The United Nations are also considering the creation of two more specialized agencies, an International Health Organization and an International Trade Organization. There already exists a Provisional International Civil Aviation Organization which was set up in 1944 under United Nations auspices, and this too may be brought into relationship with the Council.[1] And there is at least one agency which, although its origins lie with the League rather than with the United Nations, may be linked with the new Organization ; this is the International Labour Organization. Other existing agencies such as the International Institute of Agriculture, the International Institute of Intellectual Co-operation, and the International Office of Public Hygiene will probably be merged into the newer United Nations agencies rather than given an independent status in the economic and social machine.

At its thirteenth meeting, the Council appointed a committee to negotiate agreements with the specialized agencies. This committee consists of the President of the Council and representatives of the United States, the United Kingdom, the Soviet Union, France, China, Belgium, Canada, Chile, Colombia, Czechoslovakia, and Norway. The Committee is still at work.

A similar committee was set up at the same time to arrange for the collaboration, in a consultative capacity, of such non-governmental organizations as the World Federation of Trade Unions, the International Co-operative Alliance, the International Federation of Women, and the major independent trade union groupings such as the American Federation of Labour. The Charter lays down that while the Council may negotiate directly with international organizations, it may only make arrangements with national non-governmental organizations after consultation with the government concerned.

The Council is authorized to allow representatives of the specialized agencies to participate without vote in its discussions and in those of its

[1] An International Refugee Organization is also under consideration.

Commissions, and it will also send representatives to participate in the discussions of the agencies. It must invite the participation of any member state which is particularly concerned in any matter under discussion, when that state is not already represented on the Council ; but the invited state shall have no vote.

The Council may arrange to obtain reports from both member states and specialized agencies on the steps they have taken to carry out its recommendations and those of the General Assembly. It will pass its comments on these reports to the Assembly. It will assist the Security Council, if requested to do so, by providing information and in other ways. It will prepare reports and initiate studies in all social and economic fields.

The Economic and Social Council is empowered to make its own rules of procedure and to choose for itself its method of electing a President. Actually the Council decided at its first session to accept, without any important amendments, the procedural rules suggested for it by the preparatory Commission. The first President, elected by acclamation, was Sir Ramaswami Mudaliar of India ; each President will hold office for a year, and may be re-elected immediately.

The Charter provides that the Council must be convened whenever a majority of its members so demand, and the Council has further decided that normally three regular sessions will be held every year. The first session having been held in London from January 23 to February 18, 1946, the second has been convened for May in New York.

COMMISSIONS OF THE COUNCIL

Article 68 of the Charter directs that the Council " shall set up commissions in economic and social fields and for the promotion of human rights, and such other commissions as may be required for the performance of its functions."

At the first session of the Council there was considerable difficulty in reaching agreement on the way in which these Commissions would be constructed. Eventually the Council decided that provisionally the Commissions would be small " nuclear " ones of nine members each, and that these members would be selected not as representatives of nations but on the basis of their individual qualifications. Each member of the Council was allowed to nominate two persons for membership of the Commissions, and a sub-committee of the Council was established to make recommendations for the constitution of the Commissions on the basis of these nominations and of nominations from other quarters. Most of the Commissions are already in provisional existence, and are beginning their work by examining their own terms of reference.

The first Commission to be authorized by the Council was that on Human Rights ; to this is attached a sub-commission on the status of women. The Commission on Human Rights is responsible for making recommendations for :—an international bill of rights ; international declarations or conventions on civil liberties, the status of women, freedom of information and similar matters ; the protection of minorities ; and the prevention of discrimination on grounds of race, sex, language or religion.

The Economic and Employment Commission will be responsible for advising the Council on general economic matters, and in particular on : the promotion of world-wide full employment ; the prevention of economic instability ; reconstruction ; and the economic development of backward areas. It will probably have the assistance of subordinate committees on employment, balance of payment problems, and economic development.

The Statistical Commission will co-ordinate national statistics and the statistics of specialized agencies, advise member nations and organs of the United Nations on all matters relating to the collection, interpretation and dissemination of statistical material, and in general promote the improvement of statistics throughout the world.

The Commission on Narcotic Drugs will take over the work of the League of Nations " Advisory Committee on Traffic in Opium and Other Dangerous Drugs," and will advise the Council on all matters relating to the enforcement of the existing narcotics conventions, the framing of further conventions, and the general control of narcotic drugs.[1]

At the first session of the Council it was decided to set up a Temporary Transport and Communications Commission, which would take over certain functions of the League's Communications and Transit Organization, and advise the Council on international co-operation, the co-ordination of the work of the specialized agencies, and the creation of the new international machinery, in all branches of international transport and communications. The definitive composition of this Commission will not be decided before the second session of the Council.

The Council has received proposals for the establishment of a Demographic Commission and a Fiscal Commission. These will be decided upon at later sessions of the Council. A Temporary Social Commission will also be set up ; and pending the establishment of this Commission, the Council has set up temporary committees to deal with such urgent social problems as refugees, health, and the position of the specialized agencies and non-governmental organizations.

It is clear that if these Commissions are to be effective they will require a considerable staff of technical experts and research workers. It is noteworthy that the Charter lays down that the staff of the Economic and Social Council will be appointed by the Secretary-General " under regulations established by the General Assembly " in exactly the same way

[1]The composition of this Commission has already been decided. It will consist of representatives of the United States, the United Kingdom, the Soviet Union, France, China, Canada, Egypt, India, Iran, Mexico, Netherlands, Peru, Poland, Turkey and Yugoslavia.

as the main Secretariat[1]. There will presumably be no separate Director as was the case in the ILO, for the Secretary-General himself is to act as secretary to the Council.

This brief survey of the Council's functions must indicate that it is not granted any very effective powers under the terms of the Charter. It can only make recommendations to the General Assembly, which in turn is not empowered to do more than make recommendations to member states. And it is difficult to conceive of any really far-reaching measures in the economic and social field which would not be forbidden by Article 2 of the Charter, which lays down that " nothing in the present Charter shall authorize the United Nations to intervene in matters which are essentially within the domestic jurisdiction of any state, or shall require members to submit such matters for settlement under the present Charter." If the Council is to get anything worthwhile done, it must be by sheer moral influence ; and if it is to wield this insubstantial weapon with effect, it must get to work at once to win a commanding position in the eyes of the world. The Economic and Social Council can, if it chooses, be nothing more than the economic sections of the League were before it, but, if it is capable of seizing its opportunities, it may succeed in realizing the lofty aims set out in the Preamble to the Charter : " to reaffirm faith in fundamental human rights, in the dignity and worth of the human person, in the equal rights of men and women . . . to promote social progress and better standards of life in larger freedom, and for these ends . . . to employ international machinery for the promotion of the economic and social advancements of all peoples."

UNRRA

WHAT IS ITS JOB ?

Speaking over the American radio on July 23, 1942, Mr. Cordell Hull, the U.S. Secretary of State, said :

" With victory achieved our first concern must be for those whose sufferings have been almost beyond human endurance. . . . The peoples of many countries will be starving and without means of procuring food ; homeless and without means of building shelter ; their fields scorched ; their cattle slaughtered ; their tools gone ; their factories and mines destroyed ; their roads and transport wrecked. Unknown millions will be far from their homes—prisoners of war, inmates of concentration camps, forced labourers in alien lands, refugees from battle, from cruelty, from starvation. Disease and danger of disease will lurk everywhere. . . . Victory must be followed by swift and effective action to meet these pressing human needs."

UNRRA is responsible for all these tremendous tasks. In the Preamble

[1] Articles 98 and 101 of the Charter.

to the Agreement which established it, the signatory governments declare that : " . . . upon the liberation of any area . . . the population thereof shall receive aid and relief from their sufferings, food, clothing and shelter, aid in the prevention of pestilence and in the recovery of the health of the people, and preparation and arrangements shall be made for the return of prisoners and exiles to their homes and for assistance in the resumption of urgently needed agricultural and industrial production and the restoration of essential services."

The United Nations Relief and Rehabilitation Administration owes its origins to a meeting of Allied representatives in London in September 1941, which set up an inter-Allied committee (under the chairmanship of Sir Frederick Leith-Ross) to prepare estimates of the relief and rehabilitation needs of the occupied countries. The United States was not of course represented at this meeting, but it was already maintaining close contact with the Allies on relief problems, and the American Ambassador informed the meeting that the United States " stood ready at the appropriate time to consider in what respect it could co-operate in accomplishing the ends in view."

As a result of the detailed consultations on relief which took place between governments during the next two years, it was possible for the representatives of 44 United Nations to establish UNRRA in November 1943 by the simple process of assembling in Washington and signing an agreement. This is probably the only occasion in history on which an organization of the size and scope of UNRRA has been created without a preliminary international conference. And UNRRA is certainly a big enough organization. It is, of course, only a temporary creation ; it is expected to finish its work in Europe by the end of 1946, and in the Far East early in 1947.[1] Long-term projects for the prevention of famine, disease and destitution are the concern of the Economic and Social Council of the United Nations, not of UNRRA. But no other relief organization has ever tackled such huge and appalling problems. UNRRA is literally the only force which is keeping several European nations alive at this moment.

CONTROL

The Administration is controlled by a Council on which each member nation has one representative (there are at present 48 members). The Council makes its decisions by a simple majority.

The policy and programme of UNRRA are defined in the resolutions passed at the Council's meetings. There have to date been four meetings :

[1] At the UNRRA Council at Atlantic City in March 1946, Mr. Clayton, U.S. Assistant Secretary of State, pointed out that after these dates members of the United Nations would still be able to buy foodstuffs through the Combined Food Board with the aid of loans from the new International Bank for Reconstruction and Development.

the first in Atlantic City, immediately after the signing of the basic Agreement in November 1943 ; the second in Montreal in September 1944 ; the third in London in August 1945, and the fourth in Atlantic City in March 1946. This last meeting decided, in view of the critical world food situation, to remain in being so that it could reassemble quickly in an emergency.

The Council elects a Director-General, who is responsible to it for the whole work of UNRRA. The first Director-General, elected in 1943, was Mr. Herbert H. Lehman, former Governor of New York State, who was largely responsible for the creation of the UNRRA machine. His successor, elected in March 1946, was Mr. Fiorello LaGuardia, former mayor of New York City.

The Director-General controls his " army " of some ten thousand full-time workers through his deputies and heads of missions in the various countries where UNRRA is at work. His most important subordinate is his personal representative in the European Regional Office of UNRRA in London, who directs the work of all the missions in Europe. Outside Europe and apart from its main headquarters in Washington, UNRRA'S principal offices are in Shanghai, Sydney and Cairo.

UNRRA's terms of reference only permit it to begin operations in any partcular country when requested to do so either by the legal government of that country or by Allied Military Government. Its powers are not always unrestricted. Thus, in Germany UNRRA is only authorized to deal with displaced persons of Allied and pro-Allied nationality. In Italy and Austria, on the other hand, UNRRA is also responsible for feeding large sections of the population.

FINANCE

All the 48 member nations contribute towards the administrative costs of UNRRA, but the actual costs of supplies and services, which are of course vastly higher, are shared only by the 31 member nations which did not suffer invasion in the late war. In 1943 the Council asked these nations to contribute each one per cent of its national income for the year 1942-3. In 1945 the Council asked for a second contribution on the same basis.[1]

The first contributions covered the administrative costs for two years and left about £450,000,000 for operations. By the end of 1945 UNRRA had used over £400,000,000 of this ; and it is expected that the second contribution will be almost completely exhausted by the end of the present year.

Up to one-tenth of each nation's contribution is recommended to be in foreign exchange, the rest being " paid " in actual goods and services.

[1]The General Assembly of the United Nations, meeting in London in January 1946, expressed concern that certain members had not yet paid in this second contribution, and appointed a special Committee to follow the matter up.

Naturally the economic structure and resources of each member nation largely determine the nature of its contribution. Thus of the £80,000,000 which was Britain's first contribution, some three-quarters were delivered in supplies, the remainder in services such as welfare facilities, administrative assistance and shipping.

SUPPLIES

By the end of 1945 UNRRA had shipped some four million tons of supplies, with an estimated value of £270,000,000, to the devastated areas of Europe and Asia. About half of the tonnage consisted of food, feedstuffs for animals, and such personal necessities as soap. The other half was made up of industrial equipment, agricultural supplies, cloth, clothing, footwear, and medical stores. The principal recipients were the liberated countries in Eastern Europe, Greece, Yugoslavia, Albania, Czechoslovakia, Poland, Byelorussia and the Ukraine. Substantial allotments were also sent to Finland, Hungary, China, Korea, Formosa and the Philippines. In Western Europe, where the governments of the liberated nations were able to pay for relief supplies with their own money, UNRRA generally confined itself to providing emergency supplies for the devastated areas of France, Belgium, Holland, Norway and Luxembourg.

UNRRA's policy is to help the liberated peoples to help themselves, and a high proportion of the supplies shipped to Europe has therefore consisted of equipment with which production on the spot can be restarted. Horses, cattle, feedstuffs, seed, agricultural machinery, and fish to restock rivers and lakes, have been poured into Europe to enable the devastated territories to resume food production. Spare parts, lubricants, pit props, building materials and other kinds of equipment have gone in to revive industry and mining and to facilitate the rebuilding of homes. UNRRA perfers to provide raw textiles rather than finished articles of clothing, partly because raw cotton and wool are abundant while there is a world-wide shortage of clothing, partly in order to stimulate employment and manufactures in the liberated countries. But considerable quantities of clothing have also been supplied, including some 60,000 tons of used clothing collected in the United States and the British Dominions. Another substantial item in the list of UNRRA supplies is concerned with transport. Europe's plight at the end of the war was aggravated by the fact that the inland transport system of the whole continent had been reduced to a shambles. Bridges had been blown up, railway lines cut, and countless motor vehicles destroyed. In Greece, for example, only 17 per cent of the former railways, 10 per cent of the important coastal shipping, and 25 per cent of the motor transport remained in running order. UNRRA has supplied something like 50,000 vehicles and a number of railway locomotives to Europe.

In supplying food, UNNRA's aim has been to bring the basic ration in

D*

the devastated territories up to 2,000 calories, with special allowances for children and certain other categories. In many places this has meant supplying almost the whole population with almost all its food. In Athens, when UNRRA first began to operate, local stocks could only produce 250 calories for each person, and UNRRA had to provide an additional 1,750. In Western Yugoslavia it is estimated that a population of three million people is entirely dependent on UNRRA for food, and an additional two million are partly dependent.

The world-wide shortage of practically all foodstuffs, raw materials, and shipping, compelled the Allies to set up, as early as 1942, a set of " Combined Boards " which were responsible for allotting whatever was available to wherever it was most needed. The Combined Food Board is still operating. Composed of American, Canadian and British representatives, it meets in Washington at irregular intervals ; and any large-scale movement of food or feedstuffs must have its approval. Its universal authority even extends to UNRRA purchases and to the contributions in food made by member nations to UNRRA. UNRRA therefore has to argue its case before the Board in competition with all the other authorities, mostly governments, which are trying to buy food ; and in the long run UNRRA's shipments depend upon the basic world food situation. Up to April 1946 it could be said that there had been no famine in any of the areas for which UNRRA was responsible ; but the Administration's food experts were not prepared at that point to guarantee that there would be no famine, because they could not be sure that UNRRA would be able to get enough food from the supplying countries to tide over the critical period before the summer harvest.

The food crisis of 1946 is, of course, more than a relief problem. It is a matter of concern to the whole United Nations Organization, and has already been discussed in both the General Assembly and the Economic and Social Council ; other organizations such as the FAO, the Combined Food Board, the Emergency Economic Committee for Europe, and the American Famine Emergency Committee have become involved in attempts to combat it.

DISTRIBUTION OF SUPPLIES

Normally UNRRA hands over supplies in bulk to the receiving government at the most convenient port or railhead. But it is a basic rule that UNRRA will send no relief to any country which does not agree to admit UNRRA observers to check up on the distribution of supplies. These observers must be admitted in adequate numbers, and must be allowed full freedom of movement. Through its observers, UNRRA seeks to ensure that there is neither diversion of relief supplies to the " black market " nor discrimination between individual recipients on account of their race, religion, political beliefs, or comparative wealth.

A resolution of the UNRRA Council declares that relief and rehabilitation supplies must never be used as a political weapon, and that all classes of the population, irrespective of their purchasing power, must receive their fair share of essential commodities. This resolution not only prevents discrimination by receiving governments as between their individual citizens, but also discrimination by the supplying countries against individual receiving countries. Charges have been made, for example, that UNRRA has given Greece far more than the rest of the Balkans, and that Yugoslavia's present political regime has so antagonized the Administration that only a " trickle " of supplies has reached that country. In point of fact the value of the supplies shipped to Greece during 1945 was approximately £70,000,000 ; Yugoslavia also received supplies valued at £70,000,000 ; and the other countries of Eastern Europe received about £120,000,000 worth. The head of the Yugoslav government, Marshal Tito, has declared his country's debt to UNRRA on at least two occasions, saying that " UNRRA really had saved the lives of hundreds of thousands of our compatriots " and that UNRRA's help was " of vital importance and extremely precious " to Yugoslavia.

SERVICES

UNRRA provides services as well as supplies. A medical staff of over a thousand is at work in Europe, providing expert direction in the struggle to control malaria, tuberculosis and typhus. UNRRA has shipped equipment for over a thousand hospitals, and has flown in urgently needed serums, insulin, toxoid and iron lungs. A second group of UNRRA experts is engaged in supervising agricultural and industrial rehabilitation. A huge welfare staff operates special facilities for children, old people, cripples, pregnant women and nursing mothers. UNRRA has equipped milk kitchens, day nurseries, children's hostels and child welfare centres. In Italy alone UNRRA cares for about two million children.

DISPLACED PERSONS

The most important of UNRRA's services is concerned with " displaced persons." The Allies found over six million of these in Germany alone—concentration camp prisoners, slave labourers, refugees, and other people uprooted and left far from their homes by the cataclysmic effects of total war. Some of Hitler's victims have been scattered as far afield as Persia and East Africa ; and in the Far East there were also a considerable number of people displaced by the Japanese aggressions.

Unexpectedly swift progress was made in clearing the displaced persons in Germany. At first this was done by the military authorities, with assistance and advice from UNRRA ; then on October 1, 1945, UNRRA assumed the whole responsibility. By the end of 1945 over five million " D.P.s " had been returned to their homes. It was then estimated that there were about one million still in Germany, 150,000 in Austria, and smaller numbers in Italy, the Balkans and the Middle East. At this point the clearing progress began to slow down ; and at the end of March 1946 there were still 810,000 displaced persons in Germany, 82,000 in Austria, and 39,400 in Italy, the total number for all areas being 1,084,000. The nature of the displacement problem has, in fact, changed completely. The million refugees still on UNRRA's hands constitute a " hard core " which cannot be disposed of by the simple process of transporting them to their homes. For the most part they are opponents of the present political regimes in such countries as Poland, Yugoslavia, the Ukraine, and the Baltic Soviet Republics, and they are unwilling or afraid to return to their pre-war homes. Obviously UNRRA, which is to be wound up early in 1947, cannot undertake to maintain these people indefinitely, nor has it the resources to dispose of them by any other means. The whole question of the future of the refugees has therefore been taken up in the General Assembly and the Economic and Social Council, and it is now proposed that a further specialized agency be set up to handle the problems.

REFUGEES

The world has always known the refugee problem. There have been many attempts to deal with it at different times and in different parts of the world ; but the first refugee organization intended to operate on a long-term and world-wide basis was that set up by the League of Nations in 1921. In that year Dr. Fridtjof Nansen, the famous explorer and humanitarian, was appointed High Commissioner for Refugees. Dr. Nansen succeeded, largely through his own unrivalled personal standing with all governments including that of Soviet Russia, in reducing the refugee problem to manageable proportions, but this was achieved more by the co-ordination of voluntary relief work than by any large-scale contribution from the League itself. The Nansen administration's most famous creation was the " Nansen passport," which was accepted by most governments as sufficient credentials for the refugee to receive treatment as good as that given to any other foreign resident.

In 1931 the High Commissioner's Office was abolished and a smaller administration called the " Nansen International Office for Refugees " established ; this devoted itself to handling Russian, Armenian, Assyrian, Assyro-Chaldean and Saar refugees. In 1933 the League was asked to assist Jewish and other refugees from Germany, and a High Commissioner was again appointed, with his headquarters in London, to deal exclusively with the German problem. The Nansen Office remained in existence, and the two bodies operated independently of each other in their separate fields.

In 1936 the High Commissioner for German Refugees (Sir Neill Malcolm) succeeded in getting an Inter-Governmental Conference to agree on a " Provisional Arrangement " giving refugees a limited legal status. This was put into effect by France, the United Kingdom, Belgium, Denmark, Norway, Spain and Switzerland.

In 1938 a more detailed Convention on Refugees was adopted by a League conference which met at Geneva. In the same year the Assembly appointed a new High Commissioner (Sir Herbert Emerson), empowered to take over the work both of the Nansen Office and of the High Commissioner for German Refugees ; in 1939 his powers were extended to cover refugees from the Sudetenland. The emphasis was still on the coordination of unofficial voluntary attempts to resettle and maintain the refugees, and the High Commissioner's only direct function was to provide for their political and legal protection.

At the League's final Assembly meeting in April 1946, it was agreed to adopt a British proposal that the High Commissioner's appointment be extended to the end of the year, in order to give time for the establishment of a new administration.

Meanwhile, in July 1938, President Roosevelt had invited a number of governments to take part in a conference on the refugee problem at Evian. Twenty-eight nations, including a number of Latin-American states, agreed to set up a standing Inter-Governmental Committee (the IGC). A Director was appointed, but in 1939 it was arranged that Sir Herbert Emerson should thenceforward combine the office of Director under the IGC and High Commissioner under the League.

In 1943, as a result of the Anglo-American discussions in Bermuda during that year, the IGC decided to extend its scope to all European refugees, to collect funds from both governments and unofficial sources for the maintenance of refugees, to co-operate closely with UNRRA, and to invite twenty more nations to become members of the Committee.

In November 1945 the IGC held its fifth plenary session in Paris, twenty-eight states being represented.[1] The Executive Committee of the IGC was authorized to negotiate with the United Nations for the transfer of refugee relief to the Economic and Social Council, provided that arrangements should be made for the continued co-operation of states which were members of the IGC but not of the United Nations.

UNRRA's part in the handling of the refugee problem has been outlined in a previous section of this chapter, and it is only necessary here to note that UNRRA's declared policy has always been to confine itself to repatriating displaced persons who were willing to return to their homes, leaving it to the IGC to find new homes for those who were not. The

[1]The membership of the Committee was at this time 36, the members being : the United States, the Soviet Union, the United Kingdom ; Australia, Canada, India, New Zealand, South Africa; Belgium, Czechoslovakia, Denmark, Eire, Greece, Iceland, Luxembourg, Netherlands, Norway, Poland, Sweden, Switzerland ; Argentina, Bolivia, Brazil, Chile, Colombia, Dominican Republic, Ecuador, Egypt, Haiti, Honduras, Mexico, Nicaragua, Paraguay, Peru, Venezeula.

bulk of the present total of " refugees and displaced persons " with whom the United Nations now have to deal come into the second of these categories ; they are people who are either unwilling or afraid to entrust themselves to the political regimes now in power in their former countries.

The refugee problem was one of the first to engage the attention of the United Nations after the creation of the Organization. The Preparatory Commission placed the subject on the agenda of both the General Assembly and the Economic and Social Council for their first sessions. The Assembly devoted considerable time to discussions both in plenary session and in its Third (Social, Humanitarian and Cultural) Committee. It was clear from the beginning of these discussions that there was general agreement on the need for a refugee relief administration, but that there were very different opinions as to the methods it should adopt. Soviet and other East European delegations were chiefly concerned that the refugee camps should not harbour undesirables, that no propaganda against the political regimes of member nations should be allowed in them, and that they should be administered by representatives of the governments whose nationals they contained. British, American and other spokesmen pointed out that it was already agreed that war criminals, quislings and traitors would be surrendered for punishment, and that it was not consistent with the principles of toleration and human rights set out in the Charter that refugees should be placed under the administration of the very regimes to which they were opposed. Eventually the Assembly agreed to recommend the Economic and Social Council to set up a special committee to examine the refugee question. This the Council duly did, and a committee on which twenty nations[1] were represented was convened in London in April 1946. Its recommendations are to be submitted not later than July.

This committee has now recommended that the new refugee administration shall be a specialized agency akin to UNRRA and UNESCO, and not an integral part of the United Nations Organization. This decision was supported by Soviet, American, Chinese, East European and Latin-American delegates, and opposed by four members of the British Commonwealth, the Netherlands and the Lebanon. France and Belgium abstained from voting.

If and when this new agency takes over from UNRRA and the IGC their present responsibilities for refugees, it will be the first international refugee organization to undertake directly the maintenance of a large number of refugees, and its operating costs will undoubtedly be far higher than those of the High Commissioner's organization, the Nansen Office or the IGC. The decision to establish it as a specialized agency is therefore

[1]Of these, 13 were members of the Council (United States, Soviet Union, United Kingdom, China, France, Canada, Belgium, Colombia, Czechoslovakia, Lebanon, Peru, Ukraine and Yugoslavia), 7 were not (Australia, New Zealand, Netherlands, Brazil, Dominican Republic, Byelorussia and Poland).

of some importance, as it will probably mean that a number of members of the United Nations will decline to contribute towards the costs, on the grounds that they would only be subsidizing their political opponents if they did so.

ESTIMATED NUMBERS OF REFUGEES AND DISPLACED PERSONS PLACED BEFORE THE SPECIAL COMMITTEE BY UNRRA:—

Nationality	Total for Europe and Middle East	*Present Location*		
		Germany	Austria	Italy
All nationalities	1,084,000	810,500	82,000	39,400
Polish	616,400	514,319	19,699	16,620
Yugoslav	58,200	20,268	23,617	9,292
Baltic (Lettish, Lithuanian, Estonian)	174,400	164,850	2,888	423
Stateless	33,200	21,531	4,793	5,294
Not yet classified by nationality	117,500	62,883	22,798	41

Other totals for all areas include 11,900 Czechoslovaks, 1,400 French, 28,200 Greeks, 5,500 Italians, 2,500 Dutch, 9,500 Russians, and smaller numbers of other nationalities. Displaced persons are reported not only in Germany, Austria and Italy, but also in Albania, Czechoslovakia, Denmark, France, Greece, Netherlands, Norway, Sweden, Switzerland, Egypt, Cyprus, Palestine, Iran, India, and East Africa. There is also an estimated total of 1,400,000 displaced persons in the Far East, but most of these should be more easily repatriated than those in Europe and the Middle East.

THE FOOD AND AGRICULTURE ORGANIZATION

HOT SPRINGS AND AFTER

In February 1943 the President of the United States invited 44 nations to send representatives to a conference on food and agriculture at Hot Springs, Virginia, in May of that year. The conference sat from May 18 to June 3, and passed a number of important resolutions which were embodied in a " Final Act of the United Nations Conference on Food and Agriculture."

The most important decision was to establish a permanent Food and Agriculture Organization of the United Nations (FAO), whose main task would be to "assist the several governments and authorities in making surveys of nutritional needs, in helping develop new food-distribution programmes, in disseminating information concerning those programmes, and in aiding to co-ordinate efforts in this field."

The Hot Springs Conference also created an interim Commission, which was instructed to draft a constitution for the FAO and submit it for the approval of the governments concerned, to draft a formal declaration of mutual obligations in the field of food and agriculture which could be signed by all member nations of the FAO, and to "make such proposals or reports as were necessary to give effect to the recommendations of the Conference."

This Interim Commission began work in July 1943, in Washington. All 44 nations were represented on it. Mr. Lester B. Pearson (Canada) was chairmen, with Mr. P. W. Tsou (China) and Mr. P. I. Chegula (Soviet Union) as vice-chairmen. By August 1944 the Commission had achieved agreement on a constitution for the FAO, and on a commission report ; both of these were then submitted to the 44 governments for approval. By August 1945, sufficient governments had announced their adherence to the proposed constitution for preparations to be made for the First Conference of the FAO, which was held in Quebec in the autumn. On October 16 the representatives of 30 governments signed the new constitution, and a number of other nations have adhered since that date.

THE CONSTITUTION

The Food and Agriculture Organization will be controlled by a conference of delegates of all member nations, which will meet at least once a year. This conference will appoint an executive committee of from nine to fifteen members, which will act on its behalf between conference sessions. There will also be standing advisory committees on such specialized subjects as agricultural production, nutrition, forestry, fisheries, marketing and statistics. The members of these latter committees will not be representatives of governments, but will be individuals selected purely for their own qualifications.

A Director-General appointed by the conference will be responsible to it for the whole work of the FAO. He will select and organize an international staff of experts, whose allegiance will be to the F.A.O. only. The temporary headquarters of the organization will be in Washington, but the conference may decide to change this.

The expenses of the new organization were estimated by the Interim Commission at about £1,250,000 for the first five years. Contributions from member nations were worked out on somewhat the same basis as their contributions to the League of Nations, with considerable scaling-down in the case of occupied countries. The United States has been made responsible for 25 per cent of the budget, the United Kingdom for 15 per cent, the Soviet Union for 8 per cent and China for 6.5 per cent ; all the other members will pay smaller amounts.

The FAO will act as the representative both of consumers and of producers of food, timber and clothing at international conferences and before the General Assembly of the United Nations. It will collect and centralize information about food stocks, harvest prospects, nutrition, marketing and other subjects, and will provide governments with information and advice whenever they so request. Member governments undertake to reciprocate by supplying the FAO with the information it requires about their individual food resources. If members ask it to, the FAO will send missions of experts to particular areas to help improve production, distribution and nutrition.[1] It will draw up international conventions for the control of pests and diseases and for the standardization of measurements, gradings and nomenclature. It will promote and centralize research.

THE PROBLEM AND THE GOAL

The Hot Springs Conference summed up the aims of the FAO in the very first resolution contained in its Final Act :

" The goal of freedom from want of food, suitable and adequate for the health and strength of all peoples, can be achieved."

One needs only the slightest acquaintance with the present world food shortage to realize how tremendous a task the Organization is setting itself to tackle. As yet, of course, the FAO has not established itself as the supreme international food agency. The food crisis of 1946 is being tackled by a number of different oganizations—some critics complain that there are too many of them—such as the Combined Food Board, UNRRA, the Emergency Economic Committee for Europe and the United States Famine Emergency Committee. There still exists in Rome the International Institute of Agriculture founded forty years ago by David Lubin. But the FAO is intended to replace this patchwork of jarring organizations as soon as possible. The Quebec Conference appointed as Director-General Sir John Boyd Orr, who has since announced that within the next few months the Organization will put forward, both to the United Nations Organization and to the individual governments concerned, concrete proposals to ensure a long-term sufficiency of food together with satisfactory and stable price-levels. The FAO will hold its next full conference at Copenhagen in October, when these proposals will be discussed by the representatives of the member nations. There are now 44 members ; the Soviet Union and the other Soviet Republics have not yet adhered to the constitution, although they were present at Hot Springs and at the meetings of the Interim Commission. Certain states which are not at present members of the United Nations may, at the Copenhagen confer-

[1]The first of these missions has already left for Greece.

ence, be invited to join the FAO ; this would substantially increase the Organization's field of action. But it cannot be too clearly stated that the plans drawn up by the FAO can only be put into effect if there is sincere determination among the member nations to implement the pledges given at Hot Springs. As Mr. Pearson pointed out at the Quebec conference last year, " Whether the Food and Agriculture Organization amounts to anything depends on what use Governments and peoples make of it."

BRETTON WOODS

International trade cannot thrive unless there is a stable relationship between the different currencies of the various trading countries. Until 1914 the Gold Standard provided the world with a simple and comparatively stable currency mechanism ; but, after the First World War, the nations discovered one after another that the lopsided conditions created by that war had made gold useless as a basis for currency relationships. During the thirties almost all the nations had to abandon the gold standard ; and although this drastic step alleviated conditions for individual countries, the world was left without any solid mechanism for the payment of international debts. The resulting instability was felt by no country more strongly than by Britain, for Britain lives by international trade.

As early as 1942 it was suggested that the United Nations should set up specialized agencies to overcome the instability of national currencies in the post-war world, and the difficulty which would confront countries which wanted loans to finance reconstruction. Exploratory discussions between United Nations technical experts began, and resulted in proposals for the establishment of an International Monetary Fund and an International Bank for Reconstruction and Development. The object of the Fund was to be to stabilize the relative values of national currencies. The Bank would make it easier for capital to flow across national frontiers, and at the same time would stabilize the international loan market by giving guarantees to lending nations.

More than 400 delegates from 44 nations attended the United Nations Monetary and Financial Conference which met at Bretton Woods, Virginia, in July 1944. After three weeks discussion, unanimous agreement was reached on detailed plans for both Fund and Bank. The Final Act of the conference also recommended to the participating governments that they should " reduce obstacles to international trade and in other ways promote mutually advantageous international commercial relations ; bring about the orderly marketing of staple commodities at prices fair to the producer and consumer alike ; . . . and facilitate by co-operative effort the harmonization of national policies of Member States designed to promote and maintain high levels of employment and progressively rising standards of living."

During 1945 the Bretton Woods agreements were ratified by sufficient governments to take effect ; all the principal United Nations except the Soviet Union and the other Soviet Republics have now adhered to the plan. Each member nation appointed Governors for the Fund and the Bank as provided in the agreements, and these Governors, assembled at Savannah, Georgia, in March 1946, elected executive directors and set the wheels of the two agencies in motion. There is bound to be a delay of several months before the lending operations of the Bank or the stabilizing influence of the Fund can get under way ; but both will probably be in operation by the end of 1946.

The Bretton Woods agreements have been the subject of lengthy and vigorous discussion, both in Britain and elsewhere, ever since their publication. Opponents of the plan assert, with a wealth of authoritative argument, that it will bring all the member nations under the financial control of the United States, and bind them irrevocably to gold, of which, of course, that country now has a near-monopoly. The supporters of the Bretton Woods agreements generally admit that American hegemony is inevitable to a limited extent, but insist that some sacrifice of national independence in the field of finance is inevitable unless we wish to court disaster by perpetuating the present monetary anarchy. No account of the debate on the agreements would be complete without a brief reference to the work of the late Lord Keynes, who took the leading role both among the defenders of Bretton Woods in this country and among the British delegates to both conferences. Keynes was largely responsible for such concessions to the British point of view as appear in the final framework of the Fund and the Bank.

THE INTERNATIONAL MONETARY FUND

The member nations will set up a permanent international fund, partly of gold, partly of the various national currencies of the members. From this fund the member nations can then buy limited amounts of foreign currencies, to pay off legitimate trading debts. They will buy these foreign currencies by paying in their own currencies.

To maintain the stability of the world currency market and to encourage international trade, member nations undertake not to change the par values of their own currencies by more than 10 per cent without the consent of the Fund, to make proceeds of international transactions freely convertible into other currencies as soon as possible, and to refrain from discriminatory currency arrangements and multiple currency practice.

If all the nations represented at Bretton Woods eventually join the Fund, the total subscribed capital will be $8,800,000,000.[1] The largest allotment is that of the United States, $2,750,000,000 ; Britain's share is $1,300,000,000, and that of the Soviet Union, which has not yet been taken up, $1,200,000,000. Members must pay in gold a minimum of either 25 per cent of the quota allotted to them, or 10 per cent of their total holdings

---

[1] A list showing individual allotments is given at the end of this section.

of gold and U.S. dollars, whichever is the smaller. The balance of each quota is to be paid in each member's own currency.

There will be no real geographical transfer of monies to effect these subscriptions. The currency portions of the quotas need only be credited to the Fund's account with any acceptable central bank within each member's own borders. The agreement does provide, however, that 90 per cent of the gold deposited must be held within the borders of the five largest subscribers.

The size of each member's quota determine three important limits : first, the amount of its resources on which the Fund can call ; second, the amount of foreign currency which it can buy from the Fund in normal circumstances ; third, its share in the control of the Fund. In general, any member in good standing can buy, with its own currency, an amount of foreign currency not exceeding one quarter of its own quota in any one year. There is one limitation to this right ; the Fund will not accept a member's currency if it already holds twice as much as the member's original quota, without special agreement. Thus, for example, India, whose quota is $400,000,000, will deposit with the Fund $100,000,000 in gold and $300,000,000 in her own currency. She can then buy $100,000,000 of foreign currencies every year ; but if she does so for five years, and if no other country has during that time bought any Indian currency off the Fund, the Fund will hold a total of $800,000,000 worth of Indian currency, and India will be allowed to make no further purchases except by special agreement or in gold.

Member nations can buy foreign currencies with gold without regard to the above limitations. They can also at any time buy back their own currencies from the Fund.

The Fund will make the following charges : firstly, a fee of between $\frac{1}{2}$ per cent and 1 per cent on each transaction ; secondly, interest charges on the amount of each member's currency held in excess of that member's original quota. Starting at $\frac{1}{2}$ per cent as soon as the excess either exceeds 25 per cent of the quota or has existed for more than three months, interest charges increase by $\frac{1}{2}$ per cent for every additional year that the excess exists and for every additional 25 per cent of the original quota. Thus the interest charge on an excess of 100 per cent after three years would be $3\frac{1}{2}$ per cent.

The object of these charges is, of course, to discourage members from dumping their own currency on the Fund and leaving it there. For this reason, it is laid down that interest charges must be paid in gold, and that if the charge rises to 5 per cent, the Fund may impose additional discouraging charges.

The control of the Fund is vested in a Board of Governors, to which each member state will appoint one Governor, with alternate Governors. Members may change or re-appoint their Governors at will. Unless otherwise specified in the original agreements, decisions of the Board of Governors will be made by a simple majority of all votes cast. But there is a system of weightage by which the voting power of each Governor varies according to the original quota subscribed to the Fund by the nation which he represents. Each member receives one vote for each $100,000 of its quota, plus a " basic ration " of 250 votes. The United States Governor therefore wields 27,750 votes ; the British Governor has 13,250 ; and the members with the smallest quotas, Panama and Liberia, each possess only 300 votes. There is also an adjustment of voting powers when the Board votes either on a request from a member to buy foreign currency beyond the normal limit, or on a proposal to restrict a member's access to the Fund because of its misbehaviour. Each member then receives one vote for every $400,000 worth of its currency which has been sold by the Fund, and loses one for every $400,000 worth of foreign currency which it has bought from the Fund with its own currency. The effect in each case is to give the creditor nations a stronger position in limiting the access to the Fund of debtor nations.

A Board of Executive Directors, consisting of 12 or more members, will supervise the operations of the Fund in between meetings of the Board of Governors. Of the Executive Directors, one shall be appointed by each of the five biggest subscribers to the Fund[1] ; two shall be elected jointly by the Latin-American nations ; and the remainder, which will not exceed five initially, by the other members. The Board of Governors is empowered to increase the number of Directors when new member states are admitted to participation in the Fund ; and the right to appoint Directors may also be given to two further individual members if the Fund's holdings of their currencies are reduced, by purchases, by a greater absolute amount than its holdings of the currencies of the five biggest subscribers. This last provision is, of course, another encouragement to members not to leave the Fund holding large quantities of their currencies.

The present Board of Executive Directors comprises representatives of the United States, Britain, China, France and India, the biggest subscribers ; Mexico and Brazil, elected by the Latin-American countries ; and Canada, Czechoslovakia, Belgium, Egypt and the Netherlands. The elected Directors serve a two-year term, but are eligible for immediate re-election ; appointed Directors may of course remain in office as long as their governments like. Like the Governors, the Executive Directors have alternates ; and, like the Governors, they make decisions by a simple

---

[1]Presumably the original intention was that these five would be the United States, the United Kingdom, the Soviet Union, France and China. But when the time came to appoint Directors the Soviet Government had not yet adhered to the Bretton Woods agreements ; and the next largest subscriber, India, was accordingly given a seat on the Board of Executive Directors along with the United States, the United Kingdom, France and China.

majority vote. Directors cast all the votes of all the countries which elected or appointed them.[1]

Day by day management of the Fund is in the hands of a Managing Director chosen by the Executive Directors.[2] He must not be a Governor or a member of the Board of Executive Directors. He acts as chairman of the latter, but will only vote if required to give a casting vote in the event of a deadlock. His staff will be recruited on as broad an international basis as possible.

The Board of Executive Directors shall decide every year how much of the Fund's profits shall be placed in reserve, and how much distributed to members.

Any member state may withdraw from the Fund if it wishes to, and will not be required to give notice. On the other hand, the Fund can first suspend and later, if necessary, expel any member which does not fulfil its obligations under the agreements. When a member state withdraws or is expelled, its account with the Fund must be settled in full, the Fund returning the member's original quota and adjusting all other outstanding balances. The whole Fund may be liquidated if the Governors so decide ; in this case the assets will be distributed among the members on a fixed schedule similar to that which originally allotted them their quotas.

The Bretton Woods agreements expressly forbade the Fund to use its resources for relief purposes or to settle the abnormal type of debt caused by war. Nor may the Fund be used for any large or sustained transfer of capital from one country to another. Its function is, in fact, simply to stabilize. More creative development is the task of the International Bank.

THE INTERNATIONAL BANK FOR RECONSTRUCTION AND DEVELOPMENT

The Bank is intended to revive production throughout the world by encouraging international investment through the customary private channels. Capital is urgently needed in many war-torn countries. There is much post-war reconstruction to be done ; equipment must be bought to enable industries to reconvert to peace-time production ; many backward areas are claimant for swift development. In the view of the Bretton Woods experts, a revival of international lending is essential to the attainment of a high level of world trade, without which prosperity will never be restored.

The Bank will have two main functions : to make direct loans to the

[1] It may be remarked that, had the Soviet Union joined the Fund, the three biggest subscribers—the United States, Britain, and the U.S.S.R.—would then have had an absolute majority of votes over all the other member States. The four biggest subscribers now possess a similar majority.

[2] M. Camille Gutt, former Belgian Finance Minister has been elected as the first Managing Director.

borrowing countries ; and to guarantee loans made by other parties. The latter will be much more important than the former, and on a far greater scale.

The structure of the Bank closely resembles that of the Fund. Only governments may own or acquire shares in it. The shares will be valued at $100,000 each, and the initial maximum issue will be one hundred thousand of them, giving a total capital of $10,000,000,000. If all the nations represented at Bretton Woods take up their shares, the working capital will then be $9,100,000,000, the remaining $900,000,000 worth of shares being kept in reserve for allotment to any further nations which may join later.[1] Members must pay in 2 per cent. of their allotted share values in either gold or U.S. dollars within two months of the opening of the Bank, and a further 18 per cent, in their own national currency, in instalments over a period which will be determined by the Bank. The remaining 80 per cent of the share values may be retained by each member, but must be made available to the Bank if required to meet the Bank's obligations.

At a later stage the Bank may decide to increase its capital. If it does so, it will fix an issue price, and offer member nations the opportunity of taking up additional amounts proportionate to their original shares. Members will not be obliged to buy these additional shares.

Like the Fund, the Bank is controlled by a Board of Governors, each member nation appointing one Governor and one alternative Governor. This Board will meet annually, and will exercise supreme authority over the Bank. It makes its decisions by a simple majority, but the voting is weighted in the same way as in the Board of Governors of the Fund. Between meetings of the Board of Governors, the Bank will be controlled by a Board of Executive Directors, of whose twelve members one will be appointed by each of the five largest shareholders, and the remaining seven will be elected, on a proportional representation system, by the remaining shareholders. This Board is at present composed of representatives of the United States, the United Kingdom, China, France and India, as being the five largest shareholders, and of Belgium, Canada, Chile, Cuba, Greece, Poland and the Netherlands.

The Board of Governors is to appoint an Advisory Council of seven or more representatives of banking, commercial, industrial, labour and agricultural interests, which will advise on general policy. Loan Committees will also be appointed to investigate specific applications for loans. Such committees will consist of experts from the Bank staff, together with one representative of the Government in whose territory the project for which the loan is sought is situated.

The Bank will not provide any nation with funds to spend on internal relief projects. It is intended to be financially self-supporting, and to encourage rather than supplant private business. It cannot consider ap-

[1] A list showing individual allotments is given at the end of this section.

plications for speculative or non-productive loans. It can only lend, or guarantee loans, for specific objects approved by the responsible committees. It may not guarantee private loans unless it is satisfied that the borrower could not get the loan on reasonable terms without a guarantee.

The agreements limit direct loans out of the Bank's own capital to less than $2,000,000,000. The remaining 80 per cent of the Bank's capital can be used either as backing for guarantees or to enable the Bank to borrow in the private capital market and so to make other loans.

Loans may be made not only to governments, but to cities, counties, responsible businesses and agriculturaland industrial enterprises, provided the governments concerned guarantee the loan. The Bank may, if it chooses, only make or guarantee a part of any loan.

The Bank will normally lend, or arrange loans, in a currency other than that of the borrower. Its purpose is principally to enable one country to make purchases in another, and for this reason it will naturally seek to provide the borrower with the currency of the country in which it wishes to buy.

On direct loans the Bank will charge a reasonable rate of interest, which it is empowered to determine for itself. When guaranteeing a loan, it will charge a commission of from 1 to 1½ per cent ; this rate may be revised after a period of ten years from the opening of the Bank.

The Bank is pledged to observe strict neutrality in politics, basing its decisions purely on a businesslike interpretation of its stated objectives, and in no way influencing the political affairs of any member. Its staff must owe their allegiance solely to the Bank, and are granted certain immunities similar to those of United Nations officials.

The Bank's provisions for liquidation and the withdrawal of members closely resemble those of the Fund. A member which withdraws cannot, however, consider itself in any way relieved of the obligations assumed by the Bank while it was a member.

The Bretton Woods agreements included an undertaking by all member nations to supply both Fund and Bank with full information about their monetary reserves, gold production, balance of payments and international investments.

QUOTAS ALLOTTED TO NATIONS REPRESENTED AT BRETTON WOODS
(In millions of U.S. dollars)

Big Five	Fund	Bank
U.S.A.	2,750	3,175
U.S.S.R.	1,200	1,200
U.K.	1,300	1,300
France	450	450
China	550	600

Western Europe

Belgium	225	225
Luxembourg	10	10
Netherlands	275	275
Norway	50	50

Eastern Europe

Czechoslovakia	125	125
Greece	40	25
Poland	125	125
Yugoslavia	60	40

Middle East and Africa

Egypt	45	40
Ethiopia	6	3
Iran	25	8
Iraq	24	6
Liberia	0.5	0.5
South Africa	100	100

Far East

Australia	200	200
India	400	400
New Zealand	50	50
Philippines	15	15

North and Central America

Canada	300	325
Costa Rica	5	2
Cuba	50	35
Dominican Republic	5	2
El Salvador	2.5	1
Guatemala	5	2
Haiti	5	2
Honduras	2.5	1
Mexico	90	65
Nicaragua	2	0.8
Panama	0.5	0.2

South America

Bolivia	10	7
Brazil	150	105
Chile	50	35

Colombia	50	35
Ecuador	5	3.2
Paraguay	2	0.8
Peru	25	17.5
Uruguay	15	10.5
Venezuela	15	10.5
	8,800	9,100

TRADE AND EMPLOYMENT PROJECTS

On February 18, 1946, the Economic and Social Council of the United Nations decided to call an international conference on trade and employment (probably in the latter part of 1947), and placed on the agenda of this conference a proposal for the creation of an International Trade Organization of the United Nations.

The antecedents of this project go back to the fourth principle enunciated in the Atlantic Charter, which commits the United Nations to furthering " the enjoyment by all States . . . of access, on equal terms, to the trade and to the raw materials of the world which are needed for their economic prosperity." This idea is reiterated in each of the Mutual Aid Agreements signed between the United States and other members of the United Nations in 1942 and later. The seventh article in each of these agreements is identical, and includes proposals for " agreed action . . . open to participation by all other countries of like mind, directed to the expansion, by appropriate international and domestic measures, of production, employment, and the exchange and consumption of goods, which are the material foundations of the liberty and welfare of all peoples ; to the elimination of all forms of discriminatory treatment in international commerce, and to the reduction of tariffs and other trade barriers ; and in general, to the attainment of all the economic objectives set forth in the Joint Declaration made on the 14th August 1941 (the Atlantic Charter)."

We have already seen that the Bretton Woods agreements also recommended to the participating governments that they should reduce obstacles to international trade, facilitate the orderly marketing of staple commodities and in other ways develop a healthy and vigorous system of trade and employment. The next official proposals in the chain of United Nations trade projects were made jointly by the United States and the United Kingdom in a paper issued on December 6, 1945, in connection with the proposed financial agreement between the two countries.

These were entitled " Proposals for Consideration by an International Conference on Trade and Employment." Referring to the need for cooperative economic measures which will achieve " fairness and equity in economic relations between states " and raise the economic standards of all peoples, the Proposals recommend " further measures dealing directly with trade barriers and discriminations which stand in the way of an expansion of multilateral trade " and " an undertaking on the part of nations to seek full employment." The two governments concerned recognize two guiding principles : first, that " in all countries high and stable employment is a main condition for the attainment of satisfactory standards of living " ; second, that " the attainment of approximately full employment by the major industrial and trading nations . . . is essential to the expansion of international trade, to the realization of the objectives of all liberal commercial and financial agreements, and therefore to the preservation of world peace and security."

The United States and the United Kingdom therefore propose the establishment of an International Trade Organization, whose purposes shall be " to facilitate access by all members, on equal terms, to the trade and to the raw materials of the world which are needed for their economic prosperity " [1] and " to promote national and international action for the expansion of the production, exchange and consumption of goods, for the reduction of tariffs and other trade barriers, and for the elimination of all forms of discriminatory treatment in international commerce." Thus the International Trade Organization will contribute " to an expanding world economy, to the establishment and maintenance in all countries of high levels of employment and real income, and to the creation of economic conditions conducive to the maintenance of world peace."

In almost every particular the Economic and Social Council has approved the Anglo-American proposals. The Council has suggested that the agenda of the forthcoming international conference should include the formulation of international agreements on high and stable employment levels, inter-governmental commodity arrangements, and restrictions, discriminations, and restrictive practices in international trade. The conference will also discuss the creation of an international trade organization competent to deal with these subjects. But the actual agenda for the conference will be prepared by a Preparatory Committee of representatives of 19 nations, which will also recommend what states, if any, other than members of the United Nations, will be invited to attend ; and this Committee was directed by the Council to " take into account the special conditions which prevail in countries whose manufacturing industry is still in its initial stages of development, and the questions that arise in connection with commodities which are subject to special problems of adjustment in international markets." This last modification was inserted at the vehement request of a group of states, chiefly Latin-American, which feel that some form of tariff protection is as essential to them now as it was at an earlier date to the United States.

The Preparatory Committee consists of representatives of the United

[1] It is of interest that the wording here is identical with that used in the Atlantic Charter.

States, the United Kingdom, the Soviet Union, France, China, Australia, Belgium, Brazil, Canada, Cuba, Czechoslovakia, India, Luxembourg, Netherlands, New Zealand, South Africa, Chile, Norway and the Lebanon.

The United States and British Governments have announced that, in order to prepare the ground thoroughly for the conference, they propose to hold a preliminary " Drafting Conference," probably in Frebruary, 1947, at which it is hoped to establish substantial agreement among some of the more important commercial nations, including all the British Dominions, Belgium, the Netherlands, France, Czechoslovakia, Cuba, China and Brazil. An invitation to this meeting has been sent to the Soviet Union.

UNESCO

The United Nations Educational, Scientific and Cultural Organization originated in a meeting of Allied Ministers of Education convened in London in 1942 by Mr. R. A. Butler, who was then President of the British Board of Education. This meeting agreed upon the general idea of the establishment of an international educational organization, and preparatory consultations between governments were set in motion. In 1944 American representatives visited London and discussed the whole project with the Council of Allied Ministers of Education, and in 1945 the Council produced an agreed draft of proposals for an Educational and Cultural Organization of the United Nations.

On November 1, 1945, representatives of 44 nations[1] assembled in London to discuss the CAME draft and an alternative draft submitted by the French Government. On November 16 they signed and published the constitution of UNESCO. The word " Scientific " was inserted in the title of the new organization on the motion of the British and American representatives, a substantial minority of nations opposing the addition but eventually agreeing to accept the new name. It was decided to hold the first UNESCO Conference in Paris towards the end of 1946 ; and a Preparatory Commission was set up to plan the Conference. This Commission delegated much of its authority to an Executive Committee, whose membership of 15 included representatives of the United States, the United Kingdom, France, China, Belgium, Brazil, Canada, Colombia, Greece, India, Mexico, Netherlands, Norway, and Poland. The fifteenth seat on the committee was left vacant in the hope that the Soviet Union, which has never expressed any antagonism towards UNESCO, would ratify the constitution and occupy the seat. The president and secretary of the constituent conference, Miss Ellen Wilkinson and Sir Alfred Zimmern, were appointed president and executive secretary of the Pre-

---

[1] The Soviet Union and the other Soviet Republics, which had requested a postponement of the constituent conference, were not represented in London.

paratory Commission ; but in February 1946 Dr. Julian Huxley was appointed to the post of executive secretary, Sir Alfred Zimmern remaining with UNESCO as an adviser.

In December 1945 the CAME met for the last time and agreed to hand over to UNESCO all the records and undertakings of its commissions on books, science, special educational problems, audio-visual aids, and the protection and restitution of cultural material.

The Preamble to the constitution of UNESCO declares : " . . . that since wars begin in the minds of men, it is in the minds of men that the defences of peace must be constructed.[1] "

" That ignorance of each other's ways and lives has been a common cause, throughout the history of mankind, of that suspicion and mistrust between the peoples of the world through which their differences have all too often broken into war."

" That the great and terrible war which has now ended was a war made possible by the denial of the democratic principles of the dignity, equality and mutual respect of men, and by the propagation, in their place, through ignorance and prejudice, of the doctrine of the inequality of men and races" and " that a peace based exclusively upon the political and economic arrangements of governments would not be a peace which could secure the unanimous, lasting and sincere support of the peoples of the world, and that the peace must therefore be founded, if it is not to fail, upon the intellectual and moral solidarity of mankind."

The first article of the constitution states that the purpose of UNESCO is " to contribute to peace and security by promoting collaboration among the nations through education, science and culture, in order to further universal respect for justice, for the rule of law and for the human rights and fundamental freedoms which are affirmed for the peoples of the world, without distinction of race, sex, language or religion, by the Charter of the United Nations."

UNESCO is an advisory and auxiliary organization ; it is specifically forbidden to intervene in matters within the domestic jurisdiction of member governments ; and its projects will in every case be based upon the voluntary co-operation of its members. Subject to these limitations, UNESCO plans to promote mutual understanding between peoples through all means of mass communication, to encourage popular education, particularly in backward parts of the world, to use its influence with its members to achieve equality of educational opportunity without regard to race, sex or social distinction, to organize international conventions for the preservation of the world's great books and works of art, and to arrange exchanges of both students and materials between member nations. UNESCO has also signed an agreement with UNRRA under which

[1] This phase was suggested by Mr. Attlee's remarks in his address of welcome to the constituent conference.

UNRRA will distribute basic teaching materials to the devastated countries together with its other relief supplies, and a joint UNESCO–UNRRA committee has been set up to supervise the collaborations of the two organizations.

UNESCO is a much more far-reaching enterprise than the former League of Nations Intellectual Co-operation Organization. The earlier organization confined itself to operations at the university and research level, and in this field its International Institute of Intellectual Co-operation at Paris did some excellent work ; but UNESCO aims at getting down to the level of the child, and believes that only when popular education is reshaped on a basis of " world loyalty " can " the defences of peace " be built " in the minds of men."

THE ILO

The International Labour Organization was established in 1919 as part of the framework of the League of Nations. The League Covenant does not directly mention the ILO, but in its twenty-third article it states that the members of the League " will endeavour to secure and maintain fair and humane conditions of labour for men, women, and children, both in their own countries and in all countries to which their commercial and industrial relations extend, and for that purpose will establish and maintain the necessary international organizations."

The Charter of the ILO was incorporated in the Peace Treaties of 1919 in the same way as the Covenant of the League, constituting chapters 12 and 13 of each Treaty. It declares that social justice is recognized as a condition of universal peace ; that conditions of labour exist involving such injustice, hardship and privations to large numbers of people as to produce unrest so great that the peace and harmony of the world are imperilled ; and that the failure of any nation to adopt humane conditions of labour is an obstacle in the way of other nations which desire to improve conditions in their own countries.

The League did not exercise direct control over the ILO, but financed it out of its own budget, with adjustments in the case of states which were members of the ILO but not of the League (the most important of these was the United States, which, however, did not join until 1934). The Charter provided that all members of the League were automatically members of the ILO, but, as the League is now defunct, the ILO has now amended its constitution so as to eliminate this and other links with its parent organization.

The supreme authority in the ILO is wielded by the International Labour Conference, which is bound in normal times to meet at least once a year. In the Conference each member state has four representatives ; two represent the national government, one the employers, and one the workers. The Conference can approve draft conventions and recommendations by a two-thirds majority, each individual representative voting singly.

Closer supervision is exercised by the Governing Body of the International Labour Office, which meets quarterly. It contains 32 members ; sixteen are representatives of governments, eight of employers and eight of workers. Of the sixteen governmental members, eight are appointed by the eight principal industrial nations and the other eight by the remaining nations. The Governing Body appoints a Director, who is responsible to it for the work of the International Labour Office, the staff of which is recruited on an international basis.

The main task of the ILO has been to frame international rules on conditions of labour, to persuade governments to accept these rules, and to supervise their application. By 1938 it had adopted 63 conventions and 56 recommendations to governments. Some 44 of the conventions had taken effect, an average of 20 governments having ratified each of them. Each member state is bound to make an annual report to the ILO on the action it has taken to give effect to the conventions to which it is a party. Complaints from member states or from representatives of employers' or workers' associations are taken up and investigated by the Organization, whose charter provides for economic pressure by other members on any state which gives serious offence.

The conventions adopted before the 1939–45 war covered such subjects as hours of work, unemployment, employment of nursing mothers and pregnant women, minimum ages for child workers, nightwork for children, weekly rests, the right of association for agricultural labour, medical examination of children for work at sea, seamen's terms of service, workmen's compensation, sickness insurance, and protection against accidents.

When Geneva became surrounded by the Axis in 1940 the ILO moved its headquarters to Montreal. In the autumn of 1941 the Conference met in New York and pledged itself to support of the economic and social clauses of the Atlantic Charter. In 1944 it met in Philadelphia, and at this meeting an important statement of principles was agreed upon. The ILO's field of responsibility was extended by this statement from the protection of labour to the wider sphere of economic and financial policy in general. The Organization sent representatives to Bretton Woods, to the meetings of the Council of UNRRA, to the Food and Agriculture conferences, and to San Francisco. The delegation sent to San Francisco affirmed the ILO's desire for close association with the United Nations Organization.

Meeting in Paris in the autumn of 1945, the International Labour Conference authorized the Governing Body to make the necessary arrangements to bring the ILO into relationship with the United Nations. This Conference also agreed upon an Instrument of Amendment to the 1916 Charter. The proposed amendments, which must be ratified by three-quarters of the member states before they take effect, are designed to eliminate the remaining connections between the ILO and the League, to provide for interim financial arrangements until some new system in which the United Nations may finance the Organization can be set up, and to permit any member of the United Nations not already represented in the ILO to join without requiring the approval of the other members.

THE FUTURE OF THE ILO

Obviously the ILO differs from UNRRA, UNESCO, the FAO and the financial agencies in that it was not set up by the United Nations, and indeed represents the 1919 structure which has otherwise ceased to exist. There is no clear indication whether the ILO will be " brought into relationship " with the United Nations as a " specialized agency." The Soviet Union's attitude to the Organization is extremely reserved. Even when automatically a member of the ILO through her membership of the League between 1934 and 1939, the Union took very little part in the Organization's activities and never ratified any of its conventions. It is of course natural that there should be a gulf between a socialist state which has eliminated the employer class and an organization which gives employers equal representation with workers. In 1943 the Soviet Union rejected an offer of a permanent seat among the principal industrial powers represented on the Governing Body. At San Francisco in 1945 she secured the omission of any direct reference to the ILO in the wording of the Charter, and this omission was repeated when the constitution of the World Federation of Trade Unions was drawn up in October 1945. There is also opposition to the ILO among trade union groups outside the Soviet Union, such as the American Congress of Industrial Organizations and the Confederation of Latin-American Workers. But both the Latin-American workers and the WFTU itself have admitted that the ILO is still the only international official body in which workers are represented with voting rights. And there is strong support for the ILO from the American Federation of Labour and the British Trade Union Congress. British statesmen have pronounced unanimously in its favour. In 1942 Mr. Bevin declared that, " There has been no other institution . . . in which it has been possible to incorporate representative elements and governments meeting in common council in the same way that it has been achieved through the machinery of the ILO. . . . It may well serve as a pointer to the parliament of man." Shortly afterwards Mr. Eden told the House of Commons that, " the ILO must be strengthened and developed." And in the General Assembly on January 17, 1946, Mr. Bevin said that, " The International Labour Office, by its methods and its power of making conventions applicable universally, can become an even more potent instrument than it has been already in creating new levels of human existence all over the world. . . .

I hope this instrument will continue its work and be brought into full use by the United Nations."

One thing is sure ; whatever part the ILO may or may not play in the United Nations Organization, it will not have the same status as it possessed *vis-à-vis* the League. In 1919 there were only three major international organs ; the League, the Permanent Court and the ILO. Today the ILO is reduced to the same level as the numerous " specialized agencies " of the United Nations, and much of its work will be handled by the Economic and Social Council. By the time its next Conference meets, in Montreal in September 1946, its fate will probably have been decided.

HEALTH

At San Francisco Chinese and Brazilian delegates urged that one of the United Nations, more urgent tasks should be the establishment of an international health organization. In February 1946 the Chinese member of the Economic and Social Council again raised the matter ; and on February 18 the Council passed a resolution calling an international conference in New York for June. The June conference will discuss " machinery for international action in the field of health." It will seek to unify the work formerly done by UNRRA, the League of Nations Health Organization, the International Office of Public Hygiene in Paris, and such regional agencies as the Pan-American Sanitary Bureau, and will facilitate the exchange of information and techniques between member nations.

A Technical Preparatory Committee, on which 16 nations were represented, met in Paris in March 1946 and produced a draft constitution for the proposed organization and a draft agenda for the June conference.

CIVIL AVIATION

A Provisional International Civil Aviation Organization was established by a conference held at Chicago in November and December, 1944, at which 52 nations were represented. The interim agreement which set up this Organization provided for an Interim Council and an Interim Assembly, and laid down a number of principles and rules for civil aviation.

NON-GOVERNMENTAL ORGANIZATIONS
THE WORLD FEDERATION OF TRADE UNIONS

Of the non-governmental organizations with which the Economic and Social Council is authorized to arrange consultations, the most vocal is the World Federation of Trade Unions (WFTU). This organization, which has replaced the earlier International Federation of Trade Unions, was conceived in February 1944, when a World Trade Union Conference met in London and resolved to create a federation which would include all the trade unions of the freedom-loving countries " regardless of considerations of race or creed or of political and religious distinctions or differences

E

in philosophical theory." A draft constitution for the Federation was prepared by an Administrative Committee, and in September 1945 a second World Trade Union Conference assembled in Paris. Delegations from 56 countries, representing 65 trade union groups, were present. On October 3 a constitution for the WFTU was adopted ; it announces the aims of the new Federation as being : " to organize and unite within its ranks the trade unions of the whole world, irrespective of considerations of race, nationality, religion or political opinion ; to assist, wherever necessary, the workers in countries socially or industrially less developed, in setting up their trade unions ; to combat war and the causes of war and to work for a stable and enduring peace by giving full support to the establishment of a powerful and effective international organization, armed with all necessary power to prevent aggression and maintain peace, and by supporting the widest possible international co-operation in the social and economic spheres ; and to represent the interests of world labour in all international agencies resting upon the agreements or conventions concluded between the United Nations and in such other international bodies as the Federation may decide."

Acting in the spirit of this last clause, the WFTU applied for representation in the United Nations Organization as soon as the San Francisco Conference had adopted its provisions for consultation with non-governmental agencies. Its demands were repeated in correspondence with the secretariat of the Preparatory Commission, and when the General Assembly met in January 1946 it was confronted with a request that the WFTU be given a seat, with full rights of membership, in both the General Assembly and the Economic and Social Council. There was strong opposition to this request, which would have been a substantial modification of the Charter itself, and the WFTU then applied for representation in the Economic and Social Council only. This application was championed by the Soviet, French and Belgian representatives in a series of vigorous debates in the General Assembly and in its committees. A majority of member nations, among which were the United States and the United Kingdom, objected to the WFTU being given a seat in the Council, but were willing to concede that the Council " should as soon as possible adopt suitable arrangements enabling the WFTU and the International Co-operative Alliance, as well as other international non-governmental organizations. . . to collaborate for purposes of consultation with the Economic and Social Council." The Assembly ruled, by 32 votes to 6, that this formula should be adopted, and instructed the Council to make similar arrangements with such national organizations as the American Federation of Labour.

OTHER NON-GOVERNMENTAL ORGANIZATIONS

Although the WFTU was the first of the non-governmental organizations to apply for a position in the framework of the United Nations, several other similar organizations have also sent in applications, some of them as early as San Francisco. The International Co-operative Alliance, which states that it represents some 80,000,000 families, was among the first; the International Chamber of Commerce pledged its collaboration to the Economic and Social Council at its meeting in London in August 1945; the International Federation of Women has also filed an application. In October 1945 a World Youth Conference, at which 62 countries were represented, assembled in London, and set up a World Federation of Democratic Youth, which will probably have its headquarters in Paris. The WFDY has added its application to those already under consideration by the Economic and Social Council.[1]

The Council decided, at its thirteenth meeting, to appoint a committee to arrange the manner in which the various non-governmental organizations shall be placed in a consultative relationship to itself. The Committee, which is still in being, consists of the President of the Council (Sir Ramaswami Mudaliar) and representatives of the United States, the United Kingdom, the Soviet Union, France, China, Cuba, Greece, Lebanon, Peru, Ukraine, and Yugoslavia.

[1] The proposed World Federation of United Nations Associations (WFUNA) will also have a strong claim for a consultative position.

CHAPTER IX

THE SECRETARIAT AND THE HEADQUARTERS

THE SECRETARY-GENERAL

On February 2, 1946, the former Foreign Minister of Norway took the following oath in the presence of the General Assembly :

" I, Trygve Lie, solemnly swear to exercise in all loyalty, discretion and conscience the functions entrusted to me as Secretary-General of the United Nations, to discharge those functions and regulate my conduct with the interests of the United Nations only in view, and not to seek or accept instructions in regard to the performance of my duties from any Government or other authority external to the Organization."

More than any other single person, the Secretary-General must represent the United Nations in the eyes of the whole world. As head of the International Secretariat, he is the channel of all communication with the various organs of the United Nations. By virtue of the powers specially given him in the Charter, he has more responsibility for the active maintenance of peace than has ever been given to the head of an international organization. The position is therefore of immense importance.

Under Articles 18 and 27 of the Charter, the choice of a candidate for the post of Secretary-General must first be made by the Security Council. Within the Council, a majority of seven, including all the five permanent members, must agree on a choice in order for it to be valid. The Council then makes its recommendation to the General Assembly, which may confirm or reject the Council's choice ; confirmation may be made by a simple majority vote, unless the Assembly itself decides that a two-thirds majority is to be required.[1] If there is a division of opinion on the candidature, the rules of procedure recommend that both Council and Assembly discuss the alternative choices in private meetings.

The Charter does not stipulate the term for which the Secretary-General is to be appointed, but it has been proposed that the initial term should be five years, without prejudice to the reappointment of the same individual to the end of that period. The Council and Assembly, may by agreement, vary the length of the term of office.

An important condition proposed by the Preparatory Commission for the Assembly's approval obliges any Secretary-General to refrain from accepting any major governmental position immediately after vacating his office. It is pointed out that the confidential information which he

[1]In the case of the first Secretary-General, Mr. Lie, the Security Council was unanimous in its recommendation, and the Assembly supported the choice by 46 votes to 3.

would inevitably have acquired during his term of office might make for embarrassment among member states if he were immediately to return to the political field in such a position as Foreign Minister.

The Secretary-General is designated by Article 97 of the Charter as the " Chief administrative officer of the Organization," and under Article 101 he is empowered to appoint the entire staff of the Secretariat, including staffs for the Security Council, the other Councils, and any other organ of the United Nations which may require its own. He alone is responsible to the Assembly and the Councils for the whole work of the Secretariat. He is instructed by Article 98 to present an annual report on the work of the United Nations to the General Assembly. He is the channel of communication through which all governments, specialized agencies, unofficial associations and individuals must approach the Organization, and is also responsible for much of the liasion between the various organs of the United Nations themselves. Under Article 98 he has the further duty of acting as secretary to all meetings of the General Assembly, the Security Council, the Economic and Social Council and the Trusteeship Council. This task involves the preparation of provisional agenda, the convening of sessions,[1] the maintenance of verbatim reports and other records, and the execution of any special decisions within the Secretariat's authority which may be made by the Assembly or the Councils. To fulfil this last duty he will necessarily require a considerable technical staff.

At each session of the General Assembly, it is the Secretary-General's responsibility to inform the Assembly of any " matters relative to the maintenance of peace and security " which are being dealt with by the Security Council. He will also inform the Assembly, or the individual member states if the Assembly is not in session, when these particular matters cease to be under the Council's consideration. This proviso, contained in Article 12 of the Charter, is intended to ensure that the Assembly will never make recommendations about any security matter which is already in the Security Council's hands.

The Secretary-General is also responsible for two stages in the process of creating and replenishing the International Court of Justice. The Statute of the Court provides that he will invite nominations for vacant judgeships, and that no place on the Court's bench shall be officially vacant until the President has transmitted the retiring judge's resignation to the Secretary-General.

Although the Charter does not specifically allot any financial functions to him, it is clear that the Secretary-General will be responsible to the Assembly for preparing the Organization's budget, for allotting its funds and controlling its expenditure, for collecting contributions from member

---

[1]Article 20 of the Charter specifically directs the Secretary-General to convene special sessions of the Assembly at the request either of the Security Council or of a majority of members.

states and for administering financial arrangements with specialized agencies.

All these administrative functions will require a high degree of skill, tact and impartiality ; but the Secretary-General is also invested with political responsibilities which present him with even more delicate problems. For Article 99 of the Charter gives him the right, and thereby implicitly imposes on him the duty, of bringing to the attention of the Security Council any matter which, in his opinion, may threaten the maintenance of international peace and security. It should be noted that this clause makes no reference to " disputes " or to " situations which might lead to disputes ; " it uses the phrase " any matter," thus leaving to the discretion of the Secretary-General an immense field of possibilities. It may well be that a dangerous situation may arise in which no member state is willing to incur the odium of accusing another member of threatening the peace ; and in such a case the Secretary-General, as an impartial individual, may have to shoulder the vast responsibility of publicly arraigning one or more nations in the eyes of the world. It is, therefore, true in fact as well as in theory that the Secretary-General of the United Nations is " the most highly qualified representative of the international spirit."[1]

AN INTERNATIONAL STAFF

All members of the Secretariat are international civil servants, and their responsibilities are exclusively to the Organization. On accepting their appointments, they are required to take an oath similar to that made by the Secretary-General before the Assembly. Article 100 of the Charter lays down that they shall not " seek or receive instructions from any government or from any other authority external to the Organization " and that they shall " refrain from any action which might reflect on their position as international officials responsible only to the Organization."

The provisional staff regulations which have since been framed expand this ruling by explaining that staff members are not expected to abandon their national sentiments or their political and religious convictions, but that they must avoid any kind of partisan public pronouncement or activity, and must not seek or accept any political office, decoration, gift, fee or honour from any national government during their term of service with the Organization.

The staff is to be appointed by the Secretary-General under regulations established by the General Assembly. Under the terms of Article 8 of the Charter, there must be no discrimination between men and women in these regulations. Under Article 101, recruiting must be on as wide a geographical basis as possible. It has been suggested that officials from the service of national governments should be seconded to the Secretariat for

[1]This phrase was used by Mr. P. H. Spaak, president of the First General Assembly, at the installation of Mr. Lie.

periods of not longer than two years, so that personal contacts between the Secretariat and national administrations may be strengthened, and a body of national officials with international experience created. With this single exception, however, the Secretariat will be recruited on as permanent a basis as possible, most members of the staff being appointed on contracts which will be subject to review every five years, but which will not be terminated unless the post concerned becomes redundant or the official in question displays obvious incapability.

Article 105 of the Charter provides that all officials of the United Nations shall enjoy, within the territories of all member states, such privileges and immunities as are necessary for the independent exercise of their functions in connection with the Organization.[1] A convention putting this article into effect in detail was concluded during the London session of the General Assembly ; and a start has been made with the process of extending the immunity system to non-member states' territory by the conclusion of an agreement with Switzerland. One feature of the immunity system would be a special United Nations passport for senior officials who may require priority in obtaining visas and other travel permits.

ORGANIZATION OF THE SECRETARIAT

The detailed organization of the Secretariat is the responsibility of the Secretary-General, and he is empowered to arrange and amend the division into departments and other matters as he thinks fit, subject only to the staff regulations laid down by the General Assembly. There will probably be considerable room for improvements in the present provisional structure as the passage of time reveals what exactly is required of the Secretariat. Meanwhile it is proposed to establish eight principal departments, which are briefly described below.

The Department of Security Council Affairs will, of course, be primarily concerned with serving the Security Council, but it will also be at the disposal of the General Assembly whenever the Assembly is dealing with the maintenance of peace and security.

The Department of Economic Affairs will handle all economic and financial matters, all questions concerning transport and communications, and statistical work. Its statistical staff will also assist the other departments with their own statistical requirements.

The Department of Social Affairs will deal with social welfare in general, human rights (including questions concerning the status of women), health, narcotic drugs, cultural matters and education.

The Economic and Social departments will be closely linked together, and will serve the Economic and Social Council and the various specialized

[1] Similar systems are already being operated by some of the specialized agencies of the United Nations such as UNRRA, the FAO and the financial agencies.

agencies, although they will also be at the disposal of other organs, particularly the Trusteeship Council.

The Department for Trusteeship and Information from Non-Self-Governing Territories will carry out the duties which the Secretariat will incur in the execution of the policy for non-self-governing territories laid down in the Charter.

The Legal Department will advise the Secretariat and the other organs on all legal and constitutional matters. It will also be responsible for the registration and drafting of treaties and for matters pertaining to the immunities and privileges of the Organization and its staff. It will not serve the International Court of Justice, which will have its own staff, but it is possible that there will be considerable interchangeability of personnel between the Department and the staff of the Court.

The Department of Public Information will handle all forms of publicity about the work and aims of the United Nations, operating in the fields of radio, the Press, films and photography, publications, reference facilities and public liaison work.

The Conference and General Services will make all necessary arrangements for meetings of the General Assembly, the Councils, and other United Nations conferences. This department will maintain liaison with governments, unofficial international organizations, diplomatic representatives, and other parties, and will deal with questions of protocol. It will also operate documents and language services, a library, a registry, and services for the handling of mail and supplies, the management of offices and buildings, and kindred matters.

The Administrative and Financial Services will probably be divided into three sections ; a Budget Office, a Personnel Office, and a Comptroller's Office which would handle all the funds of the Organization, collecting the contributions due from the member states, and operating the accounting and internal audit systems.

It was suggested at one stage that each of the principal organs of the United Nations should be given a separate department of its own. This idea has been rejected, and it is now laid down in the provisional organization that any department may at any time be called upon to provide certain services for any organ. Thus the Security Council will not only use the Department of Security Council Affairs, but will also call upon the Legal, Economic, Social and other departments for information and services. The Trusteeship Council will make use of the Economic department, and the Economic and Social Council will at times call upon the services of the Trusteeship department. This principle is in accordance with the idea of the essential unity of the whole Organization. If each organ has a separate staff, there would be much duplication of effort and undesirable division of loyalties between the departments. There is only one exception to the general rule ; this provides that the Department of Security Council

Affairs, while continuing to serve all the organs as a whole, will embody certain special staff units which will deal with its military and enforcement responsibilities, and that these units will only provide information and services for the Security Council, no other organ having the right to call upon them.

INFORMATION SERVICES

"The United Nations cannot achieve the purposes for which it has been created unless the peoples of the world are fully informed of its aims and activities."

So began the report on information services submitted to the London session of the Assembly by a committee of experts. The recommendations contained in this report are now being implemented by the Assistant Secretary-General in charge of the Department of Public Information. The general policy adopted is that the United Nations will not indulge in "propaganda," but will supplement existing national information services to the extent necessary to realize "an informed understanding of the work and purposes of the United Nations among the peoples of the world." The Press will be given the fullest possible access to the activities and official documents of the Organization. The Department of Public Information will provide full information about the United Nations both at the Organization's headquarters and at branch offices which will be set up as soon as possible. The Department will also publish pamphlets and other printed publication on the aims and activities of the United Nations. Together with its branch offices, it will actively assist and encourage all educational institutions and other organizations interested in spreading information about the United Nations. It will make available to these organizations posters, film strips, documentary films made by its own staff and by other units, and any other material which would assist them in their work.

It should also be able to analyze trends of public opinion in different parts of the world with regard to United Nations aims and activities, and to estimate the extent to which the public is acquiring an informed understanding of the Organization's work. For this purpose it will need to create a research organization.

The Department will at first work in close co-operation with existing radio organizations ; but as soon as possible the United Nations should equip itself with a radio station of its own, which would be used both for communications with member governments and for broadcasting United Nations programmes.[1] This station could also serve as a centre for existing radio networks which are willing to co-operate in diffusing United Nations radio material. The Secretary-General has already arranged for a

---

[1]The League had its own radio station (Radio-Nations) at Geneva, but owing to various difficulties full use was never made of it.

E*

group of technical experts to make concrete proposals for the establishment
and working of the radio station, and these proposals, together with an
estimated budget, will be submitted for the approval of the Assembly at
its September session.

FINANCE

Broadly speaking, member nations will contribute to the Organization
in accordance with their ability to pay. For this purpose it has been agreed
to take the scale of contributions to the Food and Agriculture Organization
as a general basis ; but the FAO scale will be superseded by a new scale
which will be fixed by the General Assembly at an early date.

Members must pay their contributions in the currency of the state in
which the United Nations has its headquarters : that is, in United States
dollars.

An annual Budget will be prepared by the Secretary-General and submitted to the General Assembly at its regular September sessions. The
Assembly will appoint a small Advisory Committee of seven members, of
whom at least two shall be financial experts of recognized standing, to
examine and report on the Budget, the auditor's reports, the budgets
of specialized agencies, and other financial questions.

Until the permanent scale of contributions and the permanent budgetary
system are established, the Organization will operate on a Working Capital
Fund, to which member nations have been asked to contribute a substantial
proportion of the whole contribution due from them on the FAO scale.
Many members have in fact already transferred the whole of their allotted
contributions for the first year to the Organization.[1]

During the London session of the Assembly there was considerable
dissension in the Fifth (Administrative and Budgetary) Committee about
the provisional estimates for the first Budget. The original proposal
amounted to $25,000,000, as compared with the sum of $8,000,000 which
used to suffice for the League and the ILO together. The Soviet delegation pressed for reductions, and was supported by several other East
European delegations. British spokesmen defended the original figure,
pointing out that the United Nations were attempting to do far more than
the League, that the value of money had been greatly diminished in recent
years, and that in any case some 30 per cent of the budget was going to be
provided by members of the British Commonwealth, who were satisfied
with the demands made of them. Eventually the estimate was reduced to
$21,500,000.

THE LEGACY OF THE LEAGUE

The League of Nations has been formally dissolved ; but it has left

[1] Allocations for the Working Capital Fund include $6,153,500 from the United
States, $3,692,750 from the United Kingdom, $1,723,000 from the Soviet Union
and $1,000,000 from China.

behind it two legacies, both of which have been inherited by the United Nations.

The first inheritance consists of the continuing functions and obligations of the League, exercised under international agreements which have not expired with the Covenant. These are principally economic and social tasks, and the Economic and Social Council has already begun to operate, through its Commissions, such League functions as the epidemiological service, the work of the Opium Section, and the various statistical and research services based on Geneva.

The second and more tangible inheritance consists of the real assets of the League, including the fine buildings in Geneva which housed it. In December 1945 the United Nations Preparatory Commission formed a small committee to negotiate with the League's Supervisory Commission for the transfer of these assets to the United Nations. In February the General Assembly agreed on the broad outlines of the transfer terms and authorized the Secretary-General to negotiate detailed agreements, appointing a second committee to assist him.

THE HEADQUARTERS

Unlike the Covenant of the League of Nations, which specifies Geneva as the permanent seat of the League, the Charter makes no reference to the site for the headquarters of the United Nations. The question was taken up by the Executive Committee of the Preparatory Commission and later by the Commission itself, and a series of meetings were held during the autumn of 1945 at which representatives from various parts of the world put forward their arguments for the siting of the headquarters in their particular localities. The proposed sites included Geneva, Danzig, Vienna, Jerusalem, Tangier, Cairo, and Bournemouth, and whole areas such as Scotland, Belgium, the Philippines and the Isle of Wight were also offered for the Commission to consider. But the greater number of the locations offered were in the United States ; there were altogether forty of these, with an additional five in Canada and along the United States—Canada border. The Preparatory Commission decided in the end to restrict its choice to the United States. There were, of course, arguments in favour of continuing to use Geneva which was already equipped with buildings and other facilities ; but there were also arguments against this choice ; war-torn Europe was not in a fit state to handle large-scale assemblies of diplomats, and a return to Geneva would find favour neither in the United States nor in the Soviet Union. The Preparatory Commission therefore decided in December 1945 to send a Committee of twelve representatives of member states to visit the United States and report on the sites offered.

This Committee returned in January and made its report to the General Assembly. It announced that it had rejected all the sites specifically

offered, and had chosen instead an area some thirty miles north of New
York City, lying partly in New York State and partly in the Stamford and
Greenwich district of Connecticut.[1] The General Assembly appointed a
special Permanent Headquarters Committee to discuss this report, and this
committee, after considerable discussion, agreed with the choice of the
Stamford-Greenwich site. On February 16 the Assembly passed a resolution confirming this decision, and approving also the Committee's suggestion that the interim headquarters be in New York City and the
immediate neighbourhood.

In view of the decision on the interim headquarters, the Secretariat began
to move to New York immediately after the end of the London session of
the Assembly, and it is now established in a group of buildings centred on
Hunter College in the Bronx borough of the city. Here the Security
Council has also been meeting, and it is presumed that the Council and the
Secretariat will remain at Hunter College until August 1946. In September, when the General Assembly meets for the Second Part of its First
Session, it will use the New York City building on the 1939 World's Fair
site in Flushing Meadows, Long Island, and the Secretariat will then
occupy the Sperry Gyroscope Plant at Lake Success, twenty-two miles
from New York.

Meanwhile a Headquarters Planning Commission, composed of experts
nominated by the Secretary-General with the approval of the General
Assembly, is already at work in New York preparing recommendations
about both temporary and permanent housing and other facilities.

Once the permanent seat of the Organization has been definitely designated and its boundaries agreed upon, a treaty will be concluded between
the United Nations and the host country, vesting full ownership of all
land and buildings in the agreed area in the United Nations, and providing
that the " zone " shall be under the exclusive control of the Organization.
The headquarters area, with the air above it, will be inviolable ; it is, however, intended that the law of the United States and the authority of its
courts shall continue to apply to the zone, and United States police will
probably be supplied, at the request of the Secretary-General, to maintain
order. The United Nations will be entitled to construct and maintain its
own radio station or stations, its own railway station and its own airport.
The United States will undertake to allow unimpeded passage to and from
the zone across its territory for all representatives of member states, regardless of the relations existing between their governments and that of the
United States ; and many other minor privileges, facilities, and immunities will also be granted to accredited representatives of the United
Nations on American territory. The payment made to the United States
for the land and buildings will be set off against the contributions due from
her to the funds of the United Nations ; and if at any time the United

[1] The counties involved are Westchester, N.Y., and Fairfield, Conn.

Nations should cease to use the zone, the United States will repay a fair sum on account of the value of the land and buildings returned to her.

It is, of course, not absolutely certain as yet that the permanent headquarters of the Organization will be where it is now planned. A remarkable amount of vociferous opposition to the use of the Stamford–Greenwich site has been put up by certain local inhabitants. Further, the high costs of living in New York and its immediate neighbourhood are adversely affecting the opinions of many member nations, and it is too early to rule out the possibility that a change may be made in the choice of a permanent site before the Stamford–Greenwich area is ever occupied. Meanwhile the question of the utilization of the Geneva buildings is still unsettled, although there is a strong feeling that a European sub-headquarters for the United Nations, economic and social work will be sited in them.

SECRETARY-GENERAL
(with an Executive Assistant in the rank of Director)

DEPARTMENTS, each headed by an ASSISTANT SECRETARY-GENERAL

SECURITY COUNCIL AFFAIRS	ECONOMIC AFFAIRS	SOCIAL AFFAIRS	TRUSTEESHIP AND INFORMATION FROM NON-SELF-GOVERNING TERRITORIES	PUBLIC INFORMATION	LEGAL	CONFERENCE AND GENERAL SERVICES	ADMINISTRATIVE AND FINANCIAL SERVICES
Matters relating to peace and security; Special unit for Security Council's military responsibilities.	Economic & financial questions; Transport and communications; Statistics.	Health and Narcotic Drugs; Social welfare; Cultural and Educational matters Human rights.		Press and Radio; Films and Photography; Publications, Exhibitions, Public Liaison.	Drafting of Treaties; Immunities and Privileges; Protocol; Registration of Treaties: Other Legal and Constitutional matters.	Conferences, Assembly and Council Meetings; relations with Governments and unofficial organizations; Documents; Languages; Buildings, etc.	Budget Office; Personnel Office; Comptroller's Office: collection of national contributions; custody of funds, accounting, internal audit, payrolls; staff funds, etc.

CHAPTER X

CAN THE UNITED NATIONS SUCCEED ?

GROWING PAINS

ALTHOUGH there were one or two awkward moments during the General Assembly's London session in January and February 1946, the Assembly emerged comparatively unscathed from its first trials. It had in fact achieved a great deal from the creative point of view ; it had chosen the Security Council and the Economic and Social Council, participated in the elections for Secretary-General and for the International Court, created the Commission on Atomic Energy, drawn up a whole volume of regulations for the guidance of the Secretariat and the Councils, and agreed on recommendations about refugees, cereals, war criminals, and several lesser matters. The weary delegates felt quite rightly that they had put through an immense construction job at a speed unrivalled in diplomatic records.

Unfortunately the Security Council could not make any similar boast. Before the Council met, it was generally believed on all sides that if any serious issue arose before the Council had got firmly into the saddle the consequences would be disastrous. For, until Article 43 of the Charter had been put into effect, the Council's authority existed only on paper. Under Article 43, the Security Council is required to negotiate agreements with all the Member States, specifying the nature and extent of the armed forces which they will thenceforward place at its disposal. The technical details of the agreements are now being worked out by the Military Staff Committee, which consists of military representatives of the five permanent members of the Council ; and no announcement has yet been made of the successful conclusion of any agreement. Meanwhile, the Charter expressly provides, in Article 106, that until Article 43 takes effect the five permanent members of the Security Council shall " consult with one another and, as occasion requires, with other Members of the United Nations, with a view to such joint action on behalf of the Organization as may be necessary for the purpose of maintaining international peace and security."

So, if the Charter were to be interpreted literally, all disputes and dangerous situations arising in the immediate future should be referred not to the Security Council but to its five permanent members ; and this would correspond with the realities of the present situation, for it is the five Great Powers which are now occupying most of the territories whose possession is disputed [1] ; their armies are the dominant factor in the ex-enemy countries, and they alone are in a position to suppress outbursts of violence anywhere in the world. Moreover, the five Powers are playing

[1] Trieste, South Tyrol, Transylvania, and others.

the decisive role in the formulation of the treaties of peace and in all the readjustments that these will involve.

There is, however, no simple process by which a suppliant can present his case to the Big Five for their consideration under Article 106. The language of the Charter suggests that the five Powers themselves must take the initiative in intervening in any matter which they may consider a threat to peace and security. And if they do not do so, there is nothing in the Charter which specifically forbids the presentation of a case to the Security Council.

The Council met for the first time on January 17, 1946, in London. The first meeting naturally confined itself to constituent and procedural questions. The second meeting, on January 25, found itself faced with not one but three major international issues, all of which were in effect accusations against Great Powers, and two of which were raised by a Great Power and one of its close associates. The infant Council was thus placed in an extremely difficult position at the very beginning of its life. Not only had it had no chance to implement Article 43, but its Military Staff Committee had not even been formed. It was therefore in no position to exercise the immense responsibilities placed upon it by the Charter, unless it could rely on its moral authority alone to ensure that its decisions were carried out. During these first anxious days many people feared that the Council would have to give a verdict which it could not possibly enforce, and that its prestige would then instantly sink to the same level as that of the League Council after the Abyssinian fiasco. Had this happened, it would have been very difficult for the Security Council to re-establish its authority even after it had assumed control of adequate military forces.

The first of the three cases laid before the second meeting was that of Iran, which complained that, " owing to interference of the Soviet Union, through the medium of their officials and armed forces, in the internal affairs of Iran, a situation has arisen which may lead to international friction." It had been known for some time that the Iranian Government were considering appealing to the United Nations, through either the Assembly or the Security Council, on the grounds that Soviet forces in Persian Azerbaijan had prevented the entry of Iranian troops sent to suppress the local rebels ; and the Iranian complaint, submitted on January 19, provoked a swift reaction. On January 21 the Soviet delegation requested the Council to discuss the presence of British troops in Greece, declaring that this constituted " interference in the internal affairs of Greece . . . fraught with grave consequences both for the Greek people and for the maintenance of peace and security." Simultaneously the Ukrainian delegation asked the Council to investigate the situation in Indonesia, alleging that, " for several months military actions directed against the local population have been waged, in which regular British forces as well as Japanese enemy armed forces are taking part. . . . This situation creates a state of threat to the maintenance of international peace and security."

The debates on all three subjects in the Council were tense and stormy. The British representatives took the view that any decision which implied that the Council accepted the truth of the allegations of misuse of British troops in Greece and Indonesia would be tantamount to a slur on the national honour of the United Kingdom. Mr. Bevin demanded that the Council should either " absolve us from this charge, or brand us as being guilty " of endangering the peace. The Soviet and Ukrainian representatives found little support for their positions among other delegates ; and eventually the Greek question was closed by a statement from the President, taking note of the views expressed on all sides and making no further comment, while the debate on Indonesia was simply closed after all the resolutions put forward by various delegates had been defeated. The Iranian case proved more troublesome, for here the Soviet representative, Mr. Vishinsky, denied categorically that any dispute existed between Iran and the Soviet Union, and claimed that the Council had therefore no jurisdiction, not even to discuss the matter. After two meetings the Council agreed on a resolution taking note of the Iranian and Soviet statements, requesting the two parties to seek a solution by negotiation, and declaring that it might at any time take the whole issue up again.

While these first three cases were under discussion, two more had been laid before the Council. The first was an application from Albania for admission to the United Nations. The American and British delegates stated that they were not prepared to agree to the admission of Albania at that point, and an American motion that the question be kept on the Council's agenda and raised again after the Council had arrived in New York was carried by the seven votes necessary to uphold a procedural motion. The second of the new problems—the fifth in the whole series considered by the Council—was a request from Syria and the Lebanon that the Council recommend the " total and simultaneous evacuation " of the French and British troops from their territory. This led to another long and vigorous debate, which ended in the presentation of an American motion that the Council should take note of the statements of the parties, express its confidence that negotiations for the early withdrawal of the French and British troops would begin without delay, and request to be informed of the results of the negotiations. This motion was supported by seven members of the Council, but not by the Soviet delegate ; and, as it was a substantial issue and therefore required the concurrence of all five permanent members, it was declared not carried. The French and British delegates, however, declared that they would act in accordance with its provisions, and proceeded to open negotiations.

The concrete results of the Security Council's first metings were therefore somewhat as follows : on Greece and Indonesia the Council was unable to find enough substance in the charges brought against the United Kingdom to justify action, and both cases were declared closed. On the Iranian and the Syrian–Lebanese complaints the Council found sufficient *prima facie* grounds to make recommendations to the parties concerned and and to warn them that it would expect results from their negotiations. On the Albanian request, the Council simply postponed making a decision.

It could, then, be claimed that the Council had in no way departed from the principles of the Charter, and that, in spite of its embarrassment at having to deal with serious issues before it was in a position to enforce its decisions, it had come out of its first test unexpectedly well. During the next few weeks there were encouraging signs that the Powers were taking its recommendations seriously. French and British troops began to evacuate Syria and the Lebanon on March 11, and Syria was cleared by the end of April ; on May 3 the Council was informed that all British forces would have left the Lebanon by the end of June, and all French forces by the end of August. Soviet troops began to evacuate north-eastern Iran on March 2 ; but the position in Azerbaijan remained uncertain and it was again on the Iranian question that the Council found itself faced with its second serious test.

On March 19 the Secretary-General announced that a second Iranian complaint had been lodged with the Security Council. It repeated the charges of Soviet interference in Iran's internal affairs, and made the additional complaint that all Soviet troops should have been withdrawn from Iran by March 2 in accordance with the Anglo-Soviet-Iranian treaty of 1942. The Council was not due to meet until a week later, and during the interval the Soviet Government announced that it was beginning to withdraw its troops, and hoped to complete the withdrawal by May 6. When the Council met the Soviet delegate, Mr. Gromyko, declared that he could not take part in any discussion of the Iranian question, and when the Council decided to proceed with the discussion he left the Council room. A few days later, after several meetings which the Soviet delegate did not attend, the Council passed an American resolution expressing reliance on the Soviet assurance that the Soviet troops would be withdrawn by May 6 and asking both parties to report on that date, when the Council would resume discussion of the Iranian question and decide if any further action was necessary.

There matters rested until on April 15 Mr. Gromyko again proposed that the Council should drop the whole question of Iran ; and simultaneously the Iranian Government informed the Council that it was satisfied that Soviet troops would be unconditionally evacuated by May 6, and that it would therefore withdraw its complaint. The French delegate moved a resolution which would have had the effect of removing the whole question from the Council's agenda, but this only received three votes, and the Iranian question remained in the Council's hands. At this point Mr.

Gromyko again announced that he could take no further part in the discussion ; and, acting in accordance with this decision, no Soviet delegate attended the meeting on May 8 which was to consider the two parties' reports on the evacuation. Nor did the Soviet Government submit any report ; and the Iranian report stated that, " because of the interferences complained of " it had not been possible to ascertain whether Azerbaijan had in fact been evacuated. The ten members present at the meeting unanimously approved an American proposal to adjourn the discussion until after May 20, by which date it was hoped that a fuller report would have been received from the Iranian Government.

Meanwhile the Council had begun to discuss a resolution proposed by the Polish delegate on April 17, calling upon all members of the United Nations to sever diplomatic relations with the Franco Government in Spain. On April 29 ten members voted in favour of an Australian resolution which, while expressing the Council's " unanimous moral condemnation " of the Franco regime, proposed the setting up of a sub-committee of five to examine in detail the evidence that the regime constituted a danger to international peace and security, and to suggest practical measures for terminating it. This sub-committee was instructed to report to the Council before the end of May ; it consisted of the delegates for Australia, Brazil, China, France and Poland. Like most of the Council's sub-committees, it held its meetings in secret.

THE BIG THREE

Speaking in November 1944, Marshal Stalin said that the actions of the new world organization proposed by the Dumbarton Oaks planners would only be effective " if the great powers which have borne on their shoulders the main burden of the war against Hitlerite Germany continue to act in a spirit of unanimity and accord. . . . They will not be effective if this essential condition is violated."

Clearly the disputes which have arisen in the Security Council during the first months of its existence do not reflect " a spirit of unanimity and accord " among the three most powerful members of the United Nations. Although the first case, that of Iran, was brought before the Council by Iran herself, it seems that the Soviet Government believed that it was at the instigation of Britain ; and in any case the British and American delegates have been firmer than any others in resisting Soviet attempts to prevent the Council discussing the complaint. The Greek and Indonesian issues were raised directly by Soviet and Ukrainian delegates, and aimed directly at Britain. In the Syrian-Lebanese case the Soviet member of the Council was more outspoken in his criticism of Britain and France than the complainants themselves. The Albanian application was forwarded to the Council through Yugoslavia, and the question of Franco was raised by Poland ; and in almost every issue on which there has been a division of opinion among the United Nations, Poland and Yugoslavia have sided with the Soviet Union. Both the Albanian application and the proposal to break off diplomatic relations with the Franco Government have been vigorously supported by the Soviet representatives on the Council, while the British and American delegates have agreed in suggesting postponement of both issues.

But it is not only in the Security Council that the serious divergence of views between the Big Three has become obvious. At the very first session of the Assembly the British and American delegations voted for Mr. P. H. Spaak for the presidency of the first session, while the Soviet delegates supported Mr. Trygve Lie. Soon afterwards the Soviet spokesman asked for a few days' delay to consider the choice of non-permanent members of the Security Council, and the American and British delegations opposed this request. It is also obvious that although the Security Council's nomination of Mr. Lie for Secretary-General was presented as a unanimous decision, it was only reached after a series of difficult discussions. And in the Assembly and its committees there were several issues on which the Big Three took opposite sides, such as the refugee question, the procedure for setting up the Trusteeship Council, and the admission of the World Federation of Trade Unions to the Organization's deliberations.

These demonstrations of disunity in the Assembly were little more than symptoms ; for in the Assembly the Big Three are only three amongst fifty-one, and even if they gather around them clusters of " satellites " the real power of decision rests with the smaller nations. Moreover, the Assembly does not deal with really explosive issues. These are the concern of the Security Council alone ; and in the Council any Great Power can use its power of veto to defy the unanimous will of all the other fifty members of the United Nations. It is in the Council that the disunity of the Big Three has assumed really dangerous proportions.

Now it would have been optimistic to believe that, once the United Nations were established, there would never again be differences of opinion among the Great Powers. The United Nations came together under the tremendous pressure of a war in which the whole future of mankind was threatened. Faced with that threat, the Powers found little difficulty in framing a common policy. And now that the peril is no longer so imminent, their many differences can emerge again into the light of day.

Mr. T. V. Soong, Foreign Minister of China, once said, " Men learn to co-operate only by having to do it."[1] Other critical observers have commented that the fiercer of the arguments indulged in during the Assembly's London meetings were a heartening sign that the Assembly was really developing towards a true world parliament. Certainly there is

[1]Speech at Carnegie Hall, New York, in October 1942.

nothing dangerous in the mere existence of differences of opinion among the member states of the United Nations. The danger inherent in the present dissensions is not the possibility of disagreement ; it is the possibility of secession.

Today the United Nations Organization embraces all the major Powers of the world. It is important to remember that the League never enjoyed such universality. But it is also important to recall that the failure of the League was due not only to the absence of the United States and other Great Powers, but equally to the refusal of Britain, France and other leading member states to fulfil their obligations under the Covenant, and to the flagrant violation of the Covenant by three permanent members of the Council, Germany, Italy and Japan.

In the speech quoted above Mr. T. V. Soong went on to say, " Today those powers which did not feel the League useful to safeguard their own security . . . have to recognize that international order and collective security have become essential for the survival of strong states as well as the preservation of weaker ones. Today an aggressor left alone in his preparations can get a death jump on a strong state as well as a weak one."

There is ample evidence that Mr. Soong's statement holds as good in 1946 as it did in 1942. The menace of Nazi and Japanese aggression is temporarily lifted ; but the Damocles sword of atomic warfare hangs even more threateningly over mankind's head. There is not a state in the world which would leave the United Nations, or deliberately sabotage its working, unless driven to it by the fear of a fate worse than the reversion to international anarchy which would inevitably follow such an act.

In view of this undoubted truth, do the dissensions among the Great Powers really imply any threat to the success of the United Nations ? In other words, is any Great Power likely to find that it can do better without the Organization ?

There can be very little doubt that British policy will always favour the strengthening and development of the United Nations. The Prime Minister, Mr. Attlee, has stated that " it is the firm intention of His Majesty's Government to make the success of the United Nations the primary object of their foreign policy. . . . The security of the British Commonwealth and Empire is bound up with the success of the United Nations, and if we accept this fact we must base our policy upon it and get rid of outworn conceptions." And His Majesty's Opposition is as fully aware of the overriding importance of the Organization as is His Majesty's Government. Mr. Winston Churchill was one of the original three " founding fathers " of the United Nations. Mr. Eden has described the Organization as " the world's last chance." Indeed, there can be no serious difference of opinion among British politicians on the vital need for a strong world security organization. Britain lives by world trade, and her economic life is affected by war just as catastrophically as that of countries which are completely devastated by invasion. Britain is peculiarly vulnerable to atomic and other modern weapons. Britain is in the embarrassing position of a democracy with a colonial past, and if she is to emancipate her dependent territories there must be guarantees that they will not be engulfed by more predatory powers. The scattered members of the British Commonwealth, and the lines of communication which link them, are liable to become involved in local disturbances wherever they occur. And finally, we must remember that during the nineteenth century British sea-power maintained a *"pax britannica"* in many parts of the world where even today the smaller political units still claim British protection ; and there is no doubt that the United Kingdom would be greatly relieved if these world-wide responsibilities could be handed over to an international organization.

The United States still contains a strongly isolationist minority ; but it is now very definitely a minority. Mr. Stettinius has described isolationists, not only in America but everywhere in the world, as " vestigial remains of the pre-atomic age," and has told a British audience that " this time the United States is in it, all the way in it, and in it to stay." Like the League, the United Nations is very largely the creation of an American President ; but, unlike the League, the United Nations is assured of the enduring support of the United States. On the first anniversary of Franklin D. Roosevelt's death, President Truman declared at Hyde Park that, " We are determined to do all within our power to make the United Nations a strong and living organization, to find effective means of alleviating suffering and distress, and to deal fairly with all nations. . . . The overall task is difficult, but it can be simply stated : it is to carry forward the underlying principles and policies of Franklin Roosevelt. . . . He recognized above all that our hope for the future of civilization, for the future of life itself, lay in the success of the United Nations. . . . For these principles of international co-operation we are determined to fight with all our strength." And although there are still many Americans who are far from wholehearted in their support of the Roosevelt foreign policy, it is in general true that the United States has learnt, the hard way, that wars must be stopped before they begin.

In analyzing the Soviet attitude to the United Nations we must be both cautious and sympathetic. At San Francisco Mr. Molotov, Foreign Minister of the Soviet Union, said, " The Soviet Government is a sincere and firm champion of the establishment of a strong international organization of security. . . . In our country the whole people has been raised in the spirit of faith and devotion to the cause of establishing a sound organization of international security. . . . The Soviet Union can be relied upon in the matter of the safeguarding of peace and security of nations. This great cause is inflexibly supported by our peace-loving people, the Soviet Government, the Red Army and our great Marshal Stalin." Marshal

Stalin himself has since confirmed his attitude of whole-hearted support for the United Nations. But the Soviet Government has approached the whole question of a world security organization in a cautious spirit, which can perhaps best be illustrated by citing a leading article in the official Soviet review of international affairs, *New Times* :

" The policy of co-operation among the democratic powers in their struggle against a common enemy who menaced the whole world was a correct and wise policy. It was supported in word and deed by the masses, the common people, the world's millions. The policy of creating a United Nations Organization as an instrument for maintaining peace and security and thus promoting further co-operation on this basis was a correct and wise policy. It has the support of the masses, of the millions of common people who stand sentinel over peace. They enthusiastically hailed the birth of this international security organization based on the equality of the freedom-loving democratic nations. They expect this organization to guide itself in all its activities by the principle of the equality of states, and not by the principles of the domination of some states over others. They fully realize that only the former principle can furnish a healthy basis for the development of this international organization, and that the latter principle is fraught with the gravest danger to the organization and to all the nations of the world."[1]

The obvious inference is that the Soviet Government fears that hostile forces may gain such a preponderance in the United Nations as to be able to use the Organization as a weapon against the Soviet Union. It is significant that at San Francisco the Soviet delegates opposed a committee report which suggested that any member state which withdrew from the United Nations would thereby " put the burden of supporting international peace and security on other members." Mr. Gromyko, acting head of the Soviet delegation, declared that, " one cannot condemn beforehand the motives which may compel a state to use its right to leave the organization." A similar note of caution was struck by the Soviet member of the Assembly's Finance Committee, who, during the discussion in London on the Organization's budget, said that " comparison with UNRRA was not particularly relevant. . . . UNRRA was an organization which had proved its worth, whereas the United Nations had not yet been fully tested."

The Soviet approach to the United Nations has, in fact, always shown signs of preoccupation with the idea that the Organization might become an anti-Soviet combination headed by the United States and the United Kingdom. One must take into account the unhappy story of the League's relations with the Soviet Union. In the first years of the League its two leading members, Britain and France, were also the leading Powers in the Allied combination which was responsible for armed intervention in the

[1] *New Times* (Moscow), April 1, 1946.

Russian civil war, for the creation of a *cordon sanitaire* in Eastern Europe and for the exclusion of revolutionary Russia from the councils of Geneva. During the next few years Moscow watched the League's shameful inaction in the face of Nazi and Japanese aggressiveness ; and when in 1934 the Soviet Union entered the League she found little support for her strong anti-fascist policy in the Ethiopian and Spanish wars. And finally the League, still dominated by the same Powers which had accepted the *Anschluss*, Munich and the annexation of Albania without more than formal protests, voted for the expulsion of the Soviet Union when she invaded Finland, a measure which her Government deemed necessary for the protection of Leningrad against the German attack which was so obviously coming. It is not surprising that at San Francisco Mr. Molotov said, " The prestige of the League was especially undermined whenever uncere-monious attempts were made to turn it into a tool of various reactionary forces and privileged Powers. . . . If the sad lessons of the League must be mentioned at present, it is only in order that past errors, which must not be committed under the label of profuse new promises, may be avoided."

Already the Soviet Government has found that in any major contest in the General Assembly it is likely to be outvoted. This was probably anticipated by Soviet politicians, since in the Assembly there are altogether twenty-one American votes, and these, together with the six votes controlled by the British Commonwealth, make up a solid block which is obviously more likely to back the United States and the United Kingdom than to favour Soviet policies. At present the only votes on which the Soviet Union can rely with any confidence are the three which actually belong to Soviet Republics, and those of Poland, Yugoslavia, and, to a lesser degree, Czechoslovakia. Naturally, then, the Soviet Govern-ment is doing its best to win the support of those member states which are not inclined to line up with any particular Great Power. And naturally it has consistently emphasized the predominant role of the Security Council ; for in the Council, although here too the Soviet representatives are more often outvoted than not, the veto power enables them to prevent any important issue going against them.

It is reasonably certain that the Soviet Government will never think of leaving the United Nations unless it is convinced that to revert to interna-tional anarchy would be more tolerable than to remain within an organiza-tion dominated by its opponents. And there are signs that Soviet circles are now reasonably satisfied that the Organization will not, in fact, be used against them. An account in *New Times* of the first General As-sembly says that, " the Soviet delegation successfully defeated the attempts of those who tried to push the Soviet Union into the background . . . thereby demonstrating that serious problems of world politics cannot be solved without the Soviet Union, and still less in spite of it."[1] Soviet

[1] *New Times* (Moscow), March 1, 1946.

representatives have also expressed satisfaction about the creation of the Commission on Atomic Energy and its subordination to the Security Council.

In spite of Soviet fears, it is therefore not at all likely that the Soviet Government will consider leaving the Organization unless some quite unforeseen development occurs. The Soviet Union suffered more in the late war than either of the other members of the " Big Three " ; its roll of dead exceeded seven millions, and large areas of its territory were devastated. It has now achieved the establishment of friendly governments in the countries along its frontiers, and has recovered most of the territories lost by Tzarist Russia in the First World War. It stands to gain as much by peace, and to lose as much by war, as any country in the world. It can be anticipated that Soviet policy within the United Nations will be vigorous, and will be directed towards strengthening the Union's position relative to the other Great Powers ; but there is nothing whatever to suggest that the question of secession will arise.

THE LONG-TERM PROSPECT

Mr. Attlee has said of the United Nations that, " It is not perfect. Nothing made by human beings ever is. But there is only one way of improving it, and that is to use it and to use it to the full."

The fiercest criticism of the present form of the Organization is directed against the veto power of the five permanent members of the Security Council. Those who believe that the veto is at present indispensable point out that, in the first place, the Great Powers would not have consented to join the Organization without it ; and, in the second, it is dictated by the harsh realities of the present situation. For if a Great Power is guilty of aggression in the immediate future, it can only be brought to book by a coalition of other Great Powers, fully determined to oppose the offender ; and if such a coalition exists, the offender's veto power will not protect it, while if it does not exist, no resolution of the Council will have any deterrent effect. But then, say the critics, if the Organization does not even pretend to exercise control over the Great Powers, what is its value ? They point out that the three Axis Powers were all former permanent members of the League Council, and argue that in the present state of the world the only nations likely to become aggressors are the Great Powers themselves.

An ingenious theory has been formulated by Mr. Walter Lippmann to cover this point. Mr. Lippmann argues that, by adopting the veto clause, the United Nations have already rejected the idea of collective security. In fact, he says, the idea of having to wage total war in order to prevent total war is so costly and repulsive that it will never be applied, unless aggression has already gone so far that the peace-loving nations must unite in order to fight a war of survival like the last. When the issue is anything less than sheer survival, peaceable peoples cannot be expected to adopt a policy which is as terrifying to them as it is to the aggressors. And Mr. Lippmann holds that no world order can be well founded on the idea of masses of innocent people undertaking to be prepared to massacre other masses of innocent people. But, he argues, while rejecting collective security, the United Nations have, by creating their War Crimes Commission, committed themselves to the principle of holding individuals responsible for the violation of treaties and for breaches of the peace. And here, says Mr. Lippmann, is the nucleus of the future World State.[1]

It is true that the United Nations have published a Charter for the International Military Tribunal at Nuremberg, giving the Tribunal jurisdiction over such offences as war in violation of treaties, deportation and other wartime atrocities, and persecution whether in war or in peace. It is true that the presiding judges have stated that, " while this law is first applied against German aggressors, the law includes . . . aggression by any other nation, including those which sit here in judgment." But at present there is no sign that the Nuremberg Tribunal, however successful in its own sphere, is the precursor of any universal system for enforcing international peace by bringing the individual to justice. To bring the prisoners now in the Nuremberg dock to justice the United Nations had to wage just such a total war as Mr. Lippmann deprecates ; and there is at present no other method of securing the individual criminals responsible for " crimes against peace " than that very " massacre of innocent masses " which he very rightly denounces.

Mr. Lippmann suggests that national governments themselves be made responsible for the enforcement of international law upon individuals of whatever nationality. A more radical project has been put forward by Air Vice-Marshal Donald Bennett, who has urged " the drafting and applying of a criminal code " under which war would be " a crime of unsurpassed depravity," and " most vitally, the creation of an instrument to enforce this criminal code, automatically, immediately, and without reference to higher authority, in the manner of an ordinary policeman doing his duty." Air Vice-Marshal Bennett has already outlined a plan for an International Law Force[1] recruited on an international basis, and equipped with sufficient strength to maintain the peace of the world. It is only a few years since people used to dismiss such projects with an impatient shrug and some such phrase as " not in our lifetime ! " Today a change has come about. The advocates of a more unified world order include some of the most practical of political leaders. During the debates on foreign affairs that took place in the House of Commons in November 1945, it became clear that Britain's long-term policy now envisages the ultimate creation of a World State, and with it just such a system of international law and law

[1] " One World or None," 1946.
[1] *Freedom from War.* Pilot Press, 1946.

enforcement as Mr. Lippmann and Air Vice-Marshal Bennett propose.

In the November debates Mr. Eden said, in the name of the Opposition, that ". . . Unless we can catch up politically to the point we have reached in science, and thus command the power which at present threatens us, we are all going to be blown to smithereens . . . I want to get a world in which the relations between nations can be transformed in a given period of time—we cannot do it in a short period—as the relations between this country and Scotland and Wales have been transformed."

The Foreign Secretary, Mr. Bevin, said in the same debate, " I think it right to let the country know exactly where the surrender of sovereignty leads us. The fact is, no one ever surrenders sovereignty ; they merge it into a greater sovereignty. . . . We need a new study for the purpose of creating a world assembly elected directly from the people of the world as a whole, to whom the governments who form the United Nations are responsible. . . . I am ready to sit with anybody, of any party, of any nation, to try to devise a franchise or a constitution for a world assembly with a limited objective—the objective of peace. . . . In the meantime, there must be no weakening of the institution which was built at San Francisco. It must be the prelude to further development. This must not be considered a substitute for it, but rather a completion of a development of it, so that the benefit of the experience and administration derived in that institution may be carried on to its final end."

Such must be the aim and the goal of the United Nations. In Mr. Lippmann's words : " No one can prove how fast and how far mankind will go now to form the World State . . . but the World State is inherent in the United Nations as an oak tree is in an acorn." This is indeed a far cry from the spirit of 1919.

WHERE THE COMMON MAN COMES IN

Mr. Henry Wallace has called our age, " The Century of the Common Man." Certainly it is either going to be that or the Century of the Common Catastrophe.

The Charter of the United Nations begins with the words :

" We, the Peoples of the United Nations, determined to save succeeding generations from the scourge of war. . . ."

Contrast this with the opening words of the Covenant of the League ; " The High Contracting Parties, in order to promote international co-operation. . . ." Contrast the complete absence of any reference to the rights of the individual from the Covenant with the phrases which recur throughout the length of the Charter :

" . . . to reaffirm faith in fundamental human rights, in the dignity and worth of the human person, in the equal rights of men and women. . . ."

" . . . co-operation in promoting and encouraging respect for human rights and for fundamental freedoms for all without distinction as to race, sex, language or religion. . . ."

Yes, the sceptic may say, but, behind all this lip-service to the common man, what is the Organization prepared to do for him ? Does the Charter mean what it says, or is it just a lot of words ?

The sober truth is that the fate of the Charter lies in the hands of the common man, and not vice versa. The peoples of the United Nations built the Organization, and saved the free world in which it now exists. Whether or not the Charter is fulfilled depends on the peoples, for it is from them that it draws its power. We have seen how the League failed because the peoples of the world, having seen the Covenant signed, chose to leave it hanging in the air without making an effort to put its noble ideas into practice. We dare not let that happen again. This time the alternative is annihilation.

Today the world is still torn between different political theories, and already there are voices saying that "the wars of religion have returned." But whatever differences there may be between the two dominant systems of our time, they have one thing in common ; they are based on the common man. Liberal democracy, the general creed of the West, emphasizes political liberty, the right to criticize, the attainment through public argument of fair solutions to domestic problems, tolerance even to the point of danger, and the retention of what is good in traditional institutions. Communism, the new dominant force in Eastern Europe, rejects many of these ideals and stresses rather the importance of social and economic justice, the right to a fair share in society's material products, the need for solidarity, and acquiescence, if necessary, enforced acquiescence, in all-embracing plans made for the common good. Both systems claim to be the true champions of democracy. Whatever their differences, they both rely for their support and inspiration upon the peoples. And the peoples need peace. Here then is reason for hope ; a world organization which is truly based on the peoples of the world can overcome the imperfections of our present political systems, provided it has the backing, the intelligent and continuous backing, of the peoples.

What can the individual do ?

First, he can use every means within his power to ensure that the world organization is kept in the forefront of his nation's policies. He can criticize his leaders when they look like backsliding from their obligations under the Charter ; he can suggest the directions in which he would like to see the Organization developed. He can follow the work of the United Nations through the press, radio and reading, and he can get plenty of background information through such organizations as the United Nations Association and the Council for Education in World Citizenship. If he is well informed on the work of the United Nations and on the problems which must be solved, he will be able to give the Organization intelligent support at the times when it most needs it.

Mr. Cordell Hull, in opening the Dumbarton Oaks conference, said that, "No institution will endure unless there is behind it considered and complete public support. The will to peace must spring from the minds and hearts of men and women everywhere."

It will be objected that no amount of support from individual enthusiasts will avail if nothing is done to win over those peoples, and those individuals among the peoples, who are not already converted to the idea of a world organization. Here is the reason for the second duty which the individual can perform for the United Nations.

The United Nations already know that, "ignorance of each other's ways and lives has been a common cause, throughout the history of mankind, of that suspicion and mistrust between the peoples of the world through which their differences have all too often broken into war."[1] The Educational, Scientific and Cultural Organization (UNESCO) has been set up largely in order to fight this ignorance. The two British organizations mentioned above (UNA and CEWC) are performing admirable work in dispelling the fog of fear and prejudice which hangs between each people and its neighbours. But all these agencies can only work properly if the individual citizen gives them his fullest support. Like the United Nations Organization itself, they fall back on the common man. They can help him to make contacts with individuals in foreign countries, to try to understand the viewpoints of his overseas contacts, and to try to make them understand his; but they cannot give him the will to do so. That is up to the common man himself.

Mr. Bevin has said that, ". . . you may invent all sorts of devices to decide who is an aggressor, but after all the thought you can give to it, the only repository of faith I have been able to find to determine that is the common people. There never was a war yet which, if the facts had been put calmly before the ordinary folk, could not have been prevented. The fact is, they are kept separated from each other. . . . The common man, I think, is the great protection against war."

If this book is of any help to him in playing his vital part in the preservation of peace, it will have achieved its object.

[1] From the Constitution of UNESCO

APPENDIX A

THE COVENANT OF THE LEAGUE OF NATIONS

PREAMBLE

The high contracting Parties,

In order to promote international co-operation and to achieve international peace and security

by the acceptance of obligations not to resort to war,

by the prescription of open, just and honourable relations between nations,

by the firm establishment of the understandings of international law as the actual rule of conduct among Governments,

and by the maintenance of justice and a scrupulous respect for all treaty obligations in the dealings of organized peoples with one another,

Agree to this Covenant of the League of Nations.

ARTICLE 1

1. The original Members of the League of Nations shall be those of the Signatories which are named in the Annex to this Covenant and also such of those other States named in the Annex as shall accede without reservation to this Covenant. Such accession shall be effected by a Declaration deposited with the Secretariat within two months of the coming into force of the Covenant. Notice thereof shall be sent to all other Members of the League.

2. Any fully self-governing State, Dominion or Colony not named in the Annex may become a Member of the League if its admission is agreed to by two-thirds of the Assembly, provided that it shall give effective guarantees of its sincere intention to observe its international obligations, and shall accept such regulations as may be prescribed by the League in regard to its military, naval and air forces and armaments.

3. Any Member of the League may, after two years' notice of its intention so to do, withdraw from the League, provided that all its international obligations and all its obligations under this Covenant shall have been fulfilled at the time of its withdrawal.

ARTICLE 2

The action of the League under this Covenant shall be effected through the instrumentality of an Assembly and of a Council, with a permanent Secretariat.

ARTICLE 3

1. The Assembly shall consist of Representatives of the Members of the League.

2. The Assembly shall meet at stated intervals and from time to time as occasion may require at the Seat of the League or at such other place as may be decided upon.

3. The Assembly may deal at its meetings with any matter within the

sphere of action of the League or affecting the peace of the world.

4. At meetings of the Assembly, each Member of the League shall have one vote, and may have not more than three Representatives.

ARTICLE 4

1. The Council shall consist of Representatives of the Principal Allied and Associated Powers together with Representatives of four other Members of the League. These four Members of the League shall be selected by the Assembly from time to time in its discretion. Until the appointment of the Representatives of the four Members of the League first selected by the Assembly, Representatives of Belgium, Brazil, Spain and Greece shall be members of the Council.

2. With the approval of the majority of the Assembly, the Council may name additional Members of the League whose Representatives shall always be Members of the Council ; the Council with like approval may increase the number of Members of the League to be selected by the Assembly for representation on the Council.

2b The Assembly shall fix by a two-thirds majority the rules dealing with the election of the non-permanent Members of the Council, and particularly such regulations as relate to their term of office and the conditions of re-eligibility.

3. The Council shall meet from time to time as occasion may require, and at least once a year, at the Seat of the League, or at such other place as may be decided upon.

4. The Council may deal at its meetings with any matter within the sphere of action of the League or affecting the peace of the world.

5. Any member of the League not represented on the Council shall be invited to send a Representative to sit as a member at any meeting of the Council during the consideration of matters specially affecting the interests of that Member of the League.

6. At meetings of the Council, each Member of the League represented on the Council shall have one vote, and may have not more than one Representative.

ARTICLE 5

1. Except where otherwise expressly provided in this Covenant or by the terms of the present Treaty, decisions at any meeting of the Assembly or of the Council, shall require the agreement of all the Members of the League represented at the meeting.

2. All matters of procedure at meetings of the Assembly or of the Council, including the appointment of Committees to investigate particular matters, shall be regulated by the Assembly or by the Council and may be decided by a majority of the Members of the League represented at the meeting.

3. The first meeting of the Assembly and the first meeting of the Council shall be summoned by the President of the United States of America.

ARTICLE 6

1. The permanent Secretariat shall be established at the Seat of the League. The Secretariat shall comprise a Secretary-General and such secretaries and staff as may be required.

2. The first Secretary-General shall be the person named in the Annex ; thereafter the Secretary-General shall be appointed by the Council with the approval of the majority of the Assembly.

3. The secretaries and staff of the Secretariat shall be appointed by the Secretary-General with the approval of the Council.

4. The Secretary-General shall act in that capacity at all meetings of the Assembly and of the Council.

5. *The expenses of the League shall be borne by the Members of the League in the proportion decided by the Assembly.*

ARTICLE 7

1. The Seat of the League is established at Geneva.

2. The Council may at any time decide that the Seat of the League shall be established elsewhere.

3. All positions under or in connection with the League, including the Secretariat, shall be open equally to men and women.

4. Representatives of the Members of the League and officials of the League when engaged on the business of the League shall enjoy diplomatic privileges and immunities.

5. The buildings and other property occupied by the League or its officials or by Representatives attending its meetings shall be inviolable.

ARTICLE 8

1. The Members of the League recognize that the maintenance of peace requires the reduction of national armaments to the lowest point consistent with national safety and the enforcement by common action of international obligations.

2. The Council, taking account of the geographical situation and circumstances of each State, shall formulate plans for such reduction for the consideration and action of the several Governments.

3. Such plans shall be subject to reconsideration and revision at least every ten years.

4. After these plans have been adopted by the several Governments, the limits of armaments therein fixed shall not be exceeded without the concurrence of the Council.

5. The Members of the League agree that the manufacture by private enterprise of munitions and implements of war is open to grave objections. The Council shall advise how the evil effects attendant upon such manufacture can be prevented, due regard being had to the necessities of those Members of the League which are not able to manufacture the munitions and implements of war necessary for their safety.

6. The Members of the League undertake to interchange full and frank information as to the scale of their armaments, their military, naval and air programmes and the condition of such of their industries as are adaptable to warlike purposes.

ARTICLE 9

A permanent Commission shall be constituted to advise the Council on the execution of the provisions of Articles 1 and 8 and on military, naval and air questions generally.

ARTICLE 10

The Members of the League undertake to respect and preserve as against external aggression the territorial integrity and existing political independence of all Members of the League. In case of any such aggression or in case of any threat or danger of such aggression, the Council shall advise upon the means by which this obligation shall be fulfilled.

ARTICLE 11

1. Any war or threat of war, whether immediately affecting any of the Members of the League or not, is hereby declared a matter of concern to the whole League, and the League shall take any action that may be deemed wise and effectual to safeguard the peace of nations. In case any such emergency should arise, the Secretary-General shall, on the request of any Member of the League, forthwith summon a meeting of the Council.

2. It is also declared to be the friendly right of each Member of the League to bring to the attention of the Assembly or of the Council any circumstance whatever affecting international relations which threatens to disturb international peace or the good understanding between nations upon which peace depends.

ARTICLE 12

1. The Members of the League agree that if there should arise between them any dispute likely to lead to a rupture they will submit the matter either to arbitration *or judicial settlement* or to enquiry by the Council, and they agree in no case to resort to war until three months after the award by the arbitrators *or the judicial decision* or the report by the Council.

2. In any case under this Article the award of the arbitrators *or the judicial decision* shall be made within a reasonable time, and the report of the Council shall be made within six months after the submission of the dispute.

ARTICLE 13

1. The Members of the League agree that whenever any dispute shall arise between them which they recognize to be suitable for submission to arbitration *or judicial settlement*, and which cannot be satisfactorily settled by diplomacy, they will submit the whole subject-matter to arbitration *or judicial settlement*.

2. Disputes as to the interpretation of a treaty, as to any question of international law, as to the existence of any fact which, if established, would constitute a breach of any international obligation or as to the extent and nature of the reparation to be made for any such breach, are declared to be among those which are generally suitable for submission to arbitration *or judicial settlement*.

3. *For the consideration of any such dispute, the court to which the case is referred shall be the Permanent Court of International Justice, established in accordance with Article 14, or any tribunal agreed on by the parties to the dispute or stipulated in any convention existing between them.*

4. The Members of the League agree that they will carry out in full good faith any award *or decision* that may be rendered, and that they will not resort

F

to war against a Member of the League which complies therewith. In the event of any failure to carry out such an award *or decision*, the Council shall propose what steps should be taken to give effect thereto.

ARTICLE 14

The Council shall formulate and submit to the Members of the League for adoption plans for the establishment of a Permanent Court of International Justice. The Court shall be competent to hear and determine any dispute of an international character which the parties thereto submit to it. The Court may also give an advisory opinion upon any dispute or question referred to it by the Council or by the Assembly.

ARTICLE 15

1. If there should arise between Members of the League any dispute likely to lead to a rupture, which is not submitted to arbitration *or judicial settlement* in accordance with Article 13, the Members of the League agree that they will submit the matter to the Council. Any party to the dispute may effect such submission by giving notice of the existence of the dispute to the Secretary-General, who will make all necessary arrangements for a full investigation and consideration thereof.

2. For this purpose, the parties to the dispute will communicate to the Secretary-General, as promptly as possible, statements of their case with all the relevant facts and papers, and the Council may forthwith direct the publication thereof.

3. The Council shall endeavour to effect a settlement of the dispute, and if such efforts are successful, a statement shall be made public giving such facts and explanations regarding the dispute and the terms of settlement thereof as the Council may deem appropriate.

4. If the dispute is not thus settled, the Council either unanimously or by a majority vote shall make and publish a report containing a statement of the facts of the dispute and the recommendations which are deemed just and proper in regard thereto.

5. Any Member of the League represented on the Council may make public a statement of the facts of the dispute and of its conclusions regarding the same.

6. If a report by the Council is unanimously agreed to by the members thereof other than the Representatives of one or more of the parties to the dispute, the Members of the League agree that they will not go to war with any party to the dispute which complies with the recommendations of the report.

7. If the Council fails to reach a report which is unanimously agreed to by the members thereof, other than the Representatives of one or more of the parties to the dispute, the Members of the League reserve to themselves the right to take such action as they shall consider necessary for the maintenance of right and justice.

8. If the dispute between the parties is claimed by one of them, and is found by the Council, to arise out of a matter which by international law is solely within the domestic jurisdiction of that party, the Council shall so report, and shall make no recommendation as to its settlement.

9. The Council may in any case under this Article refer the dispute to the Assembly. The dispute shall be so referred at the request of either party to the dispute provided that such request be made within fourteen days after the submission of the dispute to the Council.

10. In any case referred to the Assembly, all the provisions of this Article and of Article 12 relating to the action and powers of the Council shall apply to the action and powers of the Assembly, provided that a report made by the Assembly, if concurred in by the Representatives of those Members of the League represented on the Council and of a majority of the other Members of the League, exclusive in each case of the Representatives of the parties to the dispute, shall have the same force as a report by the Council concurred in by all the members thereof other than the Representatives of one or more of the parties to the dispute.

ARTICLE 16

1. Should any Member of the League resort to war in disregard of its covenants under Articles 12, 13 or 15, it shall *ipso facto* be deemed to have committed an act of war against all other Members of the League, which hereby undertake immediately to subject it to the severance of all trade or financial relations, the prohibition of all intercourse between their nationals and the nationals of the covenant-breaking State, and the prevention of all financial, commercial or personal intercourse between the nationals of the covenant-breaking State and the nationals of any other State, whether a Member of the League or not.

2. It shall be the duty of the Council in such case to recommend to the several Governments concerned what effective military, naval or air force the Members of the League shall severally contribute to the armed forces to be used to protect the covenants of the League.

3. The Members of the League agree, further, that they will mutually support one another in the financial and economic measures which are taken under this Article, in order to minimise the loss and inconvenience resulting from the above measures, and that they will mutually support one another in resisting any special measures aimed at one of their number by the covenant-breaking State, and that they will take the necessary steps to afford passage through their territory to the forces of any of the Members of the League which are co-operating to protect the covenants of the League.

4. Any Member of the League which has violated any covenant of the League may be declared to be no longer a Member of the League by a vote of the Council concurred in by the Representatives of all the other Members of the League represented thereon.

ARTICLE 17

1. In the event of a dispute between a Member of the League and a State which is not a member of the League, or between States not members of the League, the State or States not members of the League shall be invited to accept the obligations of membership in the League for the purposes of such dispute, upon such conditions as the Council may deem just. If such invitation is accepted, the provisions of Articles 12 to 16 inclusive shall be applied with such modifications as may be deemed necessary by the Council.

2. Upon such invitation being given, the Council shall immediately institute an enquiry into the circumstances of the dispute and recommend such action as may seem best and most effectual in the circumstances.

3. If a State so invited shall refuse to accept the obligations of membership in the League for the purposes of such dispute, and shall resort to war against a Member of the League, the provisions of Article 16 shall be applicable as against the State taking such action.

4. If both parties to the dispute when so invited refuse to accept the obligations of membership in the League for the purposes of such dispute, the Council may take such measures and make such recommendations as will prevent hostilities and will result in the settlement of the dispute.

ARTICLE 18

Every treaty or international engagement entered into hereafter by any Member of the League shall be forthwith registered with the Secretariat and shall as soon as possible be published by it. No such treaty or international engagement shall be binding until so registered.

ARTICLE 19

The Assembly may from time to time advise the reconsideration by Members of the League of treaties which have become inapplicable and the consideration of international conditions whose continuance might endanger the peace of the world.

ARTICLE 20

1. The Members of the League severally agree that this Covenant is accepted as abrogating all obligations or understandings *inter se* which are inconsistent with the terms thereof, and solemnly undertake that they will not hereafter enter into any engagements inconsistent with the terms thereof.

2. In case any Member of the League shall, before becoming a Member of the League, have undertaken any obligations inconsistent with the terms of this Covenant, it shall be the duty of such Member to take immediate steps to procure its release from such obligations.

ARTICLE 21

Nothing in this Covenant shall be deemed to affect the validity of international engagements, such as treaties of arbitration or regional understandings like the Monroe doctrine, for securing the maintenance of peace.

ARTICLE 22

1. To those colonies and territories which as a consequence of the late war have ceased to be under the sovereignty of the States which formerly governed them and which are inhabited by peoples not yet able to stand by themselves under the strenuous conditions of the modern world, there should be applied the principle that the well-being and development of such peoples form a sacred trust of civilization and that securities for the performance of this trust should be embodied in this Covenant.

2. The best method of giving practical effect to this principle is that the

tutelage of such peoples should be entrusted to advanced nations who, by reason of their resources, their experience or their geographical position, can best undertake this responsibility, and who are willing to accept it, and that this tutelage should be exercised by them as Mandatories on behalf of the League.

3. The character of the mandate must differ according to the stage of the development of the people, the geographical situation of the territory, its economic conditions and other similar circumstances.

4. Certain communities formerly belonging to the Turkish Empire have reached a stage of development where their existence as independent nations can be provisionally recognized subject to the rendering of administrative advice and assistance by a Mandatory until such time as they are able to stand alone. The wishes of these communities must be a principal consideration in the selection of the Mandatory.

5. Other peoples, especially those of Central Africa, are at such a stage that the Mandatory must be responsible for the administration of the territory under conditions which will guarantee freedom of conscience and religion, subject only to the maintenance of public order and morals, the prohibition of abuses such as the slave trade the arms traffic and the liquor traffic, and the prevention of the establishment of fortifications or military and naval bases and of military training of the natives for other than police purposes and the defence of territory, and will also secure equal opportunities for the trade and commerce of other Members of the League.

6. There are territories such as South West Africa and certain of the South Pacific Islands, which, owing to the sparseness of their population, or their small size, or their remoteness from the centres of civilization, or their geographical contiguity to the territory of the Mandatory, and other circumstances, can be best administered under the laws of the Mandatory as integral portions of its territory, subject to the safeguards above mentioned in the interests of the indigenous population.

7. In every case of mandate, the Mandatory shall render to the Council an annual report in reference to the territory committed to its charge.

8. The degree of authority, control or administration to be exercised by the Mandatory shall, if not previously agreed upon by the Members of the League, be explicitly defined in each case by the Council.

9. A permanent Commission shall be constituted to receive and examine the annual reports of the Mandatories and to advise the Council on all matters relating to the observance of the mandates.

ARTICLE 23

Subject to and in accordance with the provisions of international conventions existing or hereafter to be agreed upon, the Members of the League :

(a) will endeavour to secure and maintain fair and humane conditions of labour for men, women and children, both in their own countries and in all countries to which their commercial and industrial relations extend, and for that purpose will establish and maintain the necessary international organizations ;

(b) undertake to secure just treatment of the native inhabitants of territories under their control ;

(*c*) will entrust the League with the general supervision over the execution of agreements with regard to the traffic in women and children, and the traffic in opium and other dangerous drugs ;

(*d*) will entrust the League with the general supervision of the trade in arms and ammunition with the countries in which the control of this traffic is necessary in the common interest ;

(*e*) will make provision to secure and maintain freedom of communications and of transit and equitable treatment for the commerce of all Members of the League. In this connection, the special necessities of the regions devastated during the war of 1914–1918 shall be borne in mind ;

(*f*) will endeavour to take steps in matters of international concern for the prevention and control of disease.

ARTICLE 24

1. There shall be placed under the direction of the League the international bureaux already established by general treaties if the parties to such treaties consent. All such international bureaux and all commissions for the regulation of matters of international interest hereafter constituted shall be placed under the direction of the League.

2. In all matters of international interest which are regulated by general conventions but which are not placed under the control of international bureaux or commissions, the Secretariat of the League shall, subject to the consent of the Council and if desired by the parties, collect and distribute all relevant information and shall render any other assistance which may be necessary or desirable.

3. The Council may include as part of the expenses of the Secretariat the expenses of any bureau or commission which is placed under the direction of the League.

ARTICLE 25

The Members of the League agree to encourage and promote the establishment and co-operation of duly authorized voluntary national Red Cross organizations having as purposes the improvement of health, the prevention of disease and the mitigation of suffering throughout the world.

ARTICLE 26

1. Amendments to this Covenant will take effect when ratified by the Members of the League whose Representatives compose the Council and by a majority of the Members of the League whose Representatives compose the Assembly.

2. No such amendments shall bind any Member of the League which signifies its dissent therefrom, but in that case it shall cease to be a Member of the League.

ANNEX TO THE COVENANT

I. Original Members of the League of Nations, Signatories of the Treaty of Peace

United States of America
Belgium

Haiti
Hejaz

Bolivia
Brazil
British Empire
  Canada
  Australia
  South Africa
  New Zealand
  India
China
Cuba
Ecuador
France
Greece
Guatemala

Honduras
Italy
Japan
Liberia
Nicaragua
Panama
Peru
Poland
Portugal
Roumania
Serb-Croat-Slovene State
Siam
Czechoslovakia
Uruguay

States invited to accede to the Covenant

Argentine Republic
Chile
Colombia
Denmark
Netherlands
Norway
Paraguay

Persia
Salvador
Spain
Sweden
Switzerland
Venezuela

II. First Secretary-General of the League of Nations
The Hon. Sir. James Eric Drummond, K.C.M.G., C.B.

APPENDIX B

THE ATLANTIC CHARTER

THE PRESIDENT OF THE UNITED STATES OF AMERICA AND THE PRIME MINISTER, MR. CHURCHILL, representing His Majesty's Government in the United Kingdom, being met together, deem it right to make known certain common principles in the national policies of their respective countries on which they base their hopes for a better future for the world.

I Their countries seek no aggrandisement, territorial or other.

II They desire to see no territorial changes that do not accord with the freely expressed wishes of the peoples concerned.

III They respect the right of all peoples to choose the form of Government under which they will live ; and they wish to see sovereign rights and self-government restored to those who have been forcibly deprived of them.

IV They will endeavour, with due respect for their existing obligations, to further the enjoyment by all states, great or small, victor or vanquished, of access, on equal terms, to the trade and to the raw materials of the world which are needed for their economic prosperity.

V They desire to bring about the fullest collaboration between all nations in the economic field with the object of securing, for all, improved labour standards, economic advancement and social security.

VI After the final destruction of the Nazi tyranny, they hope to see established a peace which will afford to all nations the means of dwelling in safety within their own boundaries, and which will afford assurance that all the men in all the lands may live out their lives in freedom from fear and want.

VII Such a peace should enable all men to traverse the high seas and oceans without hindrance.

VIII They believe that all of the nations of the world, for realistic as well as spiritual reasons, must come to the abandonment of the use of force. Since no future peace can be maintained if land, sea or air armaments continue to be employed by nations which threaten, or may threaten, aggression outside of their frontiers, they believe, pending the establishment of a wider and permanent system of general security, that the disarmament of such nations is essential. They will likewise aid and encourage all other practicable measures which will lighten for peace-loving peoples the crushing burden of armaments.

FRANKLIN D. ROOSEVELT
WINSTON S. CHURCHILL

14 August 1941

UNITED NATIONS DECLARATION, WASHINGTON, JANUARY 1st, 1942

The governments signatory hereto,

Having subscribed to a common programme of purposes and principles embodied in this joint declaration of the President of the United States of America and the Prime Minister of the United Kingdom of Great Britain and Northern Ireland dated August 14, 1941, known as the Atlantic Charter, being convinced that complete victory over their enemies is essential to defend life, liberty, independence and religious freedom, and to preserve human rights and justice in their own lands as well as in other lands, and that they are now engaged in a common struggle against savage and brutal forces seeking to subjugate the world, declare :

(1) Each government pledges itself to employ its full resources, military or economic, against those members of the Tripartite Pact and its adherents with which such government is at war.

(2) Each government pledges itself to co-operate with the governments signatory hereto and not to make a separate armistice or peace with the enemies.

The foregoing declaration may be adhered to by other nations which are, or which may be, rendering material assistance and contributions in the struggle for victory over Hitlerism.

DONE AT WASHINGTON,
JANUARY FIRST, 1942.

APPENDIX C

JOINT FOUR-NATION DECLARATION, MOSCOW, OCTOBER 30th, 1943

The Governments of the United States of America, United Kingdom, the Soviet Union and China :

united in their determination, in accordance with the Declaration by the United Nations of January 1, 1942, and subsequent declarations, to continue hostilities against those Axis powers with which they respectively are at war until such powers have laid down their arms on the basis of unconditional surrender ;

conscious of their responsibility to secure the liberation of themselves and the peoples allied with them from the menace of aggression ; recognizing the necessity of ensuring a rapid and orderly transition from war to peace and of establishing and maintaining international peace and security with the least diversion of the world's human and economic resources for armaments ;

jointly declare :

1. That their united action, pledged for the prosecution of the war against their respective enemies, will be continued for the organization and maintenance of peace and security.

2. That those of them at war with a common enemy will act together in all matters relating to the surrender and disarmament of that enemy.

3. That they will take all measures deemed by them to be necessary to provide against any violation of the terms imposed upon the enemy.

4. That they recognize the necessity of establishing at the earliest practicable date a general international organization, based on the principle of the sovereign equality of all peace-loving states, and open to membership by all such states, large and small, for the maintenance of international peace and security.

5. That for the purpose of maintaining international peace and security pending the re-establishment of law and order and the inauguration of a system of general security, they will consult with one another and as occasion requires with other members of the United Nations with a view to joint action on behalf of the community of nations.

6. That after the termination of hostilities they will not employ their military forces within the territories of other states except for the purposes envisaged in this declaration and after joint consultation.

7. That they will confer and co-operate with one another and with other members of the United Nations to bring about a practicable general agreement with respect to the regulation of armaments in the post-war period.

APPENDIX D

CHARTER OF THE UNITED NATIONS

We, the peoples of the United Nations, determined to save succeeding

F*

generations from the scourge of war, which twice in our lifetime has brought untold sorrow to mankind, and

to reaffirm faith in fundamental human rights, in the dignity and worth of the human person, in the equal rights of men and women and of nations large and small, and

to establish conditions under which justice and respect for the obligations arising from treaties and other sources of international law can be maintained, and

to promote social progress and better standards of life in larger freedom, and for these ends

to practise tolerance and live together in peace with one another as good neighbours, and

to unite our strength to maintain international peace and security, and

to ensure, by the acceptance of principles and the institution of methods, that armed force shall not be used, save in the common interest, and

to employ international machinery for the promotion of the economic and social advancement of all peoples have resolved to combine our efforts to accomplish these aims.

Accordingly, our respective Governments, through representatives assembled in the City of San Francisco, who have exhibited their full powers found to be in good and due form, have agreed to the present Charter of the United Nations and do hereby establish an international organization to be known as the United Nations.

CHAPTER I.—PURPOSES AND PRINCIPLES

Article 1

The Purposes of the United Nations are :—

1. To maintain international peace and security, and to that end : to take effective collective measures for the prevention and removal of threats to the peace and for the suppression of acts of aggression or other breaches of the peace, and to bring about by peaceful means, and in conformity with the principles of justice and international law, adjustment or settlement of international disputes or situations which might lead to a breach of the peace ;

2. To develop friendly relations among nations based on respect for the principle of equal rights and self-determination of peoples, and to take other appropriate measures to strengthen universal peace ;

3. To achieve international co-operation in solving international problems of an economic, social, cultural, or humanitarian character, and in promoting and encouraging respect for human rights and for fundamental freedoms for all without distinction as to race, sex, language, or religion ; and

4. To be a centre for harmonizing the actions of nations in the attainment of these common ends.

Article 2

The Organization and its Members, in pursuit of the purposes stated in Article 1, shall act in accordance with the following principles :—

1. The Organization is based on the principle of the sovereign equality of all its members.

2. All Members, in order to ensure to all of them the rights and benefits resulting from membership, shall fulfil in good faith the obligations assumed by them in accordance with the present Charter.

3. All Members shall settle their international disputes by peaceful means in such a manner that international peace and security and justice, are not endangered.

4. All Members shall refrain in their international relations from the threat or use of force against the territorial integrity or political independence of any State, or in any other manner inconsistent with the Purposes of the United-Nations.

5. All Members shall give the United Nations every assistance in any action it takes in accordance with the present Charter, and shall refrain from giving assistance to any State against which the United Nations is taking preventive or enforcement action.

6. The Organization shall ensure that States which are not Members of the United Nations act in accordance with these Principles so far as may be necessary for the maintenance of international peace and security.

7. Nothing contained in the present Charter shall authorize the United Nations to intervene in matters which are essentially within the domestic jurisdiction of any State or shall require the Members to submit such matters to settlement under the present Charter ; but this principle shall not prejudice the application of enforcement measures under Chapter VII.

Chapter II.—Membership

Article 3

The original members of the United Nations shall be the states which. having participated in the United Nations Conference on International Organization at San Francisco, or having previously signed the Declaration by United Nations of January 1, 1942, sign the present Charter and ratify it in accordance with Article 110.

Article 4

1. Membership in the United Nations is open to all other peace-loving states which accept the obligations contained in the present Charter and, in the judgment of the Organization, are able and willing to carry out these obligations.

2. The admission of any such state to membership in the United Nations will be effected by a decision of the General Assembly upon the recommendation of the Security Council.

Article 5

A Member of the United Nations against which preventive or enforcement action has been taken by the Security Council may be suspended from the exercise of the rights and privileges of membership by the General Assembly upon the recommendation of the Security Council. The exercise of these rights and privileges may be restored by the Security Council.

Article 6

A Member of the United Nations which has persistently violated the

Principles contained in the present Charter may be expelled from the Organization by the General Assembly upon the recommendation of the Security Council.

CHAPTER III.—ORGANS
Article 7

1. There are established as the principal organs of the United Nations : a General Assembly, a Security Council, an Economic and Social Council, a Trusteeship Council, an International Court of Justice and a Secretariat.

2. Such subsidiary organs as may be found necessary may be established in accordance with the present Charter.

Article 8

The United Nations shall place no restrictions on the eligibility of men and women to participate in any capacity and under conditions of equality in its principal and subsidiary organs.

CHAPTER IV.—THE GENERAL ASSEMBLY—COMPOSITION
Article 9

1. The General Assembly shall consist of all the Members of the United Nations.

2. Each Member shall have not more than five representatives in the General Assembly.

FUNCTIONS AND POWERS
Article 10

The General Assembly may discuss any questions or any matters within the scope of the present Charter or relating to the powers and functions of any organs provided for in the present Charter, and, except as provided in Article 12, may make recommendations to the members of the United Nations or to the Security Council or to both on any such questions or matters.

Article 11

1. The General Assembly may consider the general principles of co-operation in the maintenance of international peace and security, including the principles governing disarmament and the regulation of armaments, and may make recommendations with regard to such principles to the Members or to the Security Council or both.

2. The General Assembly may discuss any questions relating to the maintenance of international peace and security brought before it by any Member of the United Nations, or by the Security Council, or by a state which is not a member of the United Nations in accordance with Article 35, paragraph two, and, except as provided in Article 12, may make recommendations with regard to any such questions to the state or states concerned or to the Security Council or to both. Any such question, on which action is necessary, shall be referred to the Security Council by the General Assembly either before or after discussion.

3. The General Assembly may call the attention of the Security Council to situations which are likely to endanger international peace and security.

4. The powers of the General Assembly set forth in this article shall not limit the general scope of Article 10.

Article 12

1. While the Security Council is exercising in respect of any dispute or situation the functions assigned to it in the present Charter, the General Assembly shall not make any recommendations with regard to that dispute or situation unless the Security Council so requests.

2. The Secretary-General, with the consent of the Security Council, shall notify the General Assembly at each session of any matters relative to the maintenance of international peace and security which are being dealt with by the Security Council and shall similarly notify the General Assembly, or the Members of the United Nations if the General Assembly is not in session, immediately the Security Council ceases to deal with such matters.

Article 13

1. The General Assembly shall initiate studies and make recommendations for the purpose of :
   (a) Promoting international co-operation in the political field and encouraging the progressive development of international law and its codification ;
   (b) Promoting international co-operation in the economic, social, cultural, educational, and health fields, and assisting in the realization of human rights and fundamental freedoms for all without distinction as to race, sex, language, or religion.

2. The further responsibilities, functions, and powers of the General Assembly with respect to matters mentioned in paragraph 1 (b) above are set forth in Chapters IX and X.

Article 14

Subject to the provision of Article 12, the General Assembly may recommend measures for the peaceful adjustment of any situation, regardless of origin, which it deems likely to impair the general welfare or friendly relations among nations, including situations resulting from a violation of the provisions of the present Charter setting forth the Purposes and Principles of the United Nations.

Article 15

1. The General Assembly shall receive and consider annual and special reports from the Security Council ; these reports include an account of the measures that the Security Council has decided upon or taken to maintain international peace and security.

2. The General Assembly shall receive and consider reports from the other organs of the United Nations.

Article 16

The General Assembly shall perform such functions with respect to the international trusteeship system as are assigned to it under Chapters XII and XIII, including the approval of the trusteeship agreements for areas not designated as strategic.

Article 17

1. The General Assembly shall consider and approve the budget of the Organization.

2. The expenses of the Organization shall be borne by the Members as apportioned by the General Assembly.

3. The General Assembly shall consider and approve any financial and budgetary arrangements with specialized agencies referred to in Article 57 and shall examine the administrative budgets of such specialized agencies with a view to making recommendations to the agencies concerned.

VOTING

Article 18

1. Each Member of the General Assembly shall have one vote.

2. Decisions of the General Assembly on important questions shall be made by a two-thirds majority of the members present and voting. These questions shall include : recommendations with respect to the maintenance of international peace and security, the election of the non-permanent members of the Security Council, the election of the members of the Economic and Social Council, the election of members of the Trusteeship Council in accordance with paragraph 1 (c) of Article 86, the admission of new Members to the United Nations, the suspension of the rights and privileges of membership, the expulsion of Members, questions relating to the operation of the trusteeship system, and budgetary questions.

3. Decisions on other questions, including the determination of additional categories of questions to be decided by a two-thirds majority, shall be made by a majority of the members present and voting.

Article 19

A member of the United Nations which is in arrears in the payment of its financial contributions to the Organization shall have no vote in the General Assembly if the amount of its arrears equals or exceeds the amount of the contributions due from it for the preceding two full years. The General Assembly may, nevertheless, permit such a Member to vote if it is satisfied that the failure to pay is due to conditions beyond the control of the Member.

PROCEDURE

Article 20

The General Assembly shall meet in regular annual sessions and in such special sessions as occasion may require. Special sessions shall be convoked by the Secretary-General at the request of the Security Council or of a majority of the Members of the United Nations.

Article 21

The General Assembly shall adopt its own rules of procedure. It shall elect its President for each session.

Article 22

The General Assembly may establish such subsidiary organs as it deems necessary for the performance of its functions.

CHAPTER V.—THE SECURITY COUNCIL—COMPOSITION

Article 23

1. The Security Council shall consist of 11 Members of the United Nations. The Republic of China, France, the Union of Soviet Socialist Republics, the United Kingdom of Great Britain and Northern Ireland, and the United States of America shall be permanent members of the Security Council. The General Assembly shall elect six other Members of the United Nations to be non-permanent members of the Security Council, due regard being specially paid, in the first instance to the contribution of Members of the United Nations to the maintenance of international peace and security and to the other purposes of the Organization, and also to equitable geographical distribution.

2. The non-permanent members of the Security Council shall be elected for a term of two years. In the first election of the non-permanent members, however, three shall be chosen for a term of one year. A retiring member shall not be eligible for immediate re-election.

3. Each member of the Security Council shall have one representative.

FUNCTIONS AND POWERS

Article 24

1. In order to ensure prompt and effective action by the United Nations, its Members confer on the Security Council primary responsibility for the maintenance of international peace and security, and agree that in carrying out its duties under this responsibility the Security Council acts on their behalf.

2. In discharging these duties the Security Council shall act in accordance with the Purposes and Principles of the United Nations. The specific powers granted to the Security Council for the discharge of these duties are laid down in Chapters VI, VII, VIII and XII.

3. The Security Council shall submit annual and, when necessary, special reports to the General Assembly for its consideration.

Article 25

The Members of the United Nations agree to accept and carry out the decisions of the Security Council in accordance with the present Charter.

Article 26

In order to promote the establishment and maintenance of international peace and security with the least diversion for armaments of the worlds' human and economic resources, the Security Council shall be responsible for formulating, with the assistance of the Military Staff Committee referred to in Article 47, plans to be submitted to the Members of the United Nations for the establishment of a system for the regulation of armaments.

Voting

Article 27

1. Each member of the Security Council shall have one vote.
2. Decisions of the Security Council on procedural matters shall be made by an affirmative vote of seven members.
3. Decisions of the Security Council on all other matters shall be made by an affirmative vote of seven members including the concurring votes of the permanent members ; provided that, in decisions under Chapter VI and under paragraph 3 of Article 52, a party to a dispute shall abstain from voting.

Procedure

Article 28

1. The Security Council shall be so organized as to be able to function continuously. Each member of the Security Council shall for this purpose be represented at all times at the seat of the Organization.
2. The Security Council shall hold periodic meetings at which each of its members may, if it so desires, be represented by a member of the government or by some other specially designated representative.
3. The Security Council may hold meetings at such places other than the seat of the organization as in its judgment will best facilitate its work.

Article 29

The Security Council may establish subsidiary organs as it deems necessary for the performance of its functions.

Article 30

The Security Council shall adopt its own rules of procedure, including the method of selecting its President.

Article 31

Any Member of the United Nations which is not a member of the Security Council may participate, without vote, in the discussion of any question brought before the Security Council whenever the latter considers that the interests of that Member are specially affected.

Article 32

Any Member of the United Nations which is not a member of the Security Council or any state which is not a Member of the United Nations, if it is a party to a dispute under consideration by the Security Council, shall be invited to participate, without vote, in the discussion relating to the dispute.

The Security Council shall lay down such conditions as it deems just for the participation of a state which is not a Member of the United Nations.

Chapter VI.—Pacific Settlement of Disputes

Article 33

1. The parties to any dispute, the continuance of which is likely to endanger the maintenance of international peace and security, shall, first of all,

seek a solution by negotiation, inquiry, mediation, conciliation, arbitration, judicial settlement, resort to regional agencies or arrangements, or other peaceful means of their own choice.

2. The Security Council shall, when it deems necessary, call upon the parties to settle their dispute by such means.

Article 34

The Security Council may investigate any dispute, or any situation which might lead to international friction or give rise to a dispute, in order to determine whether the continuance of the dispute or situation is likely to endanger the maintenance of international peace and security.

Article 35

1. Any Member of the United Nations may bring any dispute or any situation of the nature referred to in Article 34 to the attention of the Security Council or of the General Assembly.

2. A state which is not a Member of the United Nations may bring to the attention of the Security Council or of the General Assembly any dispute to which it is a party, if it accepts in advance, for the purposes of the dispute, the obligations of pacific settlement provided in the present Charter.

3. The proceedings of the General Assembly in respect of matters brought to its attention under this article will be subject to the provisions of Articles 11 and 12.

Article 36

1. The Security Council may, at any stage of a dispute of the nature referred to in Article 33 or of a situation of like nature, recommend appropriate procedures or methods of adjustments.

2. The Security Council should take into consideration any procedures for the settlement of the dispute which have already been adopted by the parties.

3. In making recommendations under this Article the Security Council should also take into consideration that legal disputes should as a general rule be referred by the parties to the International Court of Justice in accordance with the provisions of the Statute of the Court.

Article 37

1. Should the parties to a dispute of the nature referred to in Article 33 fail to settle it by the means indicated in that article, they shall refer it to the Security Council.

2. If the Security Council deems that the continuance of the dispute is in fact likely to endanger the maintenance of international peace and security, it shall decide whether to take action under Article 36 or to recommend such terms of settlement as it may consider appropriate.

Article 38

Without prejudice to the provisions of Articles 33–37, the Security Council may, if all the parties to any dispute so request, make recommendations to the parties with a view to a pacific settlement of the dispute.

CHAPTER VII.—ACTION WITH RESPECT TO THREATS TO THE PEACE, BREACHES
OF THE PEACE, AND ACTS OF AGGRESSION

Article 39

The Security Council shall determine the existence of any threat to the
peace, breach of the peace, or act of aggression and shall make recommendations, or decide what measures shall be taken in accordance with
Articles 41 and 42, to maintain or restore international peace and security.

Article 40

In order to prevent an aggravation of the situation, the Security Council
may, before making the recommendations or deciding upon the measures
provided for in Article 39, call upon the parties concerned to comply with such
provisional measures as it deems necessary or desirable. Such provisional
measures shall be without prejudice to the rights, claims or position of the
parties concerned. The Security Council shall duly take account of failure
to comply with such provisional measures.

Article 41

The Security Council may decide what measures not involving the use of
armed force are to be employed to give effect to its decisions, and it may call
upon the Members of the United Nations to apply such measures. These
may include complete or partial interruption of economic relations and of
rail, sea, air, postal, telegraphic, radio, and other means of communication,
and the severance of diplomatic relations.

Article 42

Should the Security Council consider that measures provided for in
Article 41 would be inadequate or have proved to be inadequate, it may take
such action by air, sea, or land forces as may be necessary to maintain or
restore international peace and security. Such action may include demonstrations, blockade and other operations by air, sea or land forces of Members
of the United Nations.

Article 43

1. All Members of the United Nations, in order to contribute to the maintenance of international peace and security, undertake to make available to
the Security Council, on its call and in accordance with a special agreement
or agreements, armed forces, assistance, and facilities, including rights of
passage, necessary for the purpose of maintaining international peace and
security.

2. Such agreement or agreements shall govern the numbers and types of
forces, their degree of readiness and general location, and the nature of the
facilities and assistance to be provided.

3. The agreement or agreements shall be negotiated as soon as possible
on the initiative of the Security Council. They shall be concluded between
the Security Council and Members or between the Security Council and
groups of Members and shall be subject to ratification by the signatory
states in accordance with their respective constitutional processes.

Article 44

When the Security Council has decided to use force it shall, before calling upon a Member not represented on it to provide armed forces in fulfilment of the obligations assumed under Article 43, invite that member, if the member so desires, to participate in the decisions of the Security Council concerning the employment of contingents of that Member's armed forces.

Article 45

In order to enable the United Nations to take urgent military measures, Members shall hold immediately available national air-force contingents for combined international enforcement action. The strength and degree or readiness of these contingents and plans for their combined action shall be determined, within the limits laid down in the special agreement or agreements referred to in Article 43 by the Security Council with the assistance of the Military Staff Committee.

Article 46

Plans for the application of armed force shall be made by the Security Council with the assistance of the Military Staff Committee.

Article 47

1. There shall be established a Military Staff Committee to advise and assist the Security Council on all questions relating to the Security Council's military requirements for the maintenance of international peace and security, the employment and command of forces placed at its disposal, the regulation of armaments, and possible disarmaments.

2. The Military Committee shall consist of the Chiefs of Staff of the permanent members of the Security Council or their representatives. Any member of the United Nations not permanently represented on the Committee shall be invited by the Committee to be associated with it when the efficient discharge of the Committee's responsibilities requires the participation of that member in its work.

3. The Military Staff Committee shall be responsible under the Security Council for the strategic direction of any armed forces placed at the disposal of the Security Council. Questions relating to the command of such forces shall be worked out subsequently.

4. The Military Staff Committee, with the authorization of the Security Council and after consultation with appropriate regional agencies, may establish regional sub-committees.

Article 48

1. The action required to carry out the decisions of the Security Council for the maintenance of international peace and security shall be taken by all the Members of the United Nations or by some of them, as the Security Council may determine.

2. Such decisions shall be carried out by the Members of the United Nations directly and through their action in the appropriate international agencies of which they are members.

Article 49

The Members of the United Nations shall join in affording mutual assistance in carrying out the measures decided upon by the Security Council.

Article 50

If preventative or enforcement measures against any State are taken by the Security Council, any other State, whether a Member of the United Nations or not, which finds itself confronted with special economic problems arising from the carrying out of those measures, shall have the right to consult the Security Council with regard to a solution of those problems.

Article 51

Nothing in the present Charter shall impair the inherent right of individual or collective self-defence if an armed attack occurs against a Member of the United Nations, until the Security Council has taken the measures necessary to maintain international peace and security. Measures taken by Members in the exercise of this right of self-defence shall be immediately reported to the Security Council and shall not in any way affect the authority and responsibility of the Security Council under the present Charter to take at any time such action as it deems necessary in order to maintain or restore international peace and security.

CHAPTER VIII.—REGIONAL ARRANGEMENTS

Article 52

1. Nothing in the present Charter precludes the existence of regional arrangements or agencies for dealing with such matters relating to the maintenance of international peace and security as are appropriate for regional action, provided that such arrangements or agencies and their activities are consistent with the Purposes and Principles of the United Nations.

2. The Members of the United Nations entering into such arrangements or constituting such agencies shall make every effort to achieve pacific settlement of local disputes through such regional arrangements or by such regional agencies before referring them to the Security Council.

3. The Security Council shall encourage the development of pacific settlement of local disputes through such regional arrangements or by such regional agencies either on the initiative of the states concerned or by reference from the Security Council.

4. This Article in no way impairs the application of Articles 34 and 35.

Article 53

1. The Security Council shall, where appropriate, utilize such regional arrangements or agencies for enforcement action under its authority. But no enforcement action shall be taken under regional arrangements, or by regional agencies without the authorization of the Security Council, with the exception of measures against any enemy State, as defined in Paragraph 2 of this Article, provided for pursuant to Article 107 or in regional arrangements directed against renewal of aggressive policy on the part of any such state,

until such time as the Organization may, on request of the government-concerned, be charged with the responsibility for preventing further aggress sion by such a state.

2. The term enemy State as used in paragraph 1 of this Article applies to any state which during the Second World War has been an enemy of any signatory of the present Charter.

Article 54

The Security Council shall at all times be kept fully informed of activities undertaken or in contemplation under regional arrangements or by regional agencies for the maintenance of international peace and security.

CHAPTER IX.—INTERNATIONAL ECONOMIC AND SOCIAL CO-OPERATION

Article 55

With a view to the creation of conditions of stability and well-being which are necessary for peaceful and friendly relations among nations based on respect for the principle of equal rights and self-determination of peoples, the United Nations shall promote :—

(a) Higher standards of living, full employment, and conditions of economic and social progress and development.

(b) Solutions of international economic, social, health and related problems ; and international cultural and educational co-operation ; and

(c) universal respect for, and observance of, human rights and fundamental freedoms for all without distinction as to race, sex, language or religion.

Article 56

All Members pledge themselves to take joint and separate action in co-operation with the Organization for the achievement of the purposes set forth in Article 55.

Article 57

1. The various specialized agencies, established by inter-governmental agreement and having wide international responsibilities, as defined in their basic instruments, in economic, social, cultural, educational, health and related fields, shall be brought into relationship with the United Nations in accordance with the provisions of Article 63.

2. Such agencies thus brought into relationship with the United Nations are hereinafter referred to as specialized agencies.

Article 58

The organization shall make recommendations for the co-ordination of the policies and activities of the specialized agencies.

Article 59

The Organization shall, where appropriate, initiate negotiations among the states concerned for the creation of any new specialized agencies required for the accomplishment of the purposes set forth in Article 55.

Article 60

Responsibility for the discharge of the functions of the Organization set forth in this Chapter shall be vested in the General Assembly and, under the authority of the General Assembly, in the Economic and Social Council, which shall have for this purpose the powers set forth in Chapter X.

CHAPTER X.—THE ECONOMIC AND SOCIAL COUNCIL—COMPOSITION

Article 61

1. The Economic and Social Council shall consist of 18 Members of the United Nations elected by the General Assembly.

2. Subject to the provisions of paragraph 3, six members of the Economic and Social Council shall be elected each year for a term of three years. A retiring member shall be eligible for immediate re-election.

3. At the first election, 18 members of the Economic and Social Council shall be chosen, the term of office of six members so chosen shall expire at the end of one year, and of six other members at the end of two years, in accordance with arrangements made by the General Assembly.

4. Each member of the Economic and Social Council shall have one representative.

FUNCTIONS AND POWERS

Article 62

1. The Economic and Social Council may make or initiate studies and reports with respect to international, economic, social, cultural, educational, health and related matters, and may make recommendations with respect to any such matters to the General Assembly, to the Members of the United Nations, and to the specialized agencies concerned.

2. It may make recommendations for the purpose of promoting respect for, and observance of, human rights and fundamental freedoms for all.

3. It may prepare draft conventions for submission to the General Assembly, with respect to matters falling within its competence.

4. It may call, in accordance with the rules prescribed by the United Nations, international conferences on matters falling within its competence.

Article 63

1. The Economic and Social Council may enter into agreements with any of the agencies referred to in Article 57, defining the terms on which the agency concerned shall be brought into relationship with the United Nations. Such agreements shall be subject to approval by the General Assembly.

2. It may co-ordinate the activities of the specialized agencies through consultation with and recommendations to such agencies and through recommendations to the General Assembly and to the Members of the United Nations.

Article 64

1. The Economic and Social Council may take appropriate steps to obtain regular reports from the specialized agencies. It may make arrangements with the Members of the United Nations and with the specialized agencies to obtain reports on the steps taken to give effect to its own recommendations and to recommendations on matters falling within its competence made by the General Assembly.

2. It may communicate its observations on these reports to the General Assembly.

Article 65

The Economic and Social Council may furnish information to the Security Council and shall assist the Security Council upon its request.

Article 66

1. The Economic and Social Council shall perform such functions as fall within its competence in connection with the carrying out of the recommendations of the General Assembly.

2. It may, with the approval of the General Assembly, perform services at the request of Members of the United Nations and at the request of specialized agencies.

3. It shall perform such other functions as are specified elsewhere in the present Charter or as may be assigned to it by the General Assembly.

VOTING

Article 67

1. Each member of the Economic and Social Council shall have one vote.

2. Decisions of the Economic and Social Council shall be made by a majority of the members present and voting.

PROCEDURE

Article 68

The Economic and Social Council shall set up commissions in economic and social fields and for the promotion of human rights, and such other commissions as may be required for the performance of its functions.

Article 69

The Economic and Social Council shall invite any Member of the United Nations to participate, without vote, in its deliberations on any matter of particular concern to that Member.

Article 70

The Economic and Social Council may make arrangements for representatives of the specialized agencies to participate, without vote, in its deliberations and in those of the commissions established by it, and for its representatives to participate in the deliberations of the specialized agencies.

Article 71

The Economic and Social Council may make suitable arrangements for consultation with non-governmental organizations which are concerned with matters within its competence.

Such arrangements may be made with international organizations and, where appropriate, with national organizations after consultation with the Member of the United Nations concerned.

Article 72

1. The Economic and Social Council shall adopt its own rules of procedure including the method of selecting its President.

2. The Economic and Social Council shall meet as required in accordance with its rules, which shall include provision for the convening of meetings on request of a majority of its members.

CHAPTER   XI.—DECLARATION   REGARDING   NON-SELF-GOVERNING
TERRITORIES

Article 73

Members of the United Nations which have or assume responsibilities for the administration of territories whose peoples have not yet attained a full measure of self-government recognize the principle that the interests of the inhabitants of these territories are paramount, and accept as a sacred trust the obligation to promote to the utmost, within the system of international peace and security established by the present Charter, the well-being of the inhabitants of these territories, and to this end :—

a) To ensure, with due respect for the culture of the peoples concerned, their political, economic, social and educational advancement, their just treatment, and their protection against abuses ;

(*b*) To develop self-government, to take due account of the political aspirations of the peoples, and to assist them in the progressive development of their free political institutions, according to the particular circumstances of each territory and its peoples and their varying stages of advancement ;

(*e*) To further international peace and security ;

(*d*) To promote constructive measures of development, to encourage research, and to co-operate with one another and, when and where appropriate, with specialized international bodies with a view to the practical achievement of the social, economic and scientific purposes set forth in this Article ; and

(*c*) To transmit regularly to the Secretary-General for information purposes, subject to such limitation as security and constitutional considerations may require, statistical and other information of a technical nature relating to economic, social and educational conditions in the territories for which they are respectively responsible other than those territories to which Chapters XII and XIII apply.

Article 74

Members of the United Nations also agree that their policy in respect of the territories to which this Chapter applies, no less than in respect of their metropolitan areas, must be based on the general principle of good neighbourliness due account being taken of the interests and well-being of the rest of the world, in social, economic and commercial matters.

CHAPTER XII.—INTERNATIONAL TRUSTEESHIP SYSTEM

Article 75

The United Nations shall establish under its authority an international trusteeship system for the administration and supervision of such territories as may be placed thereunder by subsequent individual agreements. These territories are hereinafter referred to as Trust Territories.

Article 67

The basic objectives of the trusteeship system, in accordance with the Purposes of the United Nations laid down in Article 1 of the present Charter, shall be :—

(a) To further international peace and security ;

(b) To promote the political, economic, social and educational advancement of the inhabitants of the Trust Territories, and their progressive development towards self-government or independence as may be appropriate to the particular circumstances of each territory and its peoples and the freely expressed wishes of the people concerned, and as may be provided by the terms of each trusteeship agreement ;

(c) To encourage respect for human rights and for fundamental freedoms for all without distinction as to race, sex, language, or religion, and to encourage recognition of the interdependence of the peoples of world ; and

(d) To ensure equal treatment in social, economic and commercial matters for all Members of the United Nations and their nationals, and also equal treatment for the latter in the administration of justice, without prejudice to the attainment of the foregoing objectives and subject to the provisions of Article 80.

Article 77

1. The trusteeship system shall apply to such territories in the following categories as may be placed thereunder by means of trusteeship agreements :—

(a) Territories now held under mandate ;

(b) Territories which may de detached from enemy states as a result of the Second World War ; and

(c) Territories voluntarily placed under the system by states responsible for their administration.

2. It will be a matter for subsequent agreement as to which territories in the foregoing categories will be brought under the trusteeship system and upon what terms.

Article 78

The trusteeship system shall not apply to territories which have become Members of the United Nations, relationship among which shall be based on respect for the principle of sovereign equality.

Article 79

The terms of trusteeship for each territory to be placed under the trusteeship system, including any alteration or amendment, shall be agreed upon by the states directly concerned, including the mandatory power in the case of territories held under mandate by a Member of the United Nations, and shall be approved as provided for in Articles 83 and 85.

Article 80

1. Except as may be agreed upon in individual trusteeship agreements, made under Articles 77, 79, and 81, placing each territory under the trustee-

ship system, and until such agreements have been concluded, nothing in this Chapter shall be construed in or of itself to alter in any manner the rights whatsoever of any states or any peoples or the terms of existing international instruments to which Members of the United Nations may respectively be parties.

2. Paragraph 1 of this Article shall not be interpreted as giving grounds for delay or postponement of the negotiation and conclusion of agreements for placing mandated and other territories under the trusteeship system as provided for in Article 77.

Article 81

The trusteeship agreement shall in each case include the terms under which the trust territory will be administered and designate the authority which will exercise the administration of the trust territory. Such authority, hereinafter called the administering authority, may be one or more states or the Organization itself.

Article 82

There may be designated, in any trusteeship agreement, a strategic area or areas which may include part or all of the trust territory to which the agreement applies, without prejudice to any special agreement or agreements made under Article 43.

Article 83

1. All functions of the United Nations relating to strategic areas, including the approval of the terms of the trusteeship agreements and of their alteration or amendment, shall be exercised by the Security Council.

2. The basic objectives set forth in Article 76 shall be applicable to the people of each strategic area.

3. The Security Council shall, subject to the provisions of the trusteeship agreements and without prejudice to security considerations, avail itself of the assistance of the Trusteeship Council to perform those functions of the United Nations under the trusteeship system relating to political, economic, social, and educational matters in the strategic areas.

Article 84

It shall be the duty of the administering authority to ensure that the trust territory shall play its part in the maintenance of international peace and security. To this end the administering authority may make use of volunteer forces, facilities, and assistance from the trust territory in carrying out the obligations towards the Security Council undertaken in this regard by the administering authority, as well as for local defence and the maintenance of law and order within the trust territory.

Article 85

1. The functions of the United Nations with regard to trusteeship agreements for all areas not designated as strategic, including the approval of the terms of the trusteeship agreements and of their alteration or amendment, shall be exercised by the General Assembly.

2. The Trusteeship Council, operating under the authority of the General Assembly, shall assist the General Assembly in carrying out these functions.

CHAPTER XIII.—THE TRUSTEESHIP COUNCIL—COMPOSITION

Article 86

1. The Trusteeship Council shall consist of the following Members of the United Nations :—
   (a) Those Members administering trust territories ;
   (b) Such of those members mentioned by name in Article 23 as are not administering trust territories ; and
   (c) As many other Members elected for three-year terms by the General Assembly as may be necessary to ensure that the total number of members of the Trusteeship Council is equally divided between those Members of the United Nations which administer trust territories and those which do not.

2. Each member of the Trusteeship Council shall designate one specially qualified person to represent it therein.

FUNCTIONS AND POWERS

Article 87

The General Assembly and, under its authority, the Trusteeship Council, in carrying out their functions, may :—
   (a) Consider reports submitted by the administering authority ;
   (b) Accept petitions and examine them in consultation with the administering authority ;
   (c) Provide for periodic visits to the respective Trust Territories at times agreed upon with the administering authority ; and
   (d) Take these and other actions in conformity with the terms of the trusteeship agreements.

Article 88

The Trusteeship Council shall formulate a *questionnaire* on the political, economic, social and educational advancement of the inhabitants of each trust territory, and the administering authority for each trust territory within the competence of the General Assembly shall make an annual report to the General Assembly upon the basis of such a *questionnaire.*

VOTING

Article 89

1. Each member of the Trusteeship Council shall have one vote.

2. Decisions of the Trusteeship Council shall be made by a majority of the members present and voting.

PROCEDURE

Article 90

1. The Trusteeship Council shall adopt its own rules and procedure, including the method of selecting its President.

2. The Trusteeship Council shall meet as required in accordance with its rules, which shall include provision for the convening of meetings on the request of a majority of its members.

Article 91

The Trusteeship Council shall, when appropriate, avail itself of the assistance of the Economic and Social Council and of the specialized agencies in regard to matters with which they are respectively concerned.

CHAPTER XIV.—THE INTERNATIONAL COURT OF JUSTICE

Article 92

The International Court of Justice shall be the principal judicial organ of the United Nations. It shall function in accordance with the annexed Statute, which is based upon the Statute of the Permanent Court of International Justice and forms an integral part of the present Charter.

Article 93

1. All Members of the United Nations are *ipso facto* parties to the Statute of the International Court of Justice.

2. A state which is not a Member of the United Nations may become a party to the Statute of the International Court of Justice on conditions to be determined in each case by the General Assembly upon the commendation of the Security Council.

Article 94

1. Each Member of the United Nations undertakes to comply with the decision of the International Court of Justice in any case to which it is a party.

2. If any party to a case fails to perform the obligations incumbent upon it under a judgment rendered by the Court, the other party may have recourse to the Security Council, which may, if it deems necessary, make recommendations or decide upon measures to be taken to give effect to the judgment.

Article 95

Nothing in the present Charter shall prevent Members of the United Nations from entrusting the solution of their differences to other tribunals by virtue of agreements already in existence or which may be concluded in the future.

Article 96

1. The General Assembly or the Security Council may request the International Court of Justice to give an advisory opinion on any legal question.

2. Other organs of the United Nations and specialized agencies, which may at any time be so authorized by the General Assembly, may also request advisory opinions of the Court on legal questions arising within the scope of their activities.

CHAPTER XV.—THE SECRETARIAT

Article 97

The Secretariat shall comprise a Secretary-General and such staff as the Organization may require. The Secretary-General shall be appointed by the General Assembly upon the recommendation of the Security Council. He shall be the chief administrative officer of the Organization.

Article 98

The Secretary-General shall act in that capacity in all meetings of the General Assembly, of the Security Council, of the Economic and Social Council, and of the Trusteeship Council, and shall perform such other functions as are entrusted to him by these organs. The Secretary-General shall make an annual report to the General Assembly on the work of the Organization.

Article 99

The Secretary-General may bring to the attention of the Security Council any matter which in his opinion may threaten the maintenance of international peace and security.

Article 100

1. In the performance of their duties the Secretary-General and the staff shall not seek or receive instructions from any government or from any other authority external to the Organization. They shall refrain from any action which might reflect on their position as international officials, responsible only to the Organization.

2. Each Member of the United Nations undertakes to respect the exclusively international character of the responsibilities of the Secretary-General and the staff and not to seek to influence them in the discharge of their responsibilities.

Article 101

1. The staff shall be appointed by the Secretary-General under regulations established by the General Assembly.

2. Appropriate staffs shall be permanently assigned to the Economic and Social Council, the Trusteeship Council, and, as required, to other organs of the United Nations. These staffs shall form a part of the Secretariat.

3. The paramount consideration in the employment of the staff and in the determination of the conditions of service shall be the necessity of securing the highest standards of efficiency, competence and integrity. Due regard shall be paid to the importance of recruiting the staff on as wide a geographical basis as possible.

Chapter XVI.—Miscellaneous Provisions

Article 102

1. Every treaty and every international agreement entered into by any Member of the United Nations after the present Charter comes into force shall as soon as possible be registered with the Secretariat and published by it.

2. No party to any such treaty or international agreement which has not been registered in accordance with the provisions of paragraph 1 of this may invoke that treaty or agreement before any organ of the United Nations.

Article 103

In the event of a conflict between the obligations of the Members of the

United Nations under the present Charter and their obligations under any other international agreement, their obligations under the present Charter shall prevail.

Article 104

The Organization shall enjoy in the territory of each of its Members such legal capacity as may be necessary for the exercise of its functions and the fulfilment of its purposes.

Article 105

1. The Organization shall enjoy in the territory of each of its Members such privileges and immunities as are necessary for the fulfilment of its purposes.

2. Representatives of the Members of the United Nations and officials of the Organization shall similarly enjoy such privileges and immunities as are necessary for the independent exercise of their functions in connection with the Organization.

3. The General Assembly may make recommendations with a view to determining the details of the application of paragraphs 1 and 2 of this Article or may propose conventions to the Members of the United Nations for this purpose.

CHAPTER XVII.—TRANSITIONAL SECURITY ARRANGEMENTS

Article 106

Pending the coming into force of such special agreements referred to in Article 43 as in the opinion of the Security Council enable it to begin the exercise of its responsibilities under Article 42, the parties to the Four-Nation Declaration, signed at Moscow, 30th October, 1943, and France, shall, in accordance with the provisions of paragraph 5 of that Declaration, consult with one another and as occasion requires with other Members of the United Nations with a view to such joint action on behalf of the Organization as may be necessary for the purpose of maintaining international peace and security.

Article 107

Nothing in the present Charter shall invalidate or preclude action, in relation to any state which during the Second World War has been an enemy of any signatory to the present Charter, taken or authorized as a result of that war by the Governments having responsibility for such action.

CHAPTER XVIII.—AMENDMENTS

Article 108

Amendments to the present Charter shall come into force for all members of the United Nations when they have been adopted by a vote of two-thirds of the members of the General Assembly and ratified in accordance with their respective constitutional processes by two-thirds of the members of the United Nations, including all the permanent members of the Security Council.

Article 109

1. A General Conference of the Members of the United Nations for the purpose of reviewing the present Charter may be held at a date and place to be fixed by a two-thirds vote of the members of the General Assembly and by a vote of any seven members of the Security Council. Each Member of the United Nations shall have one vote in the conference.

2. Any alteration of the present Charter recommended by a two-thirds vote of the conference shall take effect when ratified in accordance with their respective constitutional processes by two-thirds of the Members of the United Nations including all the permanent members of the Security Council.

3. If such a conference has not been held before the tenth annual session of the General Assembly following the coming into force of the present Charter, the proposal to call such a conference shall be placed on the agenda of that session of the General Assembly, and the conference shall be held if so decided by a majority vote of the members of the General Assembly and by a vote of any seven members of the Security Council.

CHAPTER XIX.—RATIFICATION AND SIGNATURE

Article 110

1. The present Charter shall be ratified by the signatory states in accordance with their respective constitutional processes.

2. The ratifications shall be deposited with the Government of the United States of America, which shall notify all the signatory states of each deposit as well as the Secretary-General of the Organization when he has been appointed.

3. The present Charter shall come into force upon the deposit of ratifications by the Republic of China, France, the Union of Soviet Socialist Republics, the United Kingdom of Great Britain and Northern Ireland, and the United States of America, and by a majority of the other signatory states. A protocol of the ratifications deposited shall thereupon be drawn up by the Government of the United States of America which shall communicate copies thereof to all the signatory States.

4. The states signatory to the present Charter which ratify it after it has come into force will become original members of the United Nations on the date of the deposit of their respective ratifications.

Article 111

The present Charter, of which the Chinese, French, Russian, English and Spanish texts are equally authentic, shall remain deposited in the archives of the Government of the United States of America. Duly certified copies thereof shall be transmitted by that Government to the Governments of the other signatory states.

In faith whereof the representatives of the Governments of the United Nations[1] have signed the present Charter.

Done at the City of San Francisco the twenty-sixth day of June, one thousand nine hundred and forty-five.

APPENDIX E

INDEX TO THE CHARTER OF THE UNITED NATIONS

(*The numbers given are those of articles in the Charter*)

Admission of new Member States, 4, 18.
Aggression, measures against, 1, 39–42,53.
Air Forces, contingents to be immediately available, 45.
Amendments to the Charter, 108, 109.
Arbitration to settle disputes, 33.
Armaments, regulation of, 11, 26, 47.

Blockade, 42.
Budget, 17, 18.

[1]*Note.*—Representatives of the following Governments signed the Charter :—

China.
Union of Soviet Socialist
   Republics.
United Kingdom of Great Britain
   and Northern Ireland.
France
Argentina.
Australia.
Belgium.
Bolivia.
Brazil.
Byelo-Russian S.S.R.
Canada.
Chile.
Colombia.
Costa Rica.
Cuba.
Czechoslovakia
Denmark.
Dominican Republic
Ecuador.
Egypt.
El Salvador.
Ethiopia.
Greece.
Guatemala.

Haiti.
Honduras.
India.
Iran.
Iraq.
Lebanon.
Liberia.
Luxembourg.
Mexico.
Netherlands.
New Zealand.
Nicaragua.
Norway.
Panama;
Paraguay.
Peru.
Philippine Commonwealth.
Saudi Arabia.
Syria.
Turkey.
Ukrainian S.S.R.
Union of South Africa.
Uruguay.
Venezuela.
Yugoslavia.
United States of America.

        G*

APPENDIX F
CHRONOLOGY OF UNITED NATIONS ACTIVITIES

	Main Organization	Specialized Agencies, Etc.
1941 : August	Atlantic Charter	
September		Allied Relief Committee London (nucleus of UNRRA)
1942 : January	Declaration by United Nations, Washington	
1943 : February		Food and Agriculture Conference, Hot Springs, U.S.A.
October	Moscow Declaration	
November		UNRRA Agreement signed. 1st UNRRA Council, Atlantic City, U.S.A.
1944 : February		World Trade Union Conference, London.
April		ILO Conference, Philadelphia.
July		Financial Conference, Bretton Woods, U.S.A.
August	Dumbarton Oaks Conference	
September		2nd UNRRA Council, Montreal.
November		Civil Aviation Conference, Chicago.
1945 : February	Yalta Conference	
April	San Francisco Conference.	
June	Charter signed, San Francisco	
August	Executive Committee, London	3rd UNRRA Council, London. International Chamber of Commerce, London.
September		2nd World T.U.C., Paris;WFTUconstituted.
October		World Youth Conference, London ; WFDY constituted. ILO Conference, Paris.

November	Preparatory Commission, London	1st FAO Conference, Quebec UNESCO Constituent Conference, London
1946 : January	General Assembly, London Security Council, London Economic and Social Council, London	
February	Military Staff Committee, London	
March	Security Council, New York (and regularly every month thereafter)	Boards of Directors of International Fund and Bank, Savannah, U.S.A. 4th UNRRA Council, Atlantic City, U.S.A. Preparatory Committee for Health Conference, Paris
April	International Court, The Hague	
May	Economic and Social Council, New York	FAO Emergency Conference, New York UNRRA Council Emergency Meeting, New York ILO Governing Body, New York Civil Aviation Organization, Montreal Executive Committee, UNESCO, London
June	Commission on Atomic Energy, New York	Health Conference, New York ILO Maritime Conference, Seattle, U.S.A.
July		Preparatory Commission, UNESCO
September		ILO Conference, Montreal Preparatory Commission, for Trade Conference in 1947 United Nations Week organized by U.N. Associations in U.K. and U.S.A.

October	General Assembly New York	FAO Conference, Copenhagen or Washington
November	Trusteeship Council ?	1st UNESCO Conference, Paris Conference of World Federation of U.N. Associations ?
1947 : (Autumn)		Trade and Employment Conference

APPENDIX G

TABLE OF ORGANIZATION

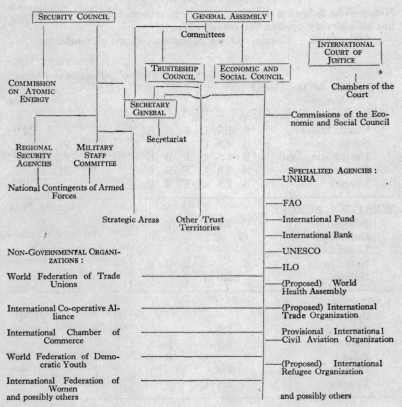

SECURITY COUNCIL

GENERAL ASSEMBLY

Committees

INTERNATIONAL COURT OF JUSTICE

TRUSTEESHIP COUNCIL

ECONOMIC AND SOCIAL COUNCIL

COMMISSION ON ATOMIC ENERGY

Chambers of the Court

SECRETARY GENERAL

————Commissions of the Economic and Social Council

Secretariat

REGIONAL SECURITY AGENCIES

MILITARY STAFF COMMITTEE

SPECIALIZED AGENCIES :
——UNRRA

National Contingents of Armed Forces

Strategic Areas   Other Trust Territories

——FAO

——International Fund

——International Bank

NON-GOVERNMENTAL ORGANIZATIONS :

——UNESCO

——ILO

World Federation of Trade Unions ——————————————— (Proposed) World Health Assembly

International Co-operative Alliance ————————————— (Proposed) International Trade Organization

International Chamber of Commerce ————————————— Provisional International Civil Aviation Organization

World Federation of Democratic Youth ————————————

International Federation of Women ————————————— (Proposed) International Refugee Organization

and possibly others   and possibly others

APPENDIX H

LIST OF SOVEREIGN STATES, SHOWING THEIR POSITIONS BOTH IN THE UNITED NATIONS AND IN THE LEAGUE

Key to Symbols :—

UNITED NATIONS :

S	Member of the Security Council (1946)
ES	Member of the Economic and Social Council (1946)
C	Represented on the International Court (1946)
F, B	Represented on the Board of Executive Directors of the International Fund or Bank (1946)
E	Member of the Executive Committee of UNESCO
T	Qualified for membership of the Trusteeship Council

LEAGUE :

PC	Permanent member of the League Council
M	League Mandatory
N	Never a member of the League

Note :—The following states are not yet members of the United Nations, but have already applied for membership:—

Afghanistan, Albania, Outer Mongolia, Siam, Transjordan.

(1) *Members of the United Nations*	Position in United Nations	Position in League
BIG FIVE		
United States	S ES C F B E T	N
Soviet Union	S ES C T	PC
United Kingdom	S ES C F B E T	PC M
France	S ES C F B E T	PC M
China	S ES C F B E T	
WESTERN EUROPE		
Belgium	ES C F B T	M
Denmark		
Luxembourg		
Netherlands	S F B E	
Norway	ES C E	
EASTERN EUROPE		
Byelorussia		N
Czechoslovakia	ES F	
Greece	ES B E	
Poland	S C B E	
Ukraine	ES	N
Yugoslavia	ES C	

MIDDLE EAST AND AFRICA								
Egypt	S		F					
Ethiopia								
Iran								
Iraq								
Lebanon	ES							N
Liberia								
Saudi Arabia								N
South Africa					T		M	
Syria								N
Turkey								

FAR EAST								
Australia	S				T		M	
India	ES		F	B	E			
New Zealand					T		M	
Philippines								N

NORTH AND CEN-TRAL AMERICA								
Canada	ES	C	F	B	E			
Costa Rica								
Cuba	ES			B				
Dominican Rep								
El Salvador		C						
Guatemala								
Haiti								
Honduras								
Mexico	S		C	F	E			
Nicaragua								
Panama								

SOUTH AMERICA								
Argentina								
Bolivia								
Brazil	S		C	F	E			
Chile	ES	C		B				
Colombia	ES			E				
Ecuador								
Paraguay								
Peru	ES							
Uruguay								
Venezuela								

(2) *Non-members*

GREAT POWERS

Germany							PC

| Italy | | PC | |
| Japan | | PC | M |

EUROPE
Albania, Austria, Bulgaria, Eire, Finland, Hungary, Portugal, Roumania, Spain, Sweden, Switzerland

ASIA
Afghanistan, Siam (Thailand)

APPENDIX I

A UNITED NATIONS WHO'S WHO

Note :—This list is confined to persons who have actually taken part in the work of United Nations organs after their creation. It does not, therefore, include such pioneers in the field of world organization as Mr. Winston Churchill, Franklin D. Roosevelt, Marshal Stalin or Field-Marshal Smuts.

Afifi Pasha, Dr. Hafez (Egypt). President of the Security Council, April 1946.

Aghnides, M. (Greece). Ambassador in London ; participated in Security Council discussions, January 1946.

Aklilu Abte-Wold (Ethiopia). Delegate to the General Assembly, January 1946.

Al Khouri, Faris (Syria). Delegate to the General Assembly and Chairman of its Administrative and Budgetary Committee, January 1946. Participated in Security Council discussions, January 1946.

Attlee, Clement (United Kingdom). Prime Minister, and Delegate to the General Assembly, January 1946.

Badawi Pasha, Dr. Abdel Hamid (Egypt). Delegate to the General Assembly and member of the Security Council ; elected to the International Court, January 1946.

Bevin, Ernest (United Kingdom). Foreign Secretary ; Delegate to the General Assembly and Security Council, January 1946.

Bidault, Georges (France). Foreign Minister ; Delegate to the General Assembly and Security Council, January 1946.

Bloom, Sol (United States). Congressman and Delegate to the General Assembly, January 1946.

Bonnet, Henri (France). Member of the Security Council, April 1946.

Boyd Orr, Sir John (United Kingdom). Director-General of the Food and Agriculture Organization.

Byrnes, James (United States). Secretary of State, and Delegate to the General Assembly and Security Council.

Cadogan, Sir Alexander (United Kingdom). Member of the Security Council, March 1946.

Connally, Senator Tom (United States). Delegate to the General Assembly, January 1946.
Creech Jones, A. (United Kingdom). Colonial Secretary, and Delegate to the General Assembly, January 1946.

Diaz, Dr. de Rosenzweig (Mexico). Member of the Security Council, January 1946.

Fraser, Peter (New Zealand). Prime Minister ; Delegate to the General Assembly and chairman of its Social, Humanitarian and Cultural Committee, January 1946.
Freitas-Valle, Senhor de (Brazil). Delegate to the General Assembly and member of the Security Council, January 1946.

Gavrilovitch, Dr. (Yugoslavia). Chairman of the Preparatory Commission's site committee, December 1945.
Gromyko, Andrey A. (Soviet Union). Delegate to the General Assembly and member of the Security Council.
Guerrero, Dr. J. Gustavo (El Salvador). Delegate to the General Assembly and first President of the International Court, April 1946.
Gusev, Feodor T. (Soviet Union). Ambassador in London ; Delegate to the General Assembly, January 1946.

Hackworth, Green H. (United States). Elected to the International Court, January 1946.
Hasluck, Paul (Australia). Member of the Security Council, May 1946.
Hassan Pasha, Mahmud (Egypt). Member of the Security Council, April 1946.
Henderson, Arthur (United Kingdom). Delegate to the General Assembly, January 1946.
Hodgson, Colonel W. R. (Australia). Member of the Security Council, March 1946.
Hussein Ala (Iran). Ambassador to the United States ; participated in discussions of Security Council, April 1946.
Huxley, Dr. Julian (United Kingdom). Secretary to UNESCO, February 1946.

Jebb, Gladwyn (United Kingdom). Executive Secretary to the Preparatory Commission, 1945.
Jimenez, Dr. Roberto (Panama). Delegate to the General Assembly and chairman of its Legal Committee, January 1946.

Kondersky, Waclaw (Poland). Delegate to the General Assembly and chairman of its Economic and Financial Committee, January 1946.
Koo, Wellington (China). Delegate to the General Assembly and Security Council, January 1946.
Krylov, Professor (Soviet Union). Elected to the International Court, January 1946.

Kuznetsov, Vasili V. (Soviet Union). Delegate to the General Assembly, January 1946.

LaGuardia, Fiorello (United States). Director-General of UNRRA, March 1946.

Lange, Dr. Oscar (Poland). Member of the Security Council, April 1946.

Lares, Dr. Roberto Picon (Venezuela). Delegate to, and Vice-President of, the General Assembly, January 1946.

Lavrentiev, Anatoli I. (Soviet Union). Delegate to the General Assembly, January 1946.

Lehmann, Herbert H. (United States). Director-General of UNRRA, 1943–1946.

Liang, Dr. (China). Chairman of the Security Council's sub-committee on procedure, April, 1946.

Lie, Trygve (Norway). Foreign Minister ; Secretary-General of the United Nations, January 1946.

Lopez, Pedro (Philippines). Delegate to the General Assembly, January 1946.

Maceachen, Dr. Roberto (Uruguay). Delegate to the General Assembly and chairman of its Trusteeship Committee, January 1946.

MacNair, Sir Arnold D. (United Kingdom). Elected to the International Court, January 1946.

McNeil, Hector (United Kingdom). Delegate to the General Assembly, January 1946.

Makin, N. J. O. (Australia). President of the Security Council, January 1946.

Manuilsky, Dr. Dmitro A. (Ukraine). Delegate to the General Assembly and chairman of its Political and Security Committees ; participated in discussions of the Security Council, January 1946.

Masaryk, Jan (Czechoslovakia). Foreign Minister, and Delegate to the General Assembly, January 1946.

Modzelewski, M. (Poland). Delegate to the General Assembly and member of the Security Council, January 1946.

Nicholls, Heaton (South Africa). High Commissioner ; Delegate to the General Assembly, January 1946.

Noel-Baker, P. J. (United Kingdom). Minister of State, and Delegate to the General Assembly, January 1946.

Paul-Boncour, Joseph (France). Delegate to the General Assembly, January 1946.

Quintana, Dr. (Argentina). Delegate to the General Assembly, January 1946.

Quo Tai-chi, Dr. (China). President of the Security Council, March 1946.

Ramaswami Mudaliar, Sir A. (India). President of the Economic and Social Council, February 1946.

Rendel, Sir George (United Kingdom). Delegate to the General Assembly; chairman of the special United Nations committee on refugees, April 1946.

Rendis, M. (Greece). Foreign Minister ; participated in discussions of Security Council, February 1946.

Roosevelt, Mrs. Eleanor (United States). Delegate to the General Assembly; chairman of the Economic and Social Council's Commission on Human Rights.

Rzymowski, Wincenty (Poland). Foreign Minister and Delegate to the General Assembly, January 1946.

Salamanca, Senor (Bolivia). Delegate to the General Assembly, January 1946.

Schermerhorn, Professor (Netherlands). Prime Minister ; Delegate to the General Assembly, January 1946.

Sophianopoulos, M. (Greece). Foreign Minister ; Delegate to the General Assembly, January 1946.

Spaak, Paul-Henri (Belgium). Foreign Minister, later Prime Minister ; President of the General Assembly, January 1946.

Stettinius, Edward R. (United States). Member of the Security Council, April 1946.

St. Laurent, L. S. (Canada). Delegate to the General Assembly, January 1946.

Taqizadeh, Seyed Hassan (Iran). Ambassador in London ; participated in discussions of the Security Council, January 1946.

Van Kleffens, Dr. E. N. (Netherlands). Member of the Security Council, 1946.

Velloso Netto, Pedro Leao (Brazil). Member of the Security Council, 1946.

Vincent-Auriol, M. (France). Member of the Security Council and Delegate to the General Assembly, January 1946.

Vishinsky, Andrey Y. (Soviet Union). Delegate to the General Assembly and member of the Security Council, January 1946.

Winant, John G. (United States). Member of the Economic and Social Council, 1946.

Wilkinson, Ellen (United Kingdom). Minister of Education ; Delegate to the General Assembly ; President of UNESCO, 1946.

Zeineddine, Farid (Syria). Delegate to the General Assembly, January 1946.

Zuleta Angel, Dr. Eduardo (Colombia). Chairman of the Preparatory Commission, 1945.

APPENDIX J

SOME SUGGESTED REFERENCES

Stationary Office publications :—

" An Introduction to the United Nations." (1945).

" Proceedings of Inter-Allied Meeting of September 24, 1941." (Cmd 6315 of 1941.)

" Final Act of the United Nations Conference on Food and Agriculture." (Cmd 6451 of 1943.)

" Agreement establishing the United Nations Relief and Rehabilitation Administration." (Cmd 6491 of 1943.)

" Resolutions and Reports adopted by the First Council of UNRRA." (Cmd 6497 of 1943.)

" Resolutions adopted by the Second Council of UNRRA." (Cmd 6566 of 1944.)

" United Nations Monetary and Financial Conference, Bretton Woods : Final Act." (Cmd 6546 of 1944.)

" Final Act of the United Nations Conference for the establishment of an Educational, Scientific and Cultural Organization." (Cmd 6711 of 1945.)

" Proposals for Consideration by an International Conference on Trade and Employment." (Cmd 6709 of 1945.)

" Final Act of a Conference on International Civil Aviation." (Cmd 6614 of 1945.)

" Documents adopted by the United Nations Conference, San Francisco June 26, 1945." (Published by H.M. Stationery Office for the United Nations Information Organization.)

(The above contains the text of the Charter and of the Statute of the International Court of Justice.)

" Commentary on the Charter of the United Nations signed at San Francisco on the 26th June, 1945." (Cmd 6666 of 1945.)

(The above contains the texts of the Charter and of the Dumbarton Oaks plan, set out on opposite pages.)

" Report of the Executive Committee to the Preparatory Commission of the United Nations." (1945.)

" Report of the Preparatory Commission of the United Nations." (1945.)

" Commentary on the Report of the Preparatory Commission of the United Nations." (Cmd 6734 of 1946.)

" Journals of the General Assembly (First Part of the First Session) January and February, 1946."

" Journals of the Security Council, January and February, 1946."

" A Report on the International Control of Atomic Energy." (1946.)

Publications of the Carnegie Endowment for International Peace, New York :—
" *International Conciliation* " :

No. 409 (Dumbarton Oaks Proposals).

No. 411 (The International Court).

No. 412 (The FAO).

No. 413 (The Charter, with explanatory notes).

No. 415 (Draft Constitution of UNESCO).

No. 417 (The United Nations and the Atomic Bomb).

No. 418 (The United States, the United Nations and the League of Nations).

No. 420 (A First Balance Sheet of the United Nations : Security Provisions, and Settlement of Disputes in the Charter and in the Covenant).

(The above series contain reproductions of important texts with explanatory notes.)

Pamphlets :—

" The Charter Explained." By Maurice Fanshawe. United Nations Association, 11 Maiden Lane, London, W.C.2.

" We The Peoples." The Story of the San Francisco Conference. United Nations Information Organization.

" The United Nations Today and Tomorrow." U.N.I.O.

" FAO : Towards a World of Plenty." U.N.I.O.

" Bretton Woods : The Story of the United Nations Monetary and Financial Conference." U.N.I.O.

" Helping the People to Help Themselves : The Story of UNRRA." U.N.I.O.

" Fifty Facts about UNRRA." Published for UNRRA by H.M. Stationery Office, London.

" The United Nations : What kind of Partnership ? " By L. M. Perez. Barnardo, London.

" The United Nations Charter : A Commentary " by Gilbert Murray, G. D. H. Cole and others. National Peace Council, London.

" A Page of British Folly." By R. F. Harrod. Macmillan, London.

(The above is a closely reasoned argument in favour of the Bretton Woods Agreements and the proposals for an International Trade Conference.)

" The Soviet Union at the San Francisco Conference." Published by " Soviet News," London.

INDEX.

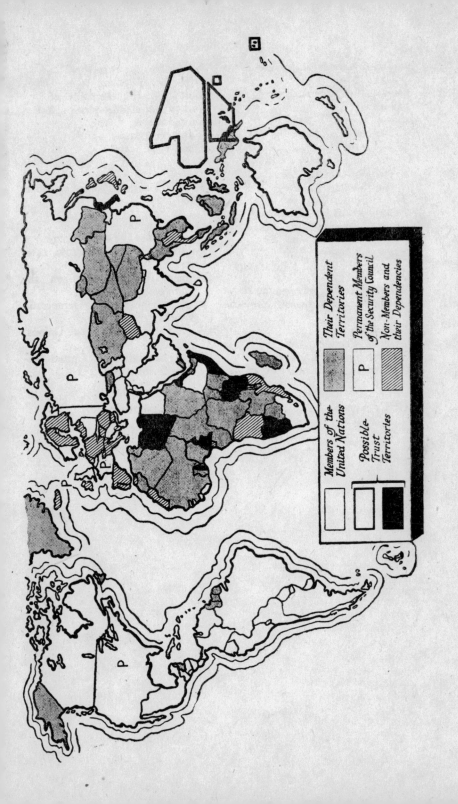

Members of the United Nations

Their Dependent Territories

Permanent Members of the Security Council P

Possible Trust Territories

Non-Members and their Dependencies